HER FINAL YEAR

A Care-Giving Memoir

and

HIS FIRST YEAR

A Journey of Recovery

by James Downey and John Bourke
with Martha John and Kathi Bourke

HFY Publishing, LLC

Published by HFY Publishing, LLC
2011 N Country Club Drive, Columbia, Missouri 65201 USA

Kindle and Amazon CreateSpace versions first printed in the
United States of America by HFY Publishing, LLC in July, 2011.

ISBN# 978-0-61551205-1   (HFY Publishing, LLC)

Table of Contents

Acknowledgments - Jim and Martha

Most of all, we would like to extend thanks to our family and friends for their support, their love, and their tolerance through the long years of our being care-providers and the recovery period after. We know that during that time we forgot birthdays and anniversaries, stepped on more than a few toes, and were not always entirely rational. Your help and forbearance made our road smoother in ways you will never know. Thank you.

And in particular, we would like to thank Martha's sister, Susan Newstead. You were always there to listen, help, and offer advice. You aided us in many ways, not the least of which was coming to provide respite care, and taking on as a solo task what two of us would normally do, in order to give us a break.

Thanks are also due to Lori, Lisa, and the rest of the staff at Missouri River Hospice. At the end of Martha Sr's journey, you made it possible for us to keep her at home with us. You taught us what to expect, how to handle it, and gave us the strength to face it without fear.

Likewise, a special thank you to Marilyn at Home Alone, who allowed us respite breaks that kept us going. It was comforting to know that Martha Sr was in good hands. And to Ruth, who was able to help us care for Martha Sr overnight towards the end.

The Alzheimer's Association in general was a help and a great resource. But in particular, we owe a debt of gratitude to the staff and volunteers at the Mid-Missouri Chapter. Having someplace to turn for support and a shoulder to cry on - a place where others understood what it was we were going through, because they had been through it - was incredibly valuable. Thank you, Linda Newkirk and Joetta Coen.

We would like to thank Kathy Brewer, Sarah Caitlin-Dupuy, Patty Gibbs, Margo Lynn Hablutzel, James Kasper, Carol Monahan, Marie Pickard, Carla Tilghman, Steve Tuck, Annie Tremmel Wilcox, and Celeste Zink, all who offered suggestions and encouragement as the writing and revision of this work progressed. The finished product is much stronger because of their feedback.

Acknowledgments - John and Kathi

A special thanks to Jim and Martha for the opportunity to collaborate on this particular journey. Your insight, advice, and hard work in making this book a reality has been invaluable.

There are no words sufficient to express the gratitude we have for family, friends, and coworkers. Your tolerance for our bewilderment, anger, despair, and irrationality..."thank you" is not enough. We're not sure what is.

A special thank you to the proprietors and employees of the Villa Rosa Restaurant in Quincy, MA, (Maria and Donna especially, for making Georgia's days a bit brighter) and Stella's Restaurant in Milton, MA (particularly Georgia and Kathy!)

Thanks to Beverly Moore, owner of Alzheimer's Coaching, Inc., who was an invaluable resource during the early days. South Shore Elder Services recommended her and without her guidance, the journey would have been a thousand times rougher. Thanks also to the staff of both the Hancock Park Adult Day Center and Hellenic House. You have our gratitude for your knowledge and empathy. Likewise a special thank you to Jeanne Johnson who offered us respite when it was so sorely needed.

ElderCareOnline was perhaps our overall one-stop resource. Thank you to all its members who listened to our concerns and frustrations, ready to give much-needed advice whenever needed.

Most of all, we wish to thank all our friends at LiveJournal, Daily Kos and ePluribus Media. All of you witnessed this journey as it happened, and provided kindness and support. We particularly wish to thank Gary Dreslinski, moderator of "The Real LJ Idol" writing contest/community, which provided Kathi with the invaluable opportunity to put what she was experiencing into words. In addition, we'd like to thank Roxy Caraway, Paul Thomas and Tanya Harned for lending a sympathetic ear as well as feedback for John's online care-giving contributions.

Last but by no means least, we are thankful to Rebecca Putnam, Donna Nichols and Debbie Brett for their feedback on the sample chapters.

How to use this book

Her Final Year/His First Year can be used in two ways. One, it can be read as a conventional memoir, to gain an overall sense of what it is like to be a care-provider for someone with dementia. You can just start at the beginning and read. This will be particularly useful for the friends and relatives of someone who is in a care-giving role, since it will give some insight into the stresses and challenges they are facing, and likely what kind of help and comfort they will need.

The other way the book can be used explains why it is structured the way it is. Every Alzheimer's patient, every family with someone who suffers from age-related dementia, will have an individual path to walk. But certain things will likely happen along the way, though sometimes in a different order or over a longer or shorter period of time. We decided to combine our experiences and collapse the time period into a more generic metaphor – a way of turning the experience universal, accessible to all.

So here you will find 12 months – twelve "stages" of care-giving, if you will. And in each month there are multiple entries, drawn from email correspondence, LiveJournal entries, and blog posts. These are all primary sources – what we were thinking and saying as we were going through the experience of care-giving (though there have been some revisions of the original entries for clarity and to comply with "fair use" doctrines). They generally follow a chronological order, but not a strict one because in some instances the things we were experiencing in one family seemed to make sense to relate to things experienced in a different order in the other family.

The idea is that someone who is in the role of being a care-giver can look through the different month descriptions and figure out about where they are, into which month or stage of care-giving their own situation best fits. Then they can read that chapter to see what we were going through at the time, and the ways we sought to cope with it.

We hope that this will provide not just information – helpful tips in terms of coping strategies, what worked or didn't work to deal with a problem – but that it will also provide something of an instant support group for a care-provider. That it will let them know that what they are experiencing is not unique, that we shared the same fears and joys, the same emotions and stresses. This is why the material is all in the first-person voice of what we were experiencing at that time. It is intended to be a conversation with the reader, just as it is something of a conversation between the four different voices of the authors.

Much of this material is *intensely* personal, and some of it is more than a little embarrassing. We have decided to share it, and show it as it was, because we deeply believe that it is extremely important that anyone entering into a care-giving relationship understand the reality of what they will likely experience. You *will* make mistakes. You *will* think you are going to go crazy. You *will* sometimes feel crushed by the isolation and stress. You *will* sometimes resent, or even hate, the person for whom you are caring. You *will* get into arguments with family and friends, and say and do things you might later regret. These things are all completely normal human reactions to the situation you will be in. You have probably been told this before. But knowing that abstractly is nothing like seeing how others have actually experienced it. How *we* experienced it.

Following *Her Final Year* is a shorter book titled *His First Year*. This is a much more straight-forward memoir, and all the entries are in actual chronological order over the span of a single year. It recounts the recovery period for the care-giver, the process of re-defining your role in the world, of coming to understand a bit about what you have been through and how it has changed you. It may be shorter than the first part of the book, but it is just as important from our perspective. Why? Well, because no matter how intense the care-giving experience will be, it will eventually come to an end. Life will go on.

Foreword

Two roads diverged in a wood, and I –
I took the one less traveled by,
And that has made all the difference.
 – Robert Frost, **"The Road Not Taken"**

We often hear that life is a journey, and it's the journey that matters – the path and the experiences – more than anything else. The family faced with a loved one struggling against the onset of Alzheimer's Disease often faces new, unexpected twists and turns in their journey.

Both Jim's and John's families faced this several times throughout the care-giving experience. When their loved ones were in the early stages, minor changes to daily life were required – a small diversion to the normal routine, a minor turn in the road. As the disease progressed and care-giving needs changed, the roads diverged from their original paths. Both families opted to care for their loved one at home throughout all or as much of the process as possible. For the Downey/John family, Martha Sr's initial frailty was taken into consideration and routines adjusted accordingly. For the Bourke/Smith family, Georgia's mobility factored in and new routines came into play – running errands, visits to friends or jobs around the house became somewhat regulated and structured into routines, but slowly changed as some aspects became increasingly difficult to pursue or continue.

Every week, sometimes every day, little changes to daily habits provided further course corrections as each family charted a new path into unfamiliar territory. At some point, care-giving began to have more of an impact in terms of time and availability requirements; this led to, and was exacerbated by, changes in income – which also had repercussions into areas like the personal health and health insurance options of the care-givers, in addition to altering options that normally required a small financial outlay. In short, everything had an effect – the small changes compounded, built one upon the other in a spiral of change and isolation.

This is why we have written this memoir – to offer some perspective on those changes, as we were going through them. The changes we experienced were both positive and negative, and they were always individual, sometimes having an impact on one partner but not the other, sometimes having an impact on everyone but in completely different ways. No single decision is "right" or "wrong" – there is only the best decision made at the time, and for the individual situation. No other family entering into the care-giving experience will have the exact same reactions, just as none will face the exact same stresses and challenges. But in seeing what we experienced, and the decisions we each made, over the arc of care-giving and then recovery, perhaps you will be better able to understand your own path, choose your own road.

Martha Sr.   Georgia

Introduction

Jim's story:

My wife, Martha John ("Martha Jr" henceforth), and I moved to Columbia, Missouri in 1992. It had been Martha Jr's hometown, was close to mine (St. Louis), and would be suitable for starting my book conservation business. Being in Columbia also meant that we would be close to Martha Jr's mother, who was in her seventies and starting to have some health issues. Through the decade of the '90s as we were busy with our professional lives (I expanded my book conservation business and opened a large art gallery in 1996, my wife went into partnership with another architect) we saw Martha Sr frequently, and saw that she was having increasing problems with a number of health issues, as well as some memory problems. But it was mostly minor things, and she was happy to continue to live on her own. We did tell her that when she wanted, we would sell our home and move in with her (the family home where she had lived since the 1950s).

That time came in 2001-2002, after Martha Sr had a couple of minor auto accidents. Shortly thereafter, she stopped driving – but as we were there with her, it was a minimal disruption in her life. Both my wife and I had a fair amount of flexibility in our schedules, so we could run errands with Martha Sr whenever necessary.

Things continued along fairly smoothly. Martha Sr got along fine on her own during the day, was perfectly capable of seeing to her own meals, though we helped her whenever she wanted as she had started needing to rely on a walker for stability in getting around. But then in January 2004 I came home one afternoon to find her on the floor of her bedroom. She had been trying to move a stack of books from one side of the room to the other, and had left her walker. She had lost her balance, fallen, and broken her hip.

It was a fairly routine break, though, and surgery to repair the hip went well. But now Martha Sr was in her mid 80s. The hospital-ization also took a real toll on Martha Sr. She came home more frail, and more mentally scattered than previously. We found out later that this is a fairly common outcome of such surgery for someone her age. We shifted our schedules around, with my wife Martha Jr spending most of the daytime hours at home to help her mom recover. But that was hard on my wife, and hurt her architecture practice significantly.

The previous fall I had decided that the time had come for me to close my art gallery, and slated that for June 2004. I still had plenty of book conservation work to do, as well as a novel I had finished and wanted to get published. My wife and I talked, and decided that it made the most sense for me to just work from home, where I would be able to do the bulk of the care-giving for her mom. We didn't entirely understand what that actually meant at that time. We learned.

John's story:

I moved from Massachusetts to Oklahoma in 1997 when the company I'd been with outsourced my department. The change of scenery and opportunity to live near some good friends was an important factor in the decision, but I missed my extended family. Several of my brothers and sisters had married and were raising their own families; I was frequently absent from many of the shared events, and realized that my nieces and nephews were growing up without my getting to see them and share in their lives. When an opportunity presented itself to take a job as a consultant back in Massachusetts, I said good bye to my friends and moved back, driving a good-sized U-Haul and towing my car. I'd met Kathi online and we'd gotten to know each other well enough that, when she learned I was moving back to the area, she helped me find a place to live that would accept dogs. When I finally rolled into Milton, she met me at the house I would be renting for the next 6 months.

Rent was high, and I subsequently moved to Braintree, MA and finally to Providence, RI in an attempt to find suitable inexpensive living. Both Kathi and I loved the place in Providence, but we began to notice that it was increasingly a problem for her mother Georgia to make the trip. That was when the first hints and signs of problems began to really manifest. We'd noticed some issues before that, but chalked them up to depression and retirement.

We began to think something else was in play.

When we decided to get married, I made arrangements to move back to Milton; we thought we could find a place near Georgia that would work. Then Georgia had her first precipitous drop, and we realized that we had to accelerate our schedule. The best option would be if I moved in with them and searched for a place from there. Around the same time, my brother Michael had just announced his own engagement and planned wedding date, and we winced at how soon it was. We were going to have to marry before that in order to comply with Georgia's wishes that Kathi and I were married before I could move in with them. We arranged for a small ceremony, by necessity making it very limited in scope, and married in April of 2003.

By then, the likelihood of Alzheimer's – or at least some form of dementia – was obvious.

As a consultant who worked from my home office whenever I wasn't on-site with a client, and with my previous experience working with Alzheimer's patients, we decided that I'd take on the role and responsibility of keeping an eye on Kathi's mom. Once the diagnosis of Alzheimer's was made, we discussed the various options and committed ourselves to caring for Georgia at home for as long as possible.

As with Jim & Martha Jr, we didn't really understand the scope of what that commitment entailed.

How we came to know one another, and to write this book

One of the most devastating aspects of being a care-provider is the sense of isolation. The longer you are in the role, the more you start to feel cut off from friends and family. Partly this is due to the dementia your patient experiences, as it is unsettling for others to be around (and hence they don't come by as often). Partly it is just due to exhaustion – it is hard to be social when you are always ready to collapse from lack of sleep. And partly it is due to the simple intensity of the experience, which most other people do not understand unless they have been through it.

This isolation – this alienation – cuts you off from your usual support mechanisms, and tends to feed upon itself.

In an attempt to counter this, both John and Jim started blogging about their experiences as care-providers. Some of these blog posts were put up at the political site Daily Kos, where each of us had been active in discussing politics. We each saw the other's postings about the experience, and started participating in discussions together on the topic. Soon we realized that we had a great deal in common, though the details of our care-giving experiences differed here and there.

Those blog posts got a fair amount of attention from the Daily Kos community, even though they were not strictly related to the ostensible focus of the site. We discovered that there were a lot of people who either had been through similar experiences, or expected to do so one day, or had a family member who was going through it. We found that there was a great need for information, for community, for help in combating the isolation.

In the months which followed the end of our respective care-providing, we continued to share notes about the process of recovery. And one of the things that each of us was considering was how to do something to help others who would be in a care-giving role. Specifically, we were each thinking of what we could do to help other men who found themselves in this role, since most of the memoir material available was written from the point-of-view of a woman care-provider. We thought we should combine our efforts, and use the material we had been writing as the basis of a book.

This book is the result. Additional supporting information, images and links can be found on the associated website at:
www.herfinalyear.com

Her Final Year
A Care-Giving Memoir

and

His First Year
A Journey of Recovery

January
Suspicions that something is wrong

From the New York Times, 13 July 2010:[1]

> The current formal criteria for diagnosing Alzheimer's require steadily progressing dementia – memory loss and an inability to carry out day-to-day activities, like dressing or bathing – along with a pathologist's report of plaque and another abnormality, known as tangles, in the brain after death.
>
> But researchers are now convinced that the disease is present a decade or more before dementia.
>
> "Our thinking has changed dramatically," said Dr. Paul Aisen, an Alzheimer's researcher at the University of California, San Diego, and a member of one of the groups formulating the new guidelines. "We now view dementia as a late stage in the process."
>
> The new guidelines include criteria for three stages of the disease: preclinical disease, mild cognitive impairment due to Alzheimer's disease and, lastly, Alzheimer's dementia. The guidelines should make diagnosing the final stage of the disease in people who have dementia more definitive.

But this isn't how the disease was viewed, or understood, just a decade ago. As with cancer a generation previously, there was a reluctance to discuss a diagnosis of Alzheimer's "too soon." Because there was little or nothing that could really be done for the Alzheimer's patient. A diagnosis of Alzheimer's meant little more than consigning a patient to a modern madhouse. So people would tend to write off memory problems as nothing more than typical aging, for as long as they could.

Georgia's first obvious sign was the computer at work. She was unable to figure it out, and it frustrated her.

Throughout the course of the disease progression, until shortly before she entered the nursing home, she kept experiencing periods where she wanted to learn how to use Kathi's computer. She even went so far as to purchase a computer learning CD from a television commercial – it was one of the two items we noticed that led to our having to remove and cancel her credit card, which was difficult for Kathi. To her, "Mom" had always been a financial whiz, in addition to a very determined and highly intelligent woman who was capable of learning anything she needed or wanted to.

She began to forget little things, and to compensate (and hide the problems) she would compartmentalize areas of her life and reduce the scope of her interactivity as needed in order to keep on top of things.

That was one of the factors that left me as a target for her frustration after I moved in with them, as I was a change element: I was a factor she couldn't directly control or limit, or hadn't included in her initial plans for how she compensated, so she appeared to feel more threatened that her slips would be detected. At least, that's how I'm interpreting some of those initial confrontations we had early on, now in retrospect.

(Kathi's LiveJournal entry. 3/15/03)
Weird

Mom *[Georgia]* is acting sort of weird this morning. I can't put a finger on it...she went to bed last night around 7. She was already up, dressed, and asleep in her chair in the living room when I came down for breakfast. When I asked her if she wanted me to make her something, she said she wasn't hungry.

I dunno, something feels weird...can't put a finger on it, don't know what exactly it is, but nevertheless, it's there...

(Kathi's LiveJournal entry. 6/9/03)
Lashing Out, 'Just Words'

One thing about Mom *[Georgia]* – she asks you to do something, you do it NOW lest you become the target of her wrath. She's always been like that. I've told John about it. Anyway, she suddenly threw a fit – how dare he NOT move when she asked him – and it escalated from there. He ended up storming out of the house with the dogs, hopped in his car, and drove off just as I pulled up. She then lashed out at me, saying that she wanted us to move out, this is HER house, there's too many people, etc., etc. She then went up to bed. John returned a few minutes later and didn't want to talk about it. We both tossed and turned all night, trying to decide what to do.

She forgot all about it yesterday. I mentioned it to her after I came home from work; she replied, "I said THAT? Doesn't he know that they're just words? I want the two of you here."

(Kathi's LiveJournal entry. 6/13/03)
Triggers

Let's just say that this past weekend her behavior's been going off the deep end more and more frequently, but at least she *[Georgia]* doesn't stay in the particular mode – she manages to "snap back" to her old self within a few minutes. I'm not even going to go into what actually happened, or else I'll be hanging onto the ceiling with my fingernails.

Comment from John: Still newlywed ourselves, Kathi and I

packed up the car and the three of us traveled out of state to attend the wedding of my brother, Michael. We quickly realized that the break in Georgia's normal routine, combined with the long drive, was an unwelcome change.

(Kathi's LiveJournal entry. 6/27/03)
Lashing Out, Not Traveling Well

Mom *[Georgia]* was another story. She began verbally attacking John for every single thing he uttered. I don't know how he managed to keep his cool.

She insulted John's parents when we got to my brother-in-law's house. She called me a bitch a half dozen times because I kept meandering between indoors and out talking to everyone rather than close myself off in a corner with her. We ended up putting her in a hotel room by herself three doors down because neither of us had the strength to look after her.

She brought over $1,000 with her. In large bills.

She didn't pack anything except for underwear and what she's wearing to the wedding. At home I tried to help her get together a couple more outfits (we're here until Sunday), but she screamed at me to stop treating her like a child. So I let her be.

(Email excerpt, Martha Jr to her sister. 8/26/05)
Rain rain, go away

You know how any change at all seems to confuse Mom *[Martha Sr]* for a while? The whole thing with her nails REALLY had her on edge on Monday. Her nail appointment was at 5:00 and we had told her that Jim would take her and I'd pick her up about 6:00 when she was done. But apparently she kept worrying about it all afternoon: when was her appointment, should she get ready, was I coming home to take her, shouldn't she be getting ready to leave, etc, etc, etc. Poor Jim was frazzled by the time he got her dropped off. Once she gets used to it, she should be alright, but it's the getting-used-to-it part that takes a while.

February
Detection, diagnoses and enabling decisions

Something's wrong, somewhere. But you don't really want to believe it. Because that would mean something you don't really want to face. So, you try and find reasons, excuses, make allowances. But still, you see a doctor...

At least in our experience with Georgia, the decision to see a doctor was a given.

Sort of.

Georgia began to get frustrated with her current doctor at the local hospital, and started talking a lot about her former doctor, who was located in the city (Boston). After going 'round and 'round with her about going in to see her doctor, and even putting in calls to her doctor and the doctor's on-call backup (neither of which was returned), I did some digging and found Georgia's old doc was still practicing, part-time, at the hospital in Boston.

We made an appointment, and Georgia was tickled that he remembered her and wanted to see her. (Tickled enough that she didn't get too upset that we made the appointment without involving her.)

That's right around the time that she made her first plummet and hit her first plateau. (At least, made a noticeable decline and hit a noticeable plateau – there were likely many minor ones that we'd missed along the way, before the various issues became blatant and unmistakable.)

(Excerpt – John's blog "A Life's Worth of Memories" 03/11/08)
"All day staring at the ceiling"

Shortly after Kathi and I began dating, Georgia left her job as a tax accountant and began spending inordinate amounts of time at home, puttering 'round. I would occasionally swing by and bring lunch, or take her out to a restaurant. She was tickled by the attention, and we often called Kathi at her work so that Georgia could say "Oh, guess where I went to lunch...and with who."

The events seemed so trivial, yet they were opportunities for Georgia to thrill and tease, and interact. It occurred to me that something might be wrong – a feeling that Kathi echoed when we discussed it, but it was something we couldn't put our fingers on. Neither could Georgia. It's a feeling that I recall clearly now whenever I listen to the song "Unwell" by Matchbox Twenty,[2] particularly the opening: *"All day staring at the ceiling / Making friends with shadows on my wall..."*

Just before I moved in, in preparation of getting married and becoming a permanent member of the family, Georgia had begun to spend very large amounts of time watching old movies, over and over and over and over again; it was a habit that she continued during the first few months of our marriage. It was a combination of the Alzheimer's Disease and the longstanding, long-suppressed depression she'd felt over the loss of her husband. It was definitely a warning sign, but it was also a source of comfort for her – she could remember the movies. Perhaps in the same way that this music helps me recall events and scenes from life and from writing, the movies served to help preserve other precious areas of her mind. She was very determined and very stubborn that way. The song seemed to echo that, as well as Georgia's attempts to describe and fight whatever was happening to her: *"Feeling like I'm headed for a breakdown..."*

She fought the onset of her illness, even though she suspected what it was and feared it – she had seen it in her brother, and couldn't bring herself to go visit him at this time even though she desperately missed him; he was her last surviving sibling, and she'd cut off communication with him years before due to a painful argument.

But I'm not crazy, I'm just a little unwell

She stopped taking all of her medication. Her doctor had stopped paying attention to her and had given her medications that she questioned, but could no longer remember why. She reminisced about the doctor she used to see, and how great he was...

(Kathi's LiveJournal entry. 5/13/03)
High blood sedimentation, low memory scores

John and I finally convinced Mom *[Georgia]* to see her old doctor at the Mass General; John took her there last week. Doctor's findings aren't promising: Her blood sedimentation level is around 69 (it's supposed to be in the teens if you're female). Anything higher means that something's going on, but it takes another battery of tests to ascertain what. She also failed both memory tests he gave her. The doc declined to diagnose anything until he gets the rest of the test results and the findings from the MRI she had back in January. Here's the kicker: He'll only talk to either John or me about it, as he's not sure Mom could comprehend anything he diagnoses. That just kills me. Her mental faculties might be faulty at this point, but she's far from not comprehending everything.

> *Comment from Martha Jr:* This can be the hard thing – deciding when to take over being the 'responsible' one. Many of the people in my support group mentioned this too – that it took a while for them to realize that they had to talk directly to the doctor, because their loved one would either not understand or, more likely, would forget what was said almost as soon as it was said. Sometimes it took a while to convince the doctor – especially if it was a general practitioner or something – that he needed to talk to them instead of to

the patient. We were fortunate in that Mom's doctor started talking to me very early, because I needed to see her into the room anyway because of her physical frailty.

(Excerpt – John's blog "A Life's Worth of Memories" 03/11/08)
"I'm not crazy, I'm just a little impaired"

Georgia knew something was wrong. She didn't want Kathi to worry. And she didn't trust her current doctor. The next line from "Unwell"[3] comes to mind: *"I'm not crazy, I'm just a little impaired..."*

Kathi and I tracked down Georgia's old doctor. He was only a few years younger than Georgia, but still practicing part-time out of a large hospital in the city. He remembered Georgia. Georgia was thrilled (perhaps a tad fearful) that we'd found him for her and set up an appointment; she went, however, and we were glad she did. A few days without her meds had cleared up her mind substantially, but much longer would likely result in catastrophe – several were not supposed to be quit "cold turkey" and several were crucial for her blood pressure and cholesterol. Her old doc cleared nearly half the meds off the list. Several were never supposed to be taken together. We were ripshit at the regular doc; we couldn't keep the old doc as Georgia's primary, but we did find a better doc locally. It was in the meeting with Georgia's old doc that we also received the dreaded suspected diagnosis of Alzheimer's Disease, possibly accompanied by one or two other dementia-inducing conditions. The road toward a full diagnosis and treatment plan began, starting with Georgia's newest doc a week or two later.

(Email excerpt, Martha Jr to the family. 11/17/05)
General update on mom

On Tuesday, Mom *[Martha Sr]* had a Cognitive Test (scheduled three months ago by Dr. S, the neurologist), followed by an appointment at Dr. S's office. It was an "on" day for her, by which I mean she was doing well and not as confused as she some-times is. As a result she did very well on her tests. The memory portions were significantly down, but everything else (judgment, abstract reasoning, etc.) was in the normal range.

The first part of the test was the "mini mental" which, I have learned, is a standard often used with Alzheimer's patients. The people in my support group can all tell me what level their loved one tests at. It's a score out of 30 and Mom got a 26 – actually a very good score. This test is often used, apparently, to determine whether someone can go into "assisted living" or must have a greater level of care.

Anyway. We went to Dr. S's office and met with his Nurse Practitioner, J. She looked at Mom's medications list and chatted with her, trying a few other physical tests on her. Then she suggested that, if we want, we could start her on Aricept, which she kept calling a 'memory drug.' She gave us information about the whole class of such drugs – three that are about the same, Aricept being the most well known – and one, Namenda (sp?), that can be a 'helper' drug or, sometimes, stand alone. For Aricept, you start with a lower dose and ramp up to the regular dose after a few weeks. It takes about six to eight weeks to reach full effectiveness. Some people don't tolerate it well (nausea). But those who do sometimes see increased memory function and, at the least, see a slowing or halting of the decline in memory.

She gave us a starter pack and told us it was our decision whether Mom should start using it. We haven't decided yet. The people in my support group all said it really is good and has had a good effect on people. But one mentioned that you need to watch out for low blood pressure.

Mom didn't seem to care whether we start it or not (and, by now, has entirely forgotten the issue). As an aside, we have noticed that any time Mom's routine is disturbed – unusual activities, vis-its, etc. – she becomes more disoriented and sometimes more cranky afterward. This one was the same. All day yesterday, Jim said, she was more confused and out-of-it, to the point where, he said, if she had taken the test that day, her result would probably have been very different.

So that's where we stand on that. We are going to let the Ginkoba run out (we're about out of it anyway) because if we start the Aricept we're supposed to stop that. But we haven't actually decided whether to start it or not. If you have some input on the issue, please let us know.

(Kathi's LiveJournal entry. 6/27/03)
Nightly Stupors and the old MRI

I am having such an incredibly difficult time doing this. Sometimes I think if I had no scruples, I'd kick her *[Georgia]* until she died just to get what will be over and done with for my anxiety's sake. I realize how selfish thinking this is; I try not to feel guilty, but every so often I'll burst into wracking sobs for no apparent reason. The past few days (last night included) I've been somewhat drinking myself to sleep – not pass out, but enough to numb myself. I almost never do this otherwise.

I didn't post this before, but we finally located the films from her last MRI and hand-delivered them to her old doctor the other night – we went into Massachusetts General Hospital and slid them under his door. I expect we'll hear from him sometime next week as to the next step. If it turns out that yes, she has dementia or (God help me) Alzheimer's, that's one thing. If, on the other hand, they don't find anything and age is just making her more and more ornery, I'm going to scream, kick, and destroy something, because I'll be damned if either John or I are her targets. I display enough of her damage, I don't need more.

(Kathi's LiveJournal entry. 6/30/03)
Good News, Bad News, and more tests

Good News: She *[Georgia]* doesn't show any signs of having a stroke, brain injury, tumor, etc.

Bad News: Her doctor wants her to undergo a PET scan for Alzheimer's as it's the only other option.

Postscript: He added that, knowing her for as long as he has, the concept of aging is not settling well with her; hence, her outbursts, etc. That is, if she doesn't have Alzheimer's.

Did I ever mention that my uncle (her only living sibling) has Alzheimer's? He's been in a nursing home for the past 6 years. I haven't seen him since he was diagnosed. We haven't had contact with his family since he started "acting weird", as Mom put it back then. She stopped talking to him because she had "no patience for his gibberish".

(John's diary. 2/7/04)
Hoppin'

– Malachy's, Quincy

Last few days pretty hectic. Stopped in here for a pint, after checking out some things at WalMart & picking up some items at Roche Bros. Georgia is home with the dogs, and Kathi is working. I'm going to pick up some extender cables at CompUSA, plus a usb-ps2 connector, so I can finish incorporating the workstations at my desk. I also have to be my filing and organizing started.

Work with X continues to have its highs and lows, though the highs are less than rewarding. No bites on the job search effort yet. And with the upsets at the house with the Alzheimer's-induced fluctuations that Georgia is undergoing, I haven't been able to work on my writing in peace.

Comment by John: This was about the time that we could still leave Georgia alone (with the dogs, at least) for short periods; the dogs seemed to help keep her focused, and she'd putter relatively safely.

The amount of time that I felt safe leaving her alone started out to be fairly large – she was doing pretty well and had a lot of autonomy – but as the disease progressed the margin of safety dwindled and we didn't feel that she could be left without company for as long a period.

Eventually, I started taking her out with me.

Kathi and I updated her wardrobe, and Georgia started coming with me to various local clients as my "assistant." She loved it.

We drove Kathi crazy, though. We started showing up at her work to show off our matching business attire...something which her mom really enjoyed doing, for various reasons I suppose.

I think Kathi vacillated between secretly enjoying the visits, sometimes envying the relationship Georgia had struck up with me, and sometimes cringing at the sudden appearance of "the Bobbsey Twins."

The effect on Georgia, however, was very positive...and it helped to expand the depth to which she trusted and felt safe in my company, which meant she'd open up and tell me things that she felt she couldn't tell her daughter – always the proud and strong Greek mom, she didn't want to have her daughter worry when or if she was having issues.

That level of trust was very helpful. If we hadn't stumbled into it, it's quite possible that Georgia would have had some more serious issues arise before either Kathi or I knew something new was happening.

One of the biggest "highs" of care-giving with Georgia at that time were the opportunities to bring her with me on consulting assignments as my assistant. She was always graceful and professional, which – for me – was like looking back into her past, and seeing the determined, intelligent woman that she'd been for her entire life.

(John's diary. 5/6/04)
Penny for your thoughts

– Villa Rosa

Kathi, Georgia & I stopped in for lunch after taking Georgia to her neurology appointment. Dr. Penny said he wasn't convinced that it was Alzheimer's, suspecting that depression plays a role.

Part and parcel with spending more time with Georgia by having

her on the occasional consulting appointment and running errands with her was that we established a better understanding of each other. One of the perks of this was helping her cope with her memory and mental lapses. I encouraged Georgia with clues and triggers to help her remember things like names. The neurologist's name – "Dr. Penny" – was one example. I placed a penny in Georgia's hand while we waited for him, after the second time she asked me his name. A minute or so later, I asked her the doctor's name. She looked at the penny in her hand and smiled. "Dr. Penny," she replied with a grin. When he entered, she didn't need to look at her hand. In fact, I think she'd pocketed the penny by that point. But she did remember his name.

Comment from John: This was one of those doubled-edged sword things. The blade cuts both ways – my helpful "hint" to Georgia to help her alleviate the stress of not remembering the doctor's name and help her feel more at ease likely factored into the doctor's evaluation, as from his perspective Georgia was able to recall his name without assistance.

I didn't really think of that at the time.

Continuation of this thought... Folks suffering from dementia, particularly in the early stages, do a lot to try and compensate as well as hide their affliction. Care-givers, in spite of the best of intentions, may be enabling a form of denial in some ways – that was the thought I was trying to articulate above, wondering if my assistance to Georgia to help her with the doctor's name was just one way of potentially helping her hide her symptoms, even though it was also a positive reinforcement of my role / relationship with her as care-giver/protector/assistant etc.

(Kathi's LiveJournal entry. 5/6/04)
Dementia Depressions, Neurology 101

I've been trying to wrap my brain this around since Mom's neurological evaluation this morning:

According to the neuro doc, she *[Georgia]* may not have Alzheimer's.

I won't go into the nitty-gritty as to what the evaluation involved. At the conclusion, though, as the three of us clustered in the doc's office, he gave us his preliminary findings:

1. There is definitely some sort of dementia going on with her. The reason why he's doubting it's Alzheimer's, though, is because she's just too articulate. She also has been in more or less the

same "pattern" for too long – she's not any worse, but neither is she better. Most Alzheimer's patients decline, plateau, decline, plateau, then start declining at a quicker rate. In other words, she should've been already beginning the quicker decline, and she's not. Not by a long shot.

2. The reason for the "other dementia"? During the physical portion of the neuro exam, she showed definite signs of something going on with her frontal lobe (the part of the brain that's behind the forehead). The MRI she's having tomorrow should verify it.

3. She's in the throes of a very deep, very longstanding depression that's never been treated. The doc said that if she had Alzheimer's, she never would've answered his questions the way she did. She understood exactly what he asked; she answered without using "word salad" (i.e., substituting words for other words, making mish-mash of grammar/phrases we'd take for granted – in other words, she understood and answered intelligently.) When he asked if there was a history of depression in the family, she said yes, everyone's suffered from it, "including my daughter" she added (thanks, Ma). Depression can mimic Alzheimer's in a lot of cases, especially the apathy part.

4. The doc stressed that it's not to say there isn't an Alzheimer's element. There may very well be, but at this point he's more concerned with the frontal lobe stuff and the depression.

Anyway, she had the blood work done after the evaluation and has the MRI tomorrow morning. He will let us know either way what the findings are.

I'm not jumping with joy over this. Dementia is dementia, whether it's Alzheimer's, Pick's Disease, Lewy Body, vascular, Huntington's ...there's too many others I could name. He's put her on 25 mg of Zoloft. I nearly burst into laughter, as I was the Zoloft Queen for too many years to count. He'll gradually increase the Zoloft – depending, of course, on how she reacts to it.

After all this, we got new shades cut for all the bathrooms, then went shopping, then lunch. And there we are.

March
Confirmation & preparation

The doctor delivers the hard fact: Alzheimer's. Now what the hell do you do?

Chances are you'll start reading, researching online resources. You'll be overwhelmed with advice and information. The task before you will seem huge, impossible. How do you make sense of everything? How do you prepare for all the challenges before you?

But because you care, because you want to do the right thing, you plow into the mass of material. Read memoirs like this one. See what advice the professionals offer. Slowly, it starts to seem like a manageable problem, though one which will leave you still feeling overwhelmed and maybe even a little angry now and then.

It takes time. To adjust your life. To adjust your mindset. To come to terms.

It may seem like you don't have that time – you're already in a care giving role. That's OK. The truth likely is that you have already started making the necessary adjustments, and the others will come along bit by bit.

One thing you want to see to almost immediately: the legal and financial stuff. Get this done early, so that you can consult with the patient if you need to, get signatures while they are still arguably competent to sign legal papers. Do you need to establish a trust to deal with financial or property matters? Is there a Will in effect? Do you have a Durable Power of Attorney for both Health and Financial decisions? Are there insurance forms which need to be filed? How about applications for government programs? Ideally, we all have this stuff resolved while we're still young and "of sound mind and body," but all too many people don't get around to it.

> *I think it can't be too important to stress just how crucial it is to have things like home ownership and property decisions identified early in the process.*

> *Financial factors pertaining to income and ownership, upkeep and maintenance become very important, very quickly.*

> *Friends of mine in Oklahoma had their mom living with them in an in-law apartment; this worked very well for them, as it gave everyone their own living space and privacy, but kept the family close when times of medical or financial duress came about.*

> *If Kathi and I had an in-law apartment for Georgia, and the house itself was in Kathi's name or if we were renting it, we wouldn't have had some of the worries. Fortunately, we were able to gather all the disparate parts and figure out what the status was, then meet with an elder attorney who helped us get everything organized.*

(Email excerpt, Martha Jr to the family. 2/24/06) Pneumonia

Just a quick note. We've been trading a cold around here for the last month or so. For about the last three weeks, Mom *[Martha Sr]* has had increasing congestion and coughing. Earlier this week she had started sounding wheezy a lot, especially when she had been coughing, of course. But we decided it was time to take her to the doctor. We got an appointment for this afternoon with Dr. M, who examined her and determined that she has a little bit of pneumonia in one portion of her right lung. He gave her a five-day course of antibiotics which he said should clear it right up, and she took the first one with her snack after we got home. Looks like we caught it early, thank goodness. We're going to try to keep her resting for a few days, and we expect a good recovery. We'll let you know if anything changes with that.

Just thought you should know.

(John's diary. 1/24/04)
Just a note

– 99 Restaurant and Pub, Pembroke

Georgia and I stopped in for lunch, leaving the dogs in the car. We'd run a few errands already, including bringing the dogs to the vet where Missy's leg and paw were examined. We'll stop in to my folks for a brief visit, then Thomas' grave. I'll fix Dad's computer while we're there. I bought this journal – plus a backup – en route.

The symbol on the front cover is the Chinese symbol for "Peace." It's a word of many functions, and subtleties of meaning. I've often used it at the closing of email messages or electronic posts.

> *Comment from John:* Thomas' grave: Thomas was my youngest sister's first child, who died two days before his second birthday.

> Part of my grieving process was to write a short story called "The Mayor of Puddlewharf Lane" which Georgia read, loved, and remembered. She even tried to help edit it; had she not been affected by the dementia, she'd have been a tremendous boon. The dementia, however, got in her way.

> She still always remembered the story, however, and got sad when the memory of my sister's son – "the little boy who died" – surfaced. Remarkably, while she made the connection between the correct sister and the loss of the child, she

was also very much socially aware and adept enough not to make offhand mention of "the little boy who died" when we were at family gatherings with my sister, who (understandably) is still grievously affected by the loss.

(John's diary. 2/1/04)
Scattered

– Applebee's, North Quincy, 2:20 pm

It's SuperBowl Sunday, and Georgia, Kathi and I have stopped in for lunch after visiting Marge, one of Georgia's friends from church. Marge had no immediate family nearby, so Georgia and Kathi – and sometimes all three of us – would visit her on Sundays after church. (We even started to bring the dogs on occasion, as Georgia had thought they'd do well visiting the other residents. She was right – the residents and the dogs loved it. But those visits were extra-tiring.) I've not been able to find a peaceful moment to journal uninterrupted since getting this journal a week ago. The home office is in the midst of renovation – Kath & I bought & assembled new workstations. Most of Saturday was a waste – I was unable to focus on any of my own tasks. So far today, I've only been able to get partway through. Kathi assisted with the workstation assembly, and we picked up a new display to help me consolidate the various systems into the single workstations. I'm looking forward to an increase in personal productivity, and an increase in organization. Finally.

(Excerpt – John's blog "A Life's Worth of Memories" 03/11/08)
"I've been talking in my sleep"

Pretty soon they'll come to get me

Georgia, at this time, had several fights with us – mostly me – trying to claim that we were trying to tell her what to do in her own house. It didn't matter that we were trying to keep her from accidentally killing us all by combining cleaning solutions or pouring strange mixtures and other things down the sinks and toilets, or that we tried to keep her from driving because she forgot to stop at stop signs and couldn't remember how to get home. These were the starting indicators of what so many others have had to go through, and it raised the spectre for the first time that we might some day face having to put her into a nursing home; Kathi and I discussed it, and decided with my past experience working with hospitals, patients and dementia in general, combined with my more flexible consulting hours and work requirements, we were going to try to take care of Georgia at home as long as possible. We didn't make it the whole journey with her, but we held out a lot longer than anyone (including ourselves) thought we would.

(Kathi's LiveJournal entry. 2/5/04)
Elder Affairs

A week from Thursday John and I have a meeting with a "Senior Resource Specialist" who works with the local Elder Affairs office regarding a plan of action should, God forbid, Mom *[Georgia]* need long-term care. Mom and I got into a rather nasty fight the other day about the house. She was lucid enough to tell me the reason why she's never put me on the deed is because (in her own words) "You've had it so easy all your life, it's about time you suffered a bit, and THIS IS THE ONLY THING I OWN!" I tried explaining to her that with the new laws coming into effect, if she ever needed to go into a nursing home, the state's going to take the house, no questions asked. "LIKE HELL THEY WILL!" Um, I don't think so. "I'M NOT GOING TO A NURSING HOME!" Um, how do you know? (Personally, I hope she's dead before she'll ever have to go there – a horrible thought, I know, but knowing her, it'd be the lesser of two evils. She'd never survive the indignity). Then, of course, my anxiety started kicking in big time, which caused me to start yelling and crying back at her, which prompted even more yelling and crying from her, and so forth...

Nevertheless, a half hour later, she forgot the exchange even happened. A blessing for her, but I'm left stewing. I still am, somewhat. Anyhow, that's what prompted John and I to make the appointment with the Senior Resource Specialist. I don't know if I can come to terms with actually losing the house. I mean, I have no great love for this place – it's too small, I've always disliked the neighborhood, it's beginning to fall apart – but yes, I did most of my growing up here. I've lived here most of my life. I've always said that when I do inherit it (I have the right of survivorship), I'm probably going to sell it. But to have the state take it away and leave John and I stranded?!? I hate sounding like a whiny little girl here, but 1) his job situation is in jeopardy; 2) I don't make enough to rent a place for myself around here (unless it's a one-room hovel), never mind for both of us plus the dogs; 3) together, we could swing it, but not in this area (read, going back to RI or something, which is out of the question because of Mom).

Cripes, I'm getting all jittery just writing about it.

(Kathi's LiveJournal entry. 2/16/04)
The Wanderer

Mom *[Georgia]* had her first bout of "wandering" today. She called me at work to tell me all about it. I didn't know whether to weep or be happy that she called me.

Piecing the story from what she told me and from what she told John (who had called her within an hour or so afterward – he called me right before I went to lunch), she decided to walk up to the corner store to get the newspapers. She made it to the next block and momentarily forgot where she was. She returned to the house. She left again, this time going down the other way and somehow made it to the store. She bought something, but couldn't remember what. She momentarily forgot where she was until she saw the gas station, but then made it back OK.

I found out what she bought: Cranberry-orange scones. They're in a white bag on the counter next to the knife block. There are crumbs all over the place. She must've eaten one for lunch because she completely disregarded the sandwich I had left her in the fridge.

When I came home, she was hanging Christmas ornaments on the pegboard where we hang the pot lids.

Her doctor's office called to confirm her appointment for tomorrow morning. She thanked them for canceling it. It took me close to a half hour to convince her that the appointment was still on. She also keeps asking when John's coming home. "Um, he's in New Jersey," I keep replying. "Oh, why don't we go down to visit him?"

And please, don't get me started about the dogs. We had to put them in a kennel for the week :(

I'm really, really hesitant about going to work tomorrow. I'm on the late shift (1-10PM). No, scratch that. I'm scared.

(Email excerpt, Jim to the family. 11/22/05)
Oh man...

Just got through talking to Martha Jr, telling her about this. You're gonna love it...

About 2:45, I heard Martha Sr rustling around over the baby monitor, no doubt pulling out the sheet I'd tucked in to restrict her from getting out of bed without me noticing. And the motion sensor alarm went off, right on cue. So I stopped doing the conservation work I was doing, went up front to her bedroom, to find her (as I expected) sitting on the side of her bed, looking around for her shoes, glasses and walker.

"Martha", I said, "you need to call and wait for someone if you want to get up."

She looked at me like I was from Pluto. "Why?"

"So you don't fall. You need to have someone with you."

"Well, I didn't want to wake anyone up."

OK, this I've heard before. I squat down in front of her, hand her her glasses and continue the conversation while I slip her shoes on. "It's OK, but you need to call. We don't want you to fall again."

She looks at me very concerned. "Since when?"

"Well, we've had to do it this way for a while now. That's why there's this sign here on your table next to the clock that says 'Call and Wait'."

"Oh." She slowly shakes her head. "But when I'm at home I don't have to do that."

Huh? "At home?"

"Yes, when I'm at home, I don't have to wait for anyone."

"But, but, this is your home."

She looks around the room. "Where I live?"

"Yes."

She looks at me, then around the room again. "Where I live everyday?"

"Um, yeah. This is where you live. It is your home. And you need to call for someone before you get up, so you don't fall. Because even with the walker, you fall if you don't have someone with you."

"Oh." She shakes her head, as though trying to clear it. I help her stand up, and we start out of the room. "Well, I just didn't want to wake anyone up."

"Well, that's thoughtful of you, but I don't usually nap in the afternoons."

"But I didn't want to wake up any of the other people."

"Um, I'm the only one here."

"You're the only one here?"

"Uh, yeah. Just me."

"Oh. OK."

Needless to say, we're ordering bedrails today...

> *Comment from John:* Georgia was, for a while, pretty steady on her feet.
>
> When she began sundowning, rummaging, and experiencing moments of disorientation, she was still able to navigate stairs and walk around.
>
> We didn't want to take the chance that she'd walk out of her room and trip at the top of the stairs, so our strategy involved putting a child safety gate at the top of the stairs, elevated so she wouldn't trip over it, and putting a door alarm at her door frame so that it would go off if she opened her bedroom door.
>
> What we didn't realize was how many things she had hidden, packed away in multiple drawers and boxes and closets in her room, which she'd eventually decide were "junk" and end up

tossing into "the hopper" – her term for flushing things down the toilet...

(Kathi's LiveJournal entry. 2/23/04)
Explorations in Day Care

I made tentative appointments for look-sees at a couple of day centers – one tomorrow afternoon; one Wednesday. The one tomorrow is located in Boston, not too far from me, but it'll be a bitch to get to during rush hour. On the plus side, it's by far the most comprehensive place wholly dedicated to higher-functioning Alzheimer's/dementia clients. On the minus – and this is purely speculation – it looks like the kind of place where you'd pay through the nose if you're not a Boston resident. The other place is not far from where I work. It's small, about half high-functioning, half lower-functioning (I cringed, thinking how Mom *[Georgia]* threw the hissy fit when she saw all the wheelchairs at the other place), but the owner stressed how they tailor individual programs geared toward each client's ability. She asked me at length what her interests are and what her general demeanor is. I couldn't stop chuckling at the latter. The owner was nonplused. She replied, "We have a woman here who'll give your mother a run for her money." I laughed so loud that John came downstairs to see what the heck was going on.

Now, of course, comes telling her we're visiting these places. She figured it out the last time – "it's babysitting because nobody trusts old people to be by themselves and everyone goes to work and drops them off to these sad places like you do to the dogs" was how she put it. Well, um...you couldn't really argue because, in essence, she was telling the truth. The places we looked at the last time were "sad" in that most of the clients were lower-functioning, in wheelchairs, etc. Most, but not all, day care clients are one step away from being in nursing homes. There's no way to avoid that aspect of it. And Mom's not one to take anything that's sugar-coated, Alzheimer's or not. You just can't plunk her down and nicely explain the reasons why you're doing this. Conversely,

you just can't plunk her down and spell it out for her either
because she becomes verbally abusive (yes, I know it's the disease,
but I had enough of that growing up, thank you.) So, short of
strait-jacketing her....how the hell am I going to approach this???

(Email excerpt, Jim to a friend. 12/24/05)
Great Escape

I was on call last night, had nothing to drink and no antihistamines
because I didn't want to have anything clouding my mind if we
had a repeat of the night before. Martha Sr was up at 1:00, a little
early for her routine, but not that unusual. Got her back to bed,
went back to bed myself. About 5:15 I woke up, listened to her
breathing for a moment, then got up to pee. I will often wake 5 –
10 minutes before she does (and then calls), which gives me time
to use the bathroom before having to tend to her. Thought about
taking something for my headache, decided that it was a bit early
to just get up (since the caff in the pills would kick-start me),
went back to bed. Listened for a bit, but nothing from Martha
Sr, so I drifted back off into a light sleep.

Well, at 6:00 I woke, having heard something. I listened closely.
Hmm. No sound of her breathing. Got up, grabbed pants, headed
downstairs. Found Martha Sr just outside her door, laying on the
floor. Check to make sure she's OK, then ask her what happened.
Well, she called. No one came. So she got up to go to the bathroom on her own. How did she get over the railing? She crawled
out at the foot of the bed. Evidently held onto the edge of the
desk to the door, then to the radiator to where I had her walker.
Started for the bathroom, but then lost her balance and fell after
about a step (judging from how far the walker had been moved
from where I usually put it outside her door).

I helped her up, took her to the bathroom. Once I had her settled
there, woke Martha Jr, told her what happened. She came back
downstairs with me, talked with her mom. Got the same story,
though her mom was confused on whether or not she had ever

actually called before trying to get up (this has happened before, where she just thinks that she has called, hasn't actually). Tried to impress on her mom just exactly how bad an idea this was, trying to get up on her own, to marginal effect. I'm sure she will remember none of it come daylight.

It seems that the motion sensor, which would have caught her moving about the room, had died. So, fresh batteries needed in that, and it was just a case of really bad timing on them failing. And I guess we need to figure out some way of adding a foot-board to the bed, to further inhibit Martha Sr from trying to get up on her own. Or maybe shackles are called for, I don't know.

Unbelievable. Just bloody unbelievable.

(John's diary. 6/4/04)
Jobless

– Bickford's, Quincy

Georgia & I stopped in for breakfast. Odd that I haven't had the opportunity to update in a while. Friday, May 28, my employer laid off another person and myself. Although they had a past practice of including separation pay in layoffs, that was not the case in this instance.

> *Comment from John:* My manager didn't find it easy; he was very upset. Kathi and I were both quite relieved, actually. The job had become very stressful. We knew I could try to get my own side-consulting stuff done, plus I could look into some writing opportunities and perhaps even focus on the book I'd been trying to write. Also, the door was still open that the former employer might need (would probably need) my services for a few projects that I was their primary resource for, so the cash flow wasn't completely cut off; it was just seriously dented.

(John's diary. 6/6/04)
Brunch

– Finians, Quincy

Georgia & I stopped in for brunch. We just came from visiting Marge. Georgia was having a bad day at first – she'd walked out on Kathi and I at breakfast and walked home. We never did figure out what upset her. She may have forgotten; by the time Kathi had left, I showed her how I compiled pix and printed them. She found that entertaining.

(Email excerpt, Martha Jr to the family. 4/2/06)
Status report

[We'd gone on vacation, with Martha Jr's sister attending to her mom while we were gone. On the last day of our vacation, Martha Sr took a fall and injured her back. This is a follow-up about a week after we'd gotten back.]

It is rather late, and I'm REALLY sleepy, so this must be short. I want to give you all an update on Mom's condition. As you know, she *[Martha Sr]* stayed in bed much of last week due to the pain in her back from her fall. By Friday, we decided to have her use the walker instead of riding in the wheelchair when she wanted to go to the toilet or to have meals in the kitchen. We continued to keep her quiet the rest of the time, but also started having her sit up more of the day – either in bed or in the wheelchair. This was because we started hearing the heavy congestion/fluid noises in her chest, and she was coughing and/or blowing her nose a LOT. Her back seems to have gotten somewhat better; in the morning and afternoon she says it doesn't really hurt. By evening, it does, but I've begun to wonder if that isn't lung gak rather than bone cracks. Today her wheezing, coughing and so forth is pretty bad. This evening she is running a bit of fever (enough to have her hair wet with sweat and her skin clammy).

Last time I took it, it was about 99.6. We plan to call Dr. M first thing in the morning and try to get her in to see him tomorrow. This is complicated a bit by the fact that I have a doctor appointment of my own at 10:00 tomorrow morning. It will depend on when Dr. M can see her.

I'm too sleepy to say much more. We'll keep you posted.

(Email excerpt, Martha Jr to the family. 4/4/06)
Another status report

Just want to keep you up on the status of Mom *[Martha Sr]*. Frankly, I'm really getting worried. We got her in to see Dr. M on Monday afternoon because her breathing had become labored and 'gurgly' and she was coughing a lot. Sure enough, she has pneumonia, the type called "aspiration" pneumonia, where it is caused by stuff being aspirated into her lungs, mostly 'light liquids.' Unfortunately, with her frailties, there isn't a LOT we can do. We have a course of antibiotics, which we're about 1/3 of the way through. He showed Mom a way to minimize what gets aspirated when she swallows. But that is difficult for her to do and thus not very likely for her to remember or do, even with us nagging her to do that. He said that she needs to eat all her food to help regain her strength, but these two things seem to work at cross purposes; when she's having to do the special way of swallowing, she doesn't want to eat much because it is difficult. Once she gets past the pneumonia and regains some strength, she's supposed to do a lot more walking, to keep exercising her various muscle groups.

But in the day and a half since we saw him, she sounds much worse. I'm sitting here listening to her sleeping and it sounds AWFUL. The way she's snorting she MUST be aspirating all sorts of saliva and such into her lungs as she sleeps. I can't imagine that it is very restful for her, though I could be wrong on that. I'm considering calling Dr. M back tomorrow to ask "ok, when do we say 'this isn't working'?"

The problem is that she's so frail otherwise, that anything could do more harm than good. She has started complaining that her back hurts a lot. We make her sit up (in the wheelchair with pillows) because lying down contributes to her lung problems. I've come to the conclusion that the back pain isn't cracked bones but stiff muscles, because she's been holding herself so funny since she hurt herself while we were gone. Now, it hurts to move the muscles properly so she doesn't want to do that, even though that's the thing that will make them stop hurting. So she keeps holding them funny, and they stiffen up more, and hurt more. I'm going to try a hot bath, but I don't know how well she'll tolerate that, either.

So I'm running out of ideas to help her. And it is a very helpless feeling. So if you have any suggestions, please let me know.

(Email excerpt, Martha Jr to the family. 4/5/06)
Caring

Well, I think we've reached a nexus of some sort. After Mom's recent rough nights and another conversation with Dr. M this afternoon, we're shifting mindset to palliative care. She *[Martha Sr]* could still recover from this pneumonia, but she's currently quite weak and not wanting to eat much. She's been complaining of many different pains (back, side, leg, belly) at different times, and sometimes she seems to have so much trouble walking we have to help support her as she goes.

Dr. M indicated that his suggestions for what Mom should do (the different way of swallowing and the recommendation that she get more exercise) were more to have some way of motivating her to work at getting better. But if she's in pain, and if she's having so much trouble with the swallowing thing (that she doesn't want to eat at all), then we should not be afraid to back off those recommendations.

I asked Dr. M at what point do we say "this isn't working" and try to do something else? Or is there anything else to do? Frankly, he said, we are far past the point that many people throw in the towel and stop trying to do so much. What is important for her at this point is that she be as comfortable as possible, and keep up her strength as much as possible. Manage the pain, see that she eats as well as she will, and make sure her other needs are met. In short, palliative care. This could end soon, it could still take a long time, we just don't know.

We talked about palliative care in general and about hospice care (which is basically professionally managed palliative care). He said when we felt we were ready he'd start the ball rolling with that. He'd be glad to do whatever is necessary to manage her pain. Just let him know. After discussing it with Jim, I called back and left a message to start in that direction. He had already left for the day, but should call me back tomorrow about it.

So, that is where things stand now. We hope she gets better. We hope she eats well. We will do what we can to see these thing happen, but we won't beat ourselves up over them, because in the end that's no good for her either.

After talking with Dr. M and discussing it ourselves, we think this is the best course of action, and we hope you agree. We'd like to hear anything you might have to add.

Love to everyone -

(Email excerpt, Jim to the family. 4/9/06)
Update

I thought I should drop a note, let you know what I see with Martha Sr's condition.

Frankly, it is not good. We'll know more after the hospice nurse is here in the morning to do a medical work up, but it is clear that Martha Sr has slipped considerably in the last few days. Her appetite is way down (eating maybe half of what she was, even with mild encouragement from us). Even with increased pain meds, she frequently complains of being in pain (another issue we'll address in the morning with the hospice nurse assigned to us). All she wants to do is return to bed after being up briefly for meals. And her aspiration problems have continued to worsen.

I hate to be the one to bring bad news, but I think everyone should be thinking about what plans they need to make for the final days of her life. I would be surprised if we're looking at more than a matter of weeks, perhaps less. Again, this could change – she could rally – and we will know more after the morning visit with the nurse. But I think you should be prepared.

This is unfortunate news. But I want to be honest, and to let you know that we're doing everything to make sure that she is as comfortable and happy as possible.

We'll keep you posted.
Love to all...

(Email excerpt, Jim to the family. 4/10/06)
Follow-up

Well, the hospice nurse just left, and I think we have more information to work with, though nothing definitive at this point.

In sum, Martha Sr has increased congestion in her lungs, due to the lingering effects of her pneumonia, the aspiration, and general weakness. When we discussed how this is likely to play out, the nurse said that it doesn't look good, and we would likely know whether she will rally this week. If she does rally, the biggest long-term threat is likely the aspiration, since the only real intervention for that is a feeding tube inserted into Martha Sr's stomach (something which she was adamantly against when we talked with Dr. M last Monday) – and even then, that wouldn't resolve problems with saliva leaking into her lungs.

If she doesn't rally, then we're likely looking at an end sometime next week or the week after. We'll know more in a few days. For right now, the nurse will be coming by each morning in order to keep track of how Martha Sr is doing and whether there is anything more we can do to keep her comfortable. We have decided to change her pain meds slightly – to get a different formulation with a lower Tylenol component, so we can increase the dosage without worry about liver problems – but that is about the only real change from what we have been doing. In going over all of Martha Sr's eating, sleeping, et cetera, it was clear that her decreased appetite and desire to stay in bed are indications that she is moving in the direction of this being the end, but those are just indications.

So for now, Martha Sr is mostly resting and listening to books-on-tape, getting up for meals and snacks as she desires, and to use the bathroom. Generally she seems to be pain free while in bed, so long as we stay on top of her meds.

We'll certainly keep you posted as to any and all developments.

If you have questions about hospice care, I'd recommend looking at this site, which has a lot of good useful info: http://www.hospicenet.org/

Love to all.

(Email excerpt, Jim to the family. 4/12/06)
Crisis overnight

I thought I would fill you in on what happened overnight.

I went to check on Martha Sr about 1:30. Initially, she seemed to be doing OK, said she wanted to go to the bathroom. But it turned out that she was burning up with fever, incoherent, et cetera. We made a quick call to the hospice nurse on call (system worked like it is supposed to), let him know what was going on, got instructions on how to treat her and to call him back if we didn't see results almost immediately. So we got cold compresses on her head, chest, and thighs, cold water into her, and one of her painkillers with Tylenol into her. Once situated, Martha Jr managed to get a thermometer into her and it was over 102 – this after I know we had managed to get her temp down some. Within about 15 minutes we had her down to normal, and she did OK through the rest of the night.

We'll know more how she's actually doing this morning after the nurse has been here to check her. But we almost lost her last night – with that level of fever, she wouldn't have lasted long.

Love to all.

> *Comment from Jim:* had I been half an hour later in checking on her, I'm certain that it would have been too late.

(Email excerpt, Jim to the family. 4/12/06)
More info

Just thought that I would pass along what the hospice nurse had to say after her visit this morning.

Basically, Martha Sr has taken a step back, as indicated by the fever episode last night. This was due to the aspiration pneumonia. Our response to it was successful, but it might not always be sufficient in the event of additional fever spikes (which we should expect to happen). The nurse is making arrangements to get us some additional tools to work with (specifically Tylenol suppositories if Martha Sr is unable to swallow, and oxygen to have on hand to relieve gasping for breath if that should occur), but it looks like Martha Sr is now on a decided downward path. The nurse's assessment is that the end could happen anytime in the next couple of weeks.

If we do have another fever spike, and are unable to break it, then that will likely precipitate her death quickly. The good news is that this sort of death is very peaceful, with the patient just wanting to go to sleep and experiencing no pain or distress. I would confirm that this is exactly the behaviour that Martha Sr exhibited last night, before we were able to intervene.

So, there it is. We're looking at a horizon of a week or two, most likely, though the end could come quickly and unexpectedly at any time.

(Email excerpt, Jim to the family. 4/14/06)
Morning update

I thought I'd pass along an update on Martha Sr. The nurse just left a few minutes ago, and the news is about what we'd expect: Martha Sr is on a slow slide. The infection pneumonia is likely doing a little better, as evidenced by her lack of a significant fever (which is also what we've tracked over the last 24 hours). But her right lung is substantially worse, due to the aspiration. Martha Sr has had an increasing lethargy over the last 24 hours, though she very much enjoyed listening to Martha Jr's quartet practice last night. Overnight I had to wake her in order to give her some meds, and she was weak and unsteady in going to the bathroom using the walker. This morning for breakfast she was somewhat better, but just wanted to go back to bed to lie down after. Now that the nurse has come and gone, she is resting comfortably in a slight sitting position on the bed, listening to a Harry Potter book.

What we can expect is that over the next few days she will likely continue to have a slow build-up of fluid in her lungs from the aspiration. This will likely not cause her any distress, and any slight discomfort can be attended to with meds we have on hand (we've liquid morphine here now for immediate relief if needed). We're working hard to make sure that we stay on top of any pain she has, and will have oxy to help her breathing if she starts feeling short of breath.

At some point she will become too weak to be able to walk using the walker, and then will only wish to sleep. About that time there's a good chance that she will experience a rise in fever which will not respond to any treatments, and then will slip into a deep sleep, with death to follow within hours. That whole process will likely take less than 48 hours from start to finish, and the nurse didn't expect it to begin until sometime next week.

The nurse won't be back until Monday, unless something happens and we need to call her in. But if there are any significant developments with Martha Sr's condition in the course of the weekend, we'll be sure to let you know.

(Email excerpt, Jim to the family. 5/2/06)
Martha Sr update

Thought I would pass along an update on how Martha Sr is doing. The hospice nurse just left, and basically Martha Sr is doing fine, about as well as possible all things considered. In recent days her appetite has picked up some, and she felt well enough to go have her nails done yesterday afternoon. We're still contending with chronic pain, and have to be careful to stay on top of it, but we're still down in dosage from where we were when she had the pneumonia. She is sleeping well at night, and has her nap after lunch as she has done for years, but has been well enough to want to be up and reading, listening to tapes, or doing her puzzles all other times during the day. In the evenings she usually watches a movie with us or plays cards.

So for now she's stable and happy, about the best we could hope for. I'll keep you posted with occasional updates as long as this trend continues, and will alert you if she seems to be taking a downturn again.

April
Shifting Responsibility

Adults, almost by definition, are responsible for their own decisions and choices. And when you're dealing with someone who you respect – someone you love – who had a long history of being a responsible adult, there is a natural reluctance to take that responsibility away. Even when it is clear that they are no longer capable of responsibility. Or even rational decisions.

There's a whole range of ways this plays out. There are myriad legal and ethical considerations. Should the Alzheimer's patient still be in charge of their own finances? Should she still be driving? Is she capable of signing legal documents?

Those are the big ones, but it's the small ones which are harder. Harder on you, and on the patient. You don't want to take away anything prematurely. Like decisions about what to wear. Or what to eat. Or what to read. Or even when to go to the bathroom. Each of those steps seems to be a diminishing, a loss of adulthood, even a loss of dignity. And this is someone you love, perhaps someone you turned to for advice on your own decisions.

But step by step, the disease robs the patient of the ability to make even the simplest choices. Even if they don't realize that.

Martha Sr and her husband Hurst had moved into their home in the early 1950s, and had raised their family there. It is a classic 1880s historic home, and still retains a lot of the original character. She loved it, and naturally it contained a wealth of memories for her. This was the primary reason why Martha Jr and I moved into the home to care for her as she started to become frail – she couldn't stand the thought of leaving it.

But she was also worried about what would happen to the home after her death, and on multiple occasions told Martha Jr that she wanted her to have it – her two other living children were well established in their own homes, one of them (Martha Jr's sister) out in California. I think that she was worried that when the time came to divide up her estate, the house would just be sold and the proceeds split among the siblings. So, she changed her will to specify that Martha Jr should receive half ownership of the house right off the top, the rest of her estate then divided in three parts.

But this was a somewhat dicey move, since she was already exhibiting some signs of the effects of Alzheimer's. Still, the long-time family attorney went along with her wishes, and made the changes.

Then over the last several years of her life, she would repeatedly ask what was going to happen to the house, and kept suggesting that she should "talk to the attorney" to make sure that Martha Jr inherited it. It was something of a fixation for her, almost to the end. We were able to tell her that the arrangements had already been made, and that put her at ease – until the next time the matter came up.

After her passing, in order that none of the other siblings felt that we had manipulated Martha Sr into making this change, we re-jiggered the allocation of the estate so that things worked out to an equitable split, while still respecting Martha Sr's wishes that Martha Jr wound up with the house.

(John's diary. 12/8/05)
Errands and tidbits

– Finian's, Quincy

Georgia & I grabbing a quick bite, giving Kathi time to relax. We dropped off and picked up dry cleaning, turned in her license

(Georgia's), got a Mass ID (temp: the "real" will be mailed). We won't likely be home in time to turn the insurance documents back in to the company, but we'll be able to attend that in the morning.

(John's diary. 7/20/05)
Handling it better

– 99 Restaurant and Pub, Quincy

Kathi, Georgia & I. Freelance consulting work is continuing; less availability to give more time for managing Georgia, who's doc says she's progressed in the signs of dementia drastically. Got ok'd to add Acetyl L Carnitine and Alpha Lipoic acid, plus Curcumin, to her regimen. I think they're helping a little, but it's too early to be certain. Perhaps I'm just getting better at management...?

Writing is progressing, although not along as far as desired.

(Email excerpt, Jim to the family. 6/15/06)
Status Report

I thought I would pass along news on the latest developments with Martha Sr.

First off, thanks to all who called/sent items yesterday for her birthday. I think she enjoyed it quite a lot.

Last Sunday was the John Family thing down at Broadway. We took her, and for the most part it went well. She was confused and somewhat concerned about not remembering names, but did enjoy everyone coming by to visit with her briefly, and took real joy in getting a cake and having everyone sing "Happy Birthday" to her.

The hospice nurse came by for her weekly visit this morning. Before seeing Martha Sr, she spoke with us and informed us that when the current initial 90 day period for being enrolled in the hospice program is over, Martha Sr will not meet the Medicare guidelines for continuing. Basically, she is now stable enough according to their criteria (expecting death within the next six months) that she no longer qualifies. This is good in that we've managed to nurse her back from the crisis we faced in April, but means that we will lose having the nurse's weekly visits and the other support. Now, should Martha Sr's condition change, we can re-enroll her into the program at any time (with the consent of her primary care doctor, but that shouldn't be a problem), and the nurse said that she expects that will likely happen sometime in the future. Martha Sr is weaker than she was prior to the latest crisis, with additional deterioration in her mental faculties, but any continued decline is likely to be slow (unless something else happens). So that will take effect here the beginning of July, and we will continue according to how things were three months ago. I thought you would like to know.

(John's diary. 8/5/05)
Time Constraints – Withdrawal

Notified my company the other day that I'd be taking a leave of absence due to increased constraints on my availability. I'd remain available if issues arose or if they required an install or training, though I'd require at least week of advanced notice in order to schedule time.

It becomes effective August 19.

The increasing demands of care-giving severely constrained my ability to be spontaneous, or even moderately available.

I had to know when I'd be gone, for how long, and coordinate that absence with Kathi's schedule in time for her to notify and adjust her work schedule. Plus – once all that was accomplished –

we needed to know whether we'd require any other resources to help manage Georgia and schedule *those* accordingly.

Any new work would have to be brief, accomplished within a day (no overnights), and ideally in-state (or within 2 hours driving radius) so that I could still get back home in case of emergency.

Needless to say, this meant that little if any work that couldn't be accomplished remotely could be taken on.

Another big blow dealt to the financial cash flow.

(Email excerpt, Martha Jr to her sister. 6/18/06) Possibilities & planning

"If there might be a place in Columbia that you would be willing to have do respite for Mom for a week, how about checking into that possibility as a back-up in case I can't get there. I really!!!!!! think you need to have something like that available for times when you need to get away or are just too tired to cope any more. She might like the sociability of a group of people too. I also think you need to take at least a week in Portland to rest and I will do my best to get there to make it possible."

I understand the idea, but we really think that the disruption would be very detrimental to her disposition/condition. The comfort of the familiar surroundings, familiar people and regular routine we have here keeps her *[Martha Sr]* from being too discombobulated. We just don't think, at this time, that she'd do well even in a 'vacation' placement. And we'd probably spend so much time worrying about how she's doing that we wouldn't really have a break, either.

Now, at such a time as she no longer seems to know where she is or who she is with, that might be a better option. But right now, I don't see it. Thanks for the thought, though!

(John's diary. 8/15/05)
Off again

– Doubletree Hotel, Washington DC

Left Milton after midnight last night; arrived at the hotel
(Doubletree) on Roosevelt this morning just before 9:00;
changed, and was at my client's by 9:15 for class. Went well, I
think.

I should sleep soundly tonight.

> *Comment from John:* This was a second consulting company
> that I was now able to provide BI training services for, as I
> was no longer an employee of the other company.
>
> Unfortunately, this one required out-of-state travel. While
> they gave us plenty of notice so we thought we could swing
> it, this turned out to be one of only two jobs I could take on
> from them, and after that nothing more came in. The logis-
> tics were just too fluid and demanding.
>
> It was the first time since Georgia's care-giving requirements
> had increased that Kathi had to manage the start of her day,
> and it really freaked her out at the level of care needed even
> though we'd reviewed it prior to my departure. The scope
> didn't register until she was on her own with her mom.
>
> It can be a pretty unsettling place to find oneself.
>
> *Comment from Kathi:* I was petrified being totally responsi-
> ble for Mom's care when John was away. It's one thing to
> watch somebody go through the routine, but it's another to
> do it on your own without anyone telling you if you're
> doing something right or wrong. I think I was more scared
> of Mom freaking out, though, than anything else – if she did,
> what would I do? Who would I call? What if she became
> violent? What if she wandered away?

(Email excerpt, Jim to a friend. 7/25/06)
Another Great Escape

So, some time after I sent the last message, I'm in here, wrapping up my morning routine, about to go get the dog and go for an early walk, and Susan (Martha Jr's sister) walks in. I can tell something's wrong and she's come to tell me about it...

Long story short: last night Martha Sr managed to crawl out the foot of her bed again, under the safety strap we have across the bed from one rail to the other, and attempt to go to the bathroom on her own. She fell, of course, and when Susan went to see what was wrong, she found Martha Sr on the floor, shoulder injured.

Gah.

It doesn't look like there is anything seriously hurt with Martha Sr. Likely just some muscle/tendon stuff. Of course, now our care-giving work has just been dramatically increased again, at least until we get her past this initial stage coping with the pain and trauma.

Martha Sr just doesn't respond well to changes, like us being gone yesterday. And one of Susan's friends came by. So did the local in-laws. I discussed this with Susan last night as we were getting Martha Sr ready for bed, how we should expect some fallout in the form of Martha Sr being off kilter in her routines today. I didn't think it'd be so literally "fallout".

Sigh Well, if Martha Sr survives this setback, I think Martha Jr and I will need to seriously reconsider whether we can both be gone for any length of time again. An afternoon with the regular respite-worker here is one thing, but that might be the most we can risk.

Forgive the rant. I needed to vent.

Comment from Jim: It turned out that Martha Sr had actually cracked her clavicle. When she was still in pain later that morning, we decided to take her to the hospital.

(Email excerpt, Martha Jr to her sister. 7/31/06)
Frailty

Mom [Martha Sr] is seeming really frail, right now. We were going to try to get her to try using the walker today, but I think we've decided to put it off for at least a day or two. She's been more and more confused, too. Jim told me that, when she woke up before lunch today, she said something about how she was supposed to be at Ellis Fischel Cancer Center to volunteer! So I guess it's just wait and see.

(John's diary. 9/24/05)
Calolillies

– Calolillies, Quincy

Today was Ryan Joseph's christening (Mark & Liz's new baby). Didn't have anything really appropriate for Georgia to wear, so took her out shopping at Lord & Taylor. Now she has a nice, understated dress suit. We missed the Christening, unfortunately, as suit-shopping took too long. Also lost the chance to get an additional part of the gift – had to give only the teddy bear bank and a card we wrote on the way. But, we did get to visit w/family, and Georgia looked (and appeared to feel) great.

Kathi was very happy for her mom and a bit taken aback at what I'd spent – suit jacket and pants tailored on-site, shoes, and an extra shirt or two to change it up – yet she grew very quiet.

When we were alone later, she sadly said that this was now Georgia's best suit, and that it would probably be the one we'd bury her in.

I'd had a similar thought skitter across my inner thoughts a little earlier, and agreed with her.

(Email excerpt, Martha Jr to the family. 8/3/06)
Mom Update

Thought I'd touch base with you to let you know how things are at the moment with Mom *[Martha Sr]*. She's still staying in bed or the wheelchair. Her shoulder is still giving her a fair amount of pain. I finally had a chance to speak (by phone) with Dr. M this morning. He indicated that the pain from a collarbone fracture doesn't start subsiding for a couple weeks and doesn't really go away for a good six weeks. So we may not be able to try to get her up walking with the walker any time soon, since that depends so heavily on the shoulder. Caring for her in this increased invalid state is more difficult. She cannot support her own weight, even just to stand while we help her balance, so transfers from chair or bed to commode, pulling down or up her pants, etc. are difficult. Lifting her into bed is now necessary (I can do it, but Jim does it better) as is completely supporting her while she's trying to sidle from chair to bed or the like. Simply, the level of care has stepped up a notch. We need to be more vigilant about pain management as well as checking for things like pressure sores, since she spends all her time in bed or the wheel-chair.

Her left hip/thigh has been giving her a fair amount of pain as well, which makes putting her weight on it iffy, even just during transfers from bed to chair and the like. I think we may try doing a little physical therapy on her legs (exercising the muscles a little while she's lying in bed) just so they don't atrophy too much.

She's still sleeping more than she used to; and each nap is longer than it used to be. And she's been quite confused more and more. We don't quite know what that means, but we've heard some very interesting stories recently. She seems sure sometimes that she's just a visitor here, or that "here" is in a hospital. She was sure she needed to get up and go do her volunteering stint at Ellis Fischel *[a cancer hospital here where Martha Sr used to volunteer]* the other day. She seems to remember dreams and think they are real. And she continues to come up with really odd ideas. Today she was eating a yogurt (raspberry) and doing her puzzles. She has, for a while, had a fixation about picking out the seeds and wiping them on the paper towel on her place mat. Today she was putting them on the page of her puzzle book, and she told Jim that this was what you had to do to be able to work the puzzles. She got quite angry with him when he suggested he take away the (empty) yogurt container because it still had some "black things" that she needed for her puzzles!

When I spoke with Dr. M this morning, he asked why hospice had discharged Mom. When I explained that it was their decision, something about not making any measurable decline, he became annoyed and indicated that he might talk to them about that. I don't know if he will or if anything will come of it, but we may hear from them again soon. Or not.

Frankly, we just don't know where she stands. Some days she seems very clear and "with it" but these are coming fewer and farther between, and even the good times seem not to be very long. So far she always seems to know me, though Jim apparently is more of a stranger to her. (There was that one episode when she thought I was her mother for a while, but that was brief.) I wish we had a crystal ball or some other means to tell us what is in store, but we just don't. Gut feeling is that she's started another slide and may or may not pull out of this one. But we just don't know, and she has surprised (and pleased) us in the past when we've thought that.

Just thought you should be kept up to date.

(Email excerpt, Jim to the family. 8/8/06)
Day to Day

Hey everyone,

Thought I'd give a new status report on how Martha Sr is doing.

We kept her quiet last week and over the weekend, trying to get
the clavicle break to heal. But starting Sunday we started letting/
encouraging her to use her left arm for light duty. Then this
morning we got her started on using her walker again, at first just
a few steps, but then later almost from the kitchen into the bedroom. When both Martha Jr and I are home we'll be doing more
of this in the next few days, trying to help her build back strength
and independence (both of us because one person needs to have

the wheelchair right there when
she peters out).

She continues to sleep a fair
amount, but less so than last week.
And the last couple of days she
has been "tracking" a lot better,
generally knowing where she is,
who I am, what happened to her,
et cetera. There are still occasions
when she is badly confused, but
this is a big improvement over last
week. Still, this will be a day-to-
day thing.

Tomorrow Martha Jr and I are hopefully going to be able to get
her into the walk-in tub and have a bath. Perhaps also a trip to
get her hair done. We'll see how she is doing in the morning.

So, progress, though there's no saying that this will continue.
Like I said: day to day.

Thought you would like to know. Love to all.

(Email excerpt, Martha Jr to her sister. 8/9/06)
Hair Appointment

Just wanted to touch base. Mom *[Martha Sr]* is sleeping soundly on her afternoon nap, after having a "busy morning." When I went to get her up, her Depends and the sheet were wet this morning – just too full. So during breakfast I changed the bed (fortunately the under-pad kept the rest dry). After breakfast she had a bath (it took both Jim and I to help her in and out) and got dressed for the first time in a long while. She sat at the kitchen table for a little while doing puzzles, then we took her out to the car and got her in it. So far this has all been with the wheelchair. I took the walker to the hair place and got Ken (the hairdresser) to come hold the door so I could help support Mom with the walker to walk in and get in the chair. We reversed the process to leave and get in the car. When she got home we put her in the wheelchair again (which she was glad of) and she did puzzles again until lunch time. She was "just not very hungry" and only ate about half her lunch, then went to lie down. I think she was just tired out. We'll see how long she sleeps.

So anyway, she's feeling better, though she said her shoulder aches and when she walks the front of her left thigh hurts. Also she seems to have developed a sore heel, oddly enough, when she's lying in bed.

Just wanted to let you know how it went today.

(Email excerpt, Jim to the family. 8/21/06)
Past the worst

Thought I'd give an update on how Martha Sr is doing.

In a nutshell, she's doing much better physically, with some improvement (though spotty) mentally. It's now been 4 weeks since her fall, and for the most part her collarbone is healed and doesn't hurt. We've been able to scale back the amount of painkillers she's on to about pre-injury levels, just enough to cope with her routine problems. We're also making progress in getting her to use her walker more, to do more of her own personal hygiene, that sort of thing. Her appetite has improved, and she's sleeping less (though still more than previously – this is likely just an indication of the slow downhill slide). I don't think we'll completely get away from her using the wheelchair, but even her being more involved in transitioning from bed to it, or on and off the commode, is an improvement.

Her cognitive skills have improved some, though she still has episodes of confusion, sometimes severe. These seem to occur randomly, without cause or connection to anything. Just now she and I had a long talk about who is who in the family, that this is her home, et cetera. She had it in her head that she had been gone, that she 'had done something wrong.' She was relieved when I reassured her that she's not done anything wrong, and that she's been here at home all along. Her memory is about as bad as ever, though like her other faculties, there are good days and bad days.

So, while the slow slide continues, and things could always change suddenly, I think we're past the worst of the broken clavicle problem. I thought you would like to know.

Love to all...

May
Deliberate blindness

Other family members will not want to see what is happening, to see the decline – while the care-giver is becoming all too aware of the reality of the situation because they live with it every day. Furthermore, there is a well known phenomenon where an Alzheimer's patient can put on a façade of normalcy for a short period in a social situation. And the Alzheimer's patient will still remember being a fully competent adult well enough that they will want to assert their independence, even though allowing that at this stage would be neglecting to provide proper care. This can put a care-giver at odds with the rest of the family or friends of the patient, and builds resentment the care-provider feels towards the patient.

Beyond that, "May" is the month where the various stresses and strains start to manifest, having an impact on routines and alerting care-givers as to what may be in store in the future. Relationships undergo new and different types of strain, having an effect on all levels, generating inter-personal stress between husband and wife, between siblings, with co-workers and business associates. Some of those impacts and fractures will surprise you – they are often unexpected, and can come from areas that the care-givers had assumed were "stable" foundations and walls that could be relied upon for support. Particularly those who haven't been in a care-giving role for someone with dementia will just not have the tools to understand what the care-giver is going through. This contributes to misunderstanding and isolation.

Almost all affected areas will take time to heal. If they can ever heal. But you can't worry about that now – you're in the thick of things.

One thing which isn't mentioned elsewhere in this memoir is the problems which care-giving presented to Martha Jr's business. She had been in a long term architectural partnership that was well established and respected. But her time in her office, and her ability to focus on the work clients needed doing, started to suffer – yes, Jim was the primary care-provider, but there was still much which required Martha Jr's time and attention. She had the Power of Attorney, and was the only one who could sign the necessary forms for medical treatments and so forth. Plus, Jim needed some respite upon occasion to conduct his own business or just get away from the house for a bit. Further, Martha Jr was 'on call' overnight half the time – which will exhaust anyone after a while.

So, Martha Jr's energy and enthusiasm for her work dropped off, and she spent less time in the office. Her partner had cared for her own mother through hospice for cancer, and was sympathetic for a while. But since caring for Martha Sr was a matter of years, rather than months, there was tension and resentment about Martha Jr no longer pulling her share of the load. Eventually this led to the breakup of the partnership.

(Email excerpt, Martha Jr to the family. 2/16/06)
Discombobulated

Just a quick note. We've had the construction guy here for the last week working on the bathroom remodel. We've got a ways to go on it – right now there are bare walls and no fixtures.

This has apparently discombobulated Mom *[Martha Sr]* quite a bit because she is exhibiting some rather strange behaviors. Some of it may also be related to her friend Neva having died last week. At any rate, she has become more difficult and we find we must monitor her more closely. Because of her increasing 'forgetfulness' about not getting up without assistance, we had moved last week to having 'safety straps' (like loose, lightweight seatbelts) in her chairs as well as across the bed from rail to rail. This is to help her remember to call one of us if she wants to get up. The chair straps were just loosely buckled around her so that she would need to call someone.

But today we had to tighten them some. No less than three times did she try to get out of them without one of us around. The first time, she succeeded. I was outside helping the fellow who was delivering fence parts. (Jim was away at a support group meeting.) I had told her where I would be for just a bit, but when she heard the truck (she was in the chair in the front room) she 'just got curious' and had to get up to look. Apparently she wriggled out under the strap (she hasn't been able to unbuckle them) and stood up to look out the window. When she couldn't see anything from there, she moved along the couch to the other window. When I came back inside, she was sitting on the floor at the far end of the couch, having fallen. She wasn't hurt, fortunately, at least not seriously. Very contrite, 'this will make me remember not to do that.' (Suuuure it will.) That was about 11:00. At noon, she had lunch in the kitchen and, as I was about to get her up to go lie down afterward, about 1:00, we noticed she had apparently scraped her wrist when she fell and it was bleeding a little. Jim had just gotten home. So he was still in the kitchen doing other things while I was looking for the bandage stuff (which I didn't pack away very intelligently when we cleared out the bathroom). Before I got back, and with Jim standing right there, Mom tried to push herself away from the table so she could get up to go lie down. She had already forgotten I was looking for a bandage, or anything else. We got her wrist cleaned up and took her in to lie down. About 2:30 (the usual time Mom calls to get up) Jim heard her fussing with the clasp on the bed strap and went in to see what she was doing. Well she was 'just trying to get this undone so I can get up.'

I keep thinking that she can learn, in the way a child can, but she just can't. She can't remember the 'rules' long enough to abide by them. Every time her behavior slips a little further, we have to ramp the vigilance up a little more. It can be very scary to come upon her trying to stand up, because if she were to fall and seriously hurt herself while under our care, it would be our fault. I'm sure it seems 'mean' to her, but what else can we do?

Just wanted to keep you informed of what's happening.

Love to all -

(John's diary. 2/5/04)
Reality Bites

Kathi's having trouble dealing with my impending absence – it's really hard for her to "manage" Georgia. We contacted the National Alzheimer's Org at the house, & scheduled for them to call back early this week.

Still have to take care of several items...

Regarding writing, I need to take stock of my growing stock of concepts and excerpts, and begin the serious work of putting them together in a coherent form. I want to develop and complete the stories – esp. since I do believe I can make a good living as a successful writer. Unfortunately, my office at the house is compromised by Georgia's rummaging. She claims not to touch anything, but can't recall her actions – and things move and disappear. She's high-functioning enough to that since we're living in her house, her space, we have to tolerate the rummaging, and are unable to do much to protect our "stuff."

Errands for today: Library (Thomas Crane in Quincy), a hat, and perhaps a safe (or two). We also need to investigate home security systems & phone recorders. Our big concerns at this point are that someone will realize that Georgia is a susceptible "mark," and sell her a product or service that she really shouldn't have.

We saw my parents last night. Dad was very concerned about the situation with Georgia, & wanted to know how he could help. He gave us the name of a lawyer who may be able to advise us re: the house, elder care, and financial matters.

> *Comment from John:* Two important items come to mind here:

1. Georgia was always used to learning and doing things on her own, so when she saw ads on the TV for a computer learning tutor, she ordered it. Yes, she still had control of her credit cards – and knew how to use 'em.

The software was too difficult for her, which disappointed her greatly; she'd wanted to have the little victory of learning how to use Kathi's computer, and not being able to figure it out was devastating for her.

2. Always the fan of old movies, Georgia's eyes lit up with the repeated barrage of offers for collections of CDs and tapes for various old movies. She managed to order a complete collection of Shirley Temple VHS tapes without either of us noticing.

She never watched a single one of them.

(John's diary. 2/25/04)
Reality Bites

Last few days busy, and productive (at least in terms of the client's implementation). Kathi's been "managing" Georgia, albeit with some difficulty. Alzheimer's Disease is definitely one of the most difficult to deal with.

(John's diary. 3/7/04)
Inner Life

– Villa Rosa

Home (since Sat. AM) after a prolonged trip to see a client in New Jersey for their go-live. Hadn't expected to be gone the entire week. Kathi was unhappy, trying to manage Georgia by herself, but Kelly & Cheryl both helped out. Kathi, Cheryl and I took Georgia here Monday night – it was the first time Georgia met Cheryl – as a prelude to Cheryl taking Georgia out to dinner on Wed, which was Kathi's "late" night. We already knew I'd be away Wed.; I was planning to leave at 3-4 am Tues. (made it out by 4:30)

Today was a bit frustrating. I'd planned to stay home with the dogs and get some things done – lots of catching up to do – and lost a significant chunk of time when I had to run down to Allerton House (where Marge resides). I'd gone to a bookstore to get the Large Print magazine we like to leave with Marge. Georgia got impatient and insisted that she and Kathi leave immediately, which turned out to be less than 5 minutes before I returned. I'd told Marge that we would get the subscription for her, and Georgia said she'd pay for it (not that she'd remember), so – since I'd forgotten to take care of it – I felt it only right that I pick up the current newsstand version. I was angry when I got home & found that Kathi had been unable to "manage" Georgia until I returned. Drove down & dropped off the mag, saying "Thanks for wasting my time" to Kathi. Georgia asked if I brought the dogs. I told her – a bit harshly – that I'd left them home, because I'd had work to do and hadn't planned on attending save for the fact that they couldn't wait for me to return. I apologized to Marge for not submitting the subscription yet & promised to take care of it when I returned home. Kath reminded Georgia that she'd wanted to leave, not wait. I left.

I'm sure it bothered Kathi – I know she's trying, and under a bit of pressure to take on & excel as wife and daughter. I'll have to try and help her – alleviate the stress – and make some of it up to her. She does have to learn a bit more about being more "the adult daughter" and managing her mom rather than just being a "daughter/enabler."

*Serendipitous Moment: Kathi just called. I apologized for being a bit hard on her – she understood, though I'm not sure if she let the stress go or not. They're on the way here now – I ordered another Tang & Tonic for myself, a Cape Codder for Kathi and a 7-Up for Georgia.

While speaking to Kathi, I suggest she take Georgia out some-

where after we have lunch, so I can still have some "quiet time" at
the house without distraction. I think they'll hit Job Lot or
WalMart. (I'll suggest both, or just WalMart.)

(Email excerpt, Jim to Martha Jr's sister. 8/7/04)
The visit

I've been thinking about a comment you made last night, and
thought that I should drop you an email. It's about Em's most
recent visit.

First, let me stress that I'm glad that she came, and had the opportunity to spend some time with Martha Sr. It certainly brightens
Martha Sr's life to have her family around her, and that's something we all rejoice in. Em is welcome with open arms whenever
she wants to come visit, both because we love her and enjoy her
company, and for the joy it brings Martha Sr to have her here.

I know Em felt some anger about how Martha Jr and I interact
with Martha Sr, as you indicated in your comment. I don't know
the details, nor do I wish to, since Em didn't discuss the matter
with us. But while she was here, her disapproval was palpable
upon occasion, and sometimes so strong as to be hurtful. I attributed
it then, as well as now, to transference – it is not an easy thing to
see a loved one declining in physical and mental abilities, and that
frustration and anger has to vent somewhere. I doubt that she
was even aware of how it effected her at the time.

But it was there nonetheless, and as I said, sometimes so strong as
to be hurtful. Both Martha Jr and I felt it, even discussed it, and
I'm sorry if there was stress between us and Em in response. Yet
that was a natural reaction, a certain resentment we felt. It's one
thing to be here on a visit as a vacation, and to dote on Martha Sr,
another altogether to be caring for someone around the clock,
week in and week out. Em was free to come and go as she pleased,
didn't have the responsibility for being on-call, yet disapproved of
us in our routine and care of Martha Sr. It chaffed. I think that
was probably what led to Martha Jr's friction with Em.

As I know you have seen for yourself, we're doing our level best to care for Martha Sr, manage her affairs, keep up the house and grounds, and still make time to see to our own careers as best we can. While we consider the opportunity to care for her to be a great gift, it is nonetheless demanding. Your coming out to visit and help care for her, to give us a respite now and again, is a real godsend, and I cannot thank you enough for your kindness in doing so.

Well, like I said, I just thought that I should drop you an email, let you know my observations on the matter.

(John's diary. 4/4/04)
Bananas

Georgia's been OK. Subtly worsening. On Friday, while I was working upstairs and it was cold and misty outside, she decided to walk up to the store to get bananas. She hadn't seen (possibly hadn't even looked for) bananas already in the hanging basket.

When I realized she was gone, I went up to the Fruit Center – surmising that was her target. I notified a Milton police officer, providing a description, and we checked the store. A cashier recalled seeing her just minutes before. I caught up to her as she

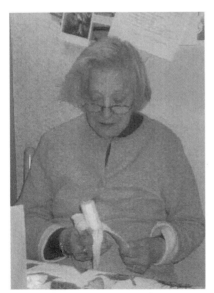

headed home, then swung back to let the Milton officer know that I'd caught up. Georgia was a bit mortified, and still speaks of the event even though she oft forgets other questions or incidents right away.

I called and told Kathi about the incident – she was at work – and she cried. It's a tough disease – on everyone. I was able to reach Rosemary, the "tutor," who was able to come watch Georgia until about 2:45. That enabled me to go to the Warwick office. I brought the dogs with me.

Georgia enjoyed the company, but after she had time to reflect (and I think realize that she was being "babysat"), she told Kathi that she didn't want Rosemary to come by anymore. We'll still bring her in – hopefully, Georgia will accept that.

(Email excerpt, Martha Jr to her sister. 8/18/05)
More Discussion

We need to talk some more about the issues of people visiting here. I know Mom *[Martha Sr]* has always had an "open house" policy of sorts, that we could all just call and say "I'm coming" and have a place to stay. But since we've moved in that really doesn't work any more. Even besides the fact that we don't have six bedrooms any more. And it especially doesn't work if someone calls Mom and tells her they're coming without talking to us as well because, as you know, Mom won't remember long enough to tell us. We need some consideration in the planning stages.

As you know, we are about at the limits of our abilities to cope with taking care of Mom 24/7. (I hate that term, but it does work.) Your visit gave us a welcome opportunity to get away and relax a little (thank you VERY MUCH). But when we're here, with any visitor, we still end up doing all the things that are necessary to keep the place going. Since Jim is home all day, he tends to bear the brunt of the 'house elf' chores, especially since his tolerance for clutter/mess is much lower than mine. Your help with Mom, keeping her occupied, etc., was very welcome, but Jim still felt a lot like a servant. (As he put it, he feels like he's running a hotel or conference center.) When other family members come, they never seem to take any responsibility for caring for Mom, so we don't even have that help. Here's something that Jim wrote to a good friend:

"My resentment level is really high, and something has to change or it's going to hurt my relationship with the rest of the family and even

my wife. I think Martha Jr is going to discuss it with her sister Susan, start there. Because while it is good for Susan to come visit and help out with her mom, I still wind up having to play housekeeper for another person. With other family members, we don't even have the benefit of them being on-call or dependably around so I can get away or do something I want to do without distraction or being tethered here. I've about reached my upper limit on putting up with it."

As you can tell, he's pretty fried. It is indicative, I think, of how stressed he is being the day-to-day carer for Mom. I asked him this morning if it would help if we got someone in to clean regularly again, and while he indicated that it might help a little, it would also be an intrusion into his private space again, and he never likes that, so it probably wouldn't help in the end.

That is one of the biggest problems, I think. He is a VERY private person and, for him, home is his refuge. It is supposed to be the place where he can get away from daily stressors but, in this case, it has *become* the major stressor. When he starts feeling like he's being asked to do even more, he starts to resent it. Another quote:

"Well, part of the problem here is that much of the rest of the family (Susan has a much more realistic idea of the current situation) thinks of Martha Sr as being in full capacity, able to invite them to come and stay, play host ... be her caring, nurturing self ... when in truth it's me and Martha Jr who are the support staff, on top of being responsible full-time for caring for Martha Sr herself."

Now, I don't want to discourage anyone from coming to visit Mom, especially not you, but we need to keep track of the fact that it is our house, too, and any additional person here means more work for us. Mom always wants to revert to the 'gracious hostess' mode, which is as it should be, except she can't actually *do* any of it so we end up doing it. And Mom has a bad habit of forgetting that Jim is actually her son-in-law and treats him rather like a servant, especially when someone else is here.

I don't know what the best resolution is, but I know we need to figure out how to make our lives less stressful. We want to continue to care for Mom as long as possible, and I don't believe it is yet time to consider another living arrangement for her. It might help when people visit, if they're not going to take some of the responsibility from us, that they stay somewhere else (like maybe with John) and just visit. That sounds a bit harsh, and I don't mean it to, but that's one option. Do you have any ideas?

> *Comment from Kathi:* We couldn't invite anyone in for the longest time because of the "Mom messes." Until it dawned on us to lock John's office door, she would go in there and shuffle through everything. Ditto with my desk, her desk, all of her books and papers, everything downstairs in the basement. The reason why I'm always on the state's lost property list is because she'd lose/tear up/who knows what with my paychecks. I'm still getting notifications from them...and to think back then that I was usually too stressed out to even realize I'd had them.

(Email excerpt, Martha Jr to her sister. 5/26/06)
Just checking in

Yesterday when I got home, I could hear Jim in the front room talking with Mom *[Martha Sr]*. I was putting my stuff down, so I couldn't listen to what they were saying, but Jim told me that she had called for me ("Martha?") – not remembering who might be home. When he got in there, she was futzing with the seatbelt in the chair, saying she needed to find out how to undo it so she could get up and go to the bathroom. They had the conversation (for about the 4,323rd time) about how she always needs someone to walk with her wherever she goes, and she denied she had ever heard of that.

After she finished in the bathroom, I took her back to the living room and got her settled in her chair, then I sat down and asked her what was going on. She said that she was provoked with Jim for telling her that she had to have someone walk with her. I told her that we'd been doing that for more than two years, and that we had discussed the necessity of it with her many times, but she was *sure* this was all news to her. So I explained again why it is necessary (because her balance is so bad, and her strength not good either, so that – even with the walker – she isn't stable enough to go by herself) and that we wanted her to be safe. I told her she is welcome to go anywhere and do anything she wants, but she just always needs someone alongside. 'But what if no one is here?' 'Someone is *always* here. ALWAYS.' She wasn't very convinced. I told her that I understood that her memory was getting worse so that she didn't remember things like this as well as she had, and that because of that she needs to trust us, that we aren't just being mean.

Comment from Kathi: reminds me when my mom's spinal stenosis got bad enough that she literally couldn't walk but kept insisting she could. She'd stand up and ask me why her legs were bothering her. When I told her it was actually her back and not her legs, she was totally dumbfounded.

June
Losing proposition

What started out as short-term memory problems and some confusion is now progressing to the point where in some important ways your loved one is no longer who they were. The disease is stealing them away, bit by bit.

And that hurts. This is actually a major part of the reason that both John and Jim became the primary care-providers for their respective mothers-in-law: it was easier on them emotionally than it was on their wives. Because losing a parent is always hard, whether it happens suddenly or over time, whereas losing an in-law just doesn't carry such emotional baggage.

Everyone responds to this type of loss differently. Friends and family members may still be in denial, though usually at this stage that is much more difficult. Some people resort to avoidance, and so drop away from your life, contributing to your isolation. Some people get angry, but it is hard to be angry at a disease and so they (unconsciously) direct their anger at the patient or even the care-givers. And care-providers themselves will experience anger, which sometimes is turned inward and manifests as health or emotional problems.

So, slowly your loved one is disappearing, and at the same time your support system (friends, family) is too. The pressure has ratcheted up a notch, and you can feel it, see it starting to have an effect. You start to look for other options, other solutions which might be able to help.

We hadn't yet learned that there were many other benefits out there that we qualified for, and wouldn't be able to find the *necessary documentation to *prove* that we qualified for (e.g., Georgia's marriage certificate to prove she was married to Kathi's father for the veteran's benefits).*

We also hadn't realized the impact that our eating out would have – the number of times we ate out had now increased to daily.

Kathi began laying out clothes for Georgia to wear, and some-times Georgia refused to wear what was chosen. Other times, I think Kathi may have been exhausted and not caught a few potential clashes...so began my instant education on the home version of "what not to wear" as I began to help Georgia select clothes and get dressed in the mornings.

On cold mornings, I'd pre-warm some of her clothes using a nearly-cylindrical heater – something that Georgia really, really liked. (Who doesn't like putting on nice warm clothes on a cold morning?) If I knew I was going to see a client and would have Georgia with me, I'd coordinate the outfits, usually putting us each into something that involved a jacket. That started our visits to Kathi at work, initially in order to ensure that I was matching us up properly and then later simply to bring a smile into her day (or to tweak her, as appropriate).

Eventually, I took over choosing Georgia's clothes for the day, and actually learned a little something about matching outfits in the process. It began slowly, with minor adjustments here and there to Kathi's selections if things didn't seem to "go" together once Georgia was dressed, and progressed to matching outfits (at least in terms of styling) when I began taking Georgia on various consulting engagements with me to give her something to do and still keep an eye on her. This was, of course, before she got enrolled into an Adult Day program.

(Email excerpt, Jim to Martha Jr's sister. 10/1/04)
Loss

"Thanks for your thoughts. I think my initial concern was Martha Jr's angry response to Mom and hoping that there is some way that the stress can be lowered and Martha Jr can find more equanimity overall. My suggestions were relevant to that."

Well, understood. You guys are all facing a loss as your mom ages and moves from this life to whatever is beyond, accentuating the emotional energy in the equation. It's easy not to realize this, because you're in the middle of it. Martha Jr sometimes expresses this in anger/frustration. You suffer migraines from worry. John *[Martha Jr's brother]* tends towards avoidance. These are natural responses, and to be expected. It's somewhat easier for me to see as an outsider of the family unit.

I think the key to dealing with these emotional winds is communication. Martha Jr mostly just wanted to vent when she initially called you, communicating her frustration at sometimes being at odds with your mom. That was a healthy outlet that I recommended, since I know how much she respects and looks up to you, and how good you are for her.

Likewise, I wanted to reassure you that our decisions on how to proceed with your mom's exercises, et cetera, were based on professional recommendations tempered with a little common sense and awareness of her needs and desires. I hate to think that you're worrying yourself into ill health when a few simple facts can clear things up.

And with John, I've tried to encourage him to just relax and spend time with his mom, taking advantage of this opportunity before it is passed. I'd hate knowing that he missed this just because of tension between him and Martha Jr, or because he doesn't want to face your mom's mortality. I never had the opportunity to know my parents as adults, let alone to share with them their 'golden years', and it would be a shame for him to miss his opportunity. And the more he and Martha Jr are together, the better it is.

"I still have that concern, but I am glad that things are going well now."

Hey, it's hard. I get frustrated, too. But I always try and explain to Martha Sr why we are doing the things we're doing, to understand from her perspective how it can be confusing and a little frightening, and we move on.

(Kathi's LiveJournal entry. 2/24/04)
Health Care, Insurance and Funding, oh my

If anything, I hope there's one thing to be learned in my ramblings as of late – when it comes time to take care of your parent(s), it pays to be prepared beforehand! And I don't mean just with the legal stuff. Learn what's available in your area. Have some idea what Medicare covers in your state (if you're in the US – I have no idea what the equivalent is in Canada, but then again you guys have socialized medicine there). Know what the qualifications are in your state for Medicaid. The rules change every year here in MA for both, so I'm presuming they also do elsewhere. What I'm finding out, sadly enough, is that there's no middle ground – you either have to be filthy rich or piss poor to receive services. That's not right. My anxiety and anger about all this means a burgeoning very angry anxious Kathi who's trying with all her might to calm herself down enough right now.

Both day care places I made appointments with yesterday aren't covered by Mom's *[Georgia]* insurance. The first one – the one in Boston – I was right about: We'd have to pay full price because we're not Boston residents. Mucho bucks. The second one – the one near where I work – isn't in the county Elder Services network, which also means we'd be paying full price.

In desperation I called Elder Services and left a message for their Care-giver Omsbudsman. This was the same person who told me earlier that Mom isn't qualified for most of their services to begin with because she's not qualified for Medicaid. But fuck, there MUST be something she's qualified for. There HAS to be, isn't there?

John and I simply can't afford the services the Senior Resource people provide. Strike One. Mom's not bad enough to warrant me placing her in one of the other day centers we looked at a few weeks ago. Strike Two. John and I can't afford to pay a home health aide out-of-pocket FT, or, hell, even PT (the starting rate around here is $15-20/hr). Strike Three. Nobody in his family wants to help us look after her (ironic how, if we had a baby, they'd be all over us though). Strike Four.

Where does that leave us? John still has no idea if he'll have more work after all this traveling is over. I can enact the Family Medical Leave Act at work, but of course I won't get paid, and it's only good for 12 weeks total. I'd still have my health/dental insurance to pay just like I did when I was out with my heel last summer.

Or...I could say "Fuck it" and spend all of Mom's money to hire somebody to look after her. That'd qualify her for Medicaid after awhile. But then we'd say goodbye to getting some necessary house repairs done and everything else around here. And hell, what about *gulp* when she dies? She has no life insurance.

(Kathi's LiveJournal entry. 4/23/04)
Classic Hollywood

Mom *[Georgia]* has been up since 3AM or so watching her classic Hollywood VHS tapes. Or so she says. Heck, maybe she's been up since 5 – who knows?

Anyway, the reason why I woke up so early was because I heard swept-away straining violins. I knew it wasn't a dream because John was already up.

The cutest thing was, both dogs were at her feet. They both looked up and waggy-thumped their tails as I came downstairs, but neither of them moved. Mom seemed completely oblivious to my presence until after I said "Good morning" and went into the kitchen. She asked me why I was awake in the middle of the night.

"Um, it's quarter past six, Mom," I said. "It's dark and rainy out. Maybe that's why you're thinking it's the middle of the night."

She paused as to think about it, looked up at the clock, looked out the window, then looked back at me. "It's morning, isn't it?"

I nodded.

BTW, I finally made a neurological appointment for her – May 6th. She hasn't had one since she was diagnosed. I'm relieved that we'll finally get some answers, but I'm also scared to fucking death.

(Email excerpt, Jim to Martha Jr. 10/9/06)
Gah!

Gah...just had a long lunch with your mom *[Martha Sr]*. She was fine before we went in the kitchen (made a stop for the toilet), but after a few minutes of her having lunch, it was clear that something was bugging her (the first evidence was her fussing with the napkin, as I mentioned when I called). I talked with her, trying to find out what was going on, and eventually got her to tell me what was bothering her. Ready for it?

She wanted "her" bib – the yellow one. The one she was wearing belonged to someone, she wasn't sure on the name. After I tried to explain that they were both hers, she got real defensive and adamant – that yellow one had been hers for years, since before she moved in here.

sigh I tried to explain that no, she'd only been using the bibs for a few months...

...she got hostile, insisted that she'd been using it for years, repeated since before she moved in here...I made the mistake of calmly trying to explain that she'd lived here for over 50 years...then we got into the whole "this house was the one I grew up in, and I remember it being moved here" routine, saying that I didn't know what I was talking about, et cetera. I was surprised at the vehemence with which she said this.

Weird. Got her in and down for her nap (she insisted that she had to go to the toilet again, though naturally didn't). With luck, it'll all be past by the time she wakes from her nap.

Love you...

(Kathi's LiveJournal entry. 6/9/04)
Setting course

Mom *[Georgia]* cannot find any of her summer clothes. I remember last year we went through a lot of her stuff and donated it. We had also bought her some new stuff. I can't find any of it. They could very well be up in the attic, too. Since last night she's been trying to convince me that I've stolen them. Um, I haven't worn anything of hers since...???

Her gait's changing. This morning she mentioned she feels like a "drunken sailor." I asked her, "In what way?" She said she feels like she's tipping over, and her hips hurt. I said that yes, her gait's starting to change (she walks at a slight tilt – has been doing so since we thought she hurt her leg last month and took her to the ER). I tried to straighten her out by placing my hands on her shoulders and leaving them there as she walked toward me. Didn't cure the "tilt" at all.

I left a message for the neuro doc.

She's also starting to have trouble choosing what to wear. Granted, even with last year's cleanout, she still has a LOT of old clothes and such scattered between 3 closets and 2 bureaus, most of it stuff she hasn't worn since Year 1. I've been trying to compartmentalize everything so that she only has to deal with 1 closet and 1 bureau. It hasn't worked because she still flings stuff all over the place. I wonder if marking separate drawers and "underwear," "shirts," etc. would help...only thing is, I also know she's not reading as much as she used to. I'm beginning to think her mind's having trouble translating whatever print she's looking at.

She's been curiously (or maybe not) interested in Reagan's death. At first she didn't realize he actually died. After she did, she kept mentioning how he used to be on "Death Valley Days", was married to Jane Wyman, his acting/broadcasting career, etc. Then she started asking what exactly he died of. I said pneumonia (which is true), but I left out the part that it was complicated by the Alzheimer's. John's reply was Alzheimer's and pneumonia. She paused and said, "That's what I have, isn't it?" I started to explain that the neuro doc didn't have a definite diagnosis, but I stopped because I thought I'd only confuse her more.

As for the care-giving part, John and I have decided that, for now, he won't be doing a high-gear job search. He can work as an independent contractor for his company from home as long as whatever he makes doesn't cut into his unemployment. This means that I'm now the primary breadwinner. At this point taking care of Mom is more important than money. We're not strapped for anything, thank goodness.

(Kathi's LiveJournal entry. 8/18/04)
Irrational Anger

She *[Georgia]* certainly had a "hair across the ass" all day today that never let up tonight. We have no idea where it sprang from. Except for her and I going out for lunch, she didn't want to do anything except sit in her chair in the living room and simmer to a boil. Didn't want dinner. John and I went out to Borders – weren't even gone an hour – she'd made herself a cup of tea in the meantime and claimed we were trying to starve her. John went up to the office. And she started in on me – "He's using you! I don't want him in this house! He's not going to run my life!" I kept benignly smiling and replying, "I'm sorry you feel that way," but that made her even more angry. At last she stomped upstairs to bed. An hour later she returns and starts in on John – "I WANT YOU OUT OF THIS HOUSE! THINGS WERE FINE UNTIL YOU CAME ALONG!" Yeah, right, and he's the cause of your dementia.

She threatened to call the police to have John forcibly removed, but it was moot since she didn't know the number, much less remember that she'd left her glasses upstairs.

On and on it went. At one point I told her that if John leaves, so do I. Start the teary fountain. John and I kept asking her why she was so upset. She couldn't remember, but was damned well not going to admit it.

"THIS IS MY HOUSE AND I CAN DO WHAT I DAMN WELL WANT! LEAVE SO I CAN DIE!"

Ah, so that's it – she's blaming our presence on her being alive. We leave, she dies. She wants to die. Or something like that.

After she went back upstairs, we called the Alzheimer's Association 24-hour hotline. A counselor called us back. Their advice? If she's still acting the same way tomorrow, don't hesitate to take her to the ER. They'll sedate her and put her on 24-hour observation. And yes, call the neuro doc and get a referral to a geriatric psychiatrist ASAP because depression + dementia = worse than dementia by itself. She poses a danger to both herself and us if her behavior continues.

And no, it's not a matter of us walking away – not that we'd actually do it. I'm legally responsible for her.

(Kathi's LiveJournal entry. 2/12/06)
Acting Out

Let's pray Mom *[Georgia]* doesn't go whacko like she did with John yesterday – rummaging everything, throwing random stuff in the washer, tearing apart what he thought were photos because Mom didn't know what they were (I'm hoping they were ads or something). I found Dad's notary public stamp shredded and scattered all over her bureau. Every time he told her not to do something, she kept screaming "It's MY house I CAN DO WHAT I WANT!"

(Email excerpt, Martha Jr to her sister. 11/30/06)
Every day is an adventure

Thanks for your call – sorry we missed it. I'm not sure when you called (the answering machine had lost track of what day and time it was) but yes, we are having a winter storm. They were so sure we were in for a lot of ice this morning that everything in the area canceled (schools, etc) and we didn't get as much as they were predicting. Just south of us did. I used the excuse to stay home. But currently there is ice and snow on the ground, sleet coming down, and dire predictions for huge amounts of snow by tomorrow. (I've heard as much as 18", but I don't believe it for a second.) It was pretty impressive yesterday when the temps started dropping – about 60 when Jim and Alwyn went on their early morning walk, dropped all day until it was about 30 at bedtime. Woke up this morning to about 22 and it hasn't gotten much warmer all day. BRRR.

Good day for a fire. Of course, Mom *[Martha Sr]* decided to obsess over some problem she thought she saw in the fireplace. Sometimes these things come entirely out of left field! It took both of us reassuring her (plus her haldol) before she calmed down.

This evening she was pretty far gone. (Sundowning.) I went to get her as usual at 8:30 to brush her teeth and get ready for bed. I was a few minutes late. She was sitting there waiting for me, with her magazines and puzzles put away. I poked the fire a bit and asked if she was ready to go brush her teeth. She said she was going to call, but couldn't remember my name to call. I told her she didn't have to call me by name. After I got her up into the wheelchair, ready to go to the bathroom, she looked thoughtful and then asked if my name was Martha. I said yes. She asked what my last name was, and I said it was the same as hers. "John?" "Yes." "Well, why is that??" "Because I'm your daughter." She thought about that for a bit and then said something like "but I thought I didn't get the name John until after you were my daughter." Huh?? So we talked about how she'd been Martha John since 1940, or for 66 years. I finally said that in 1940 she had married Hurst John and become Martha John. That rang a bell – she "had forgotten about him!"

Every day is an adventure!

Love you!!!!

(Kathi's LiveJournal entry. 9/29/05)
Losing Dad

Mom *[Georgia]* doesn't remember my dad.

She doesn't remember ever being married.

For the past half hour she's been trying to figure out why the surname she's used since 1956 isn't the same as her maiden surname. John and I tried explaining it to her. There's a photo of my dad hanging on the wall separating the kitchen from the dining room; it's been there forever. She has no idea who he is or why the photo's hanging there.

I can't cry or show any sort of distressing emotion on my face because she'll pick up on it.

(Kathi's LiveJournal entry. 12/13/05)
32 Years Ago Today: Dad's Anniversary

Grief has a life of its own. If left unchecked, it'll engulf you when you least expect it to. It doesn't care if you're in public, it doesn't care where you are in public because, dammit, if it's going to show, it'll display itself in front of an unwitting audience, come hell over high water, and not give a shit upon whom its outburst will affect!

December 13th is my bad day of the year. 32 years ago today my father died. The grief ebbs and flows; some years it bothers me less than others. Maybe it's because I don't remember him very well anymore.

The fact that I don't remember bothers me more some years than others.

My mother *[Georgia]* claims she's never had a husband. She's adamant about it.

She has no idea who the gentleman is in the photo on the wall between the kitchen and dining room. She sometimes asks us about it; John takes the roundabout route by first asking, "Now, Georgia, who was Kathi's father? You know. You know his name."

"No I don't. Kathi doesn't have a father."

"Not now she doesn't. But she did. You were married to him. What was his name?"

"I don't remember. Jack? Sam? Um, Stevie?"

"No, no, and no, Stevie was your brother. C'mon, you know."

My mother shakes her head. She goes teetering off to the living room, and, if you listen carefully, you can hear her quietly weeping. We go in and attempt to calm her down. She looks up at me. "I'm sorry. I don't remember him. If you say his name I'll know it, but other than that...I'm sorry."

Twice today she didn't recognize me until I said something.

Out of earshot she kept asking John where I was.

(Kathi's LiveJournal entry. 9/5/04)
Cuts like a knife

When John and I returned from grocery shopping earlier tonight, Mom *[Georgia]* automatically went upstairs to bed. This isn't unusual; she putters about in her room until she's tired enough to go to sleep.

John and I were putting the groceries away when she suddenly called down to ask me to come help her. I went upstairs. In her bathroom she showed me a small but clean diagonal slice almost stretching across her inner wrist. It was bleeding. She asked me to put a bandage on it.

My stomach dropped, naturally, but I didn't want to get accusatory or anything like that, so as matter-of-factly as I could I cleaned it up and put on the bandage while asking, "How did that happen?"

Immediately she replied, "Well, I didn't do it deliberately. I may not remember everything, but I'm not that stupid."

"But how did you do it?" I asked.

"Oh, I was cutting up something and the knife slipped."

Oh.

Then she started sobbing and grabbed onto me for dear life. "I want to die," she kept repeating. "I can't do anything right. I want to die."

I just held onto her and kept murmuring, "No, Mommy, you don't. Please don't say that. We want you here. The dogs want you here."

Suddenly she straightened herself out and let go of me. Her face was utter blank. "I'm OK, please don't worry. I'll see you tomorrow..." She let her voice trail off.

"I'll see you when I get home from work," I said.

"I should be here. Good night."

July
Coming to terms

"July" is coming to terms with the reality of care-giving, for everyone. You're just trying to sort out what works and what doesn't – trying to find routines which will be comfortable and comforting. In some ways, it is the longest "month" – a period when the changes brought about by dementia are fairly small from day to day. This stability can be misleading, though – the changes may be small from day to day, and your routines can be adjusted to accommodate them without real effort – but they add up.

When you are at this point, you're deeply invested in being a care-provider. You start to identify and define yourself by this role. You have been through the stage of doubting whether you can do what needs to be done, and you gain solid confidence that you and you alone understand what is really happening. You know all about the meds, all about doctors, all about the needs of your loved one for whom you are caring. You have gotten used to the responsibilities involved, and will likely resent it if anyone tries to interfere or impinge. After all, you're the one doing the care-providing – you're the one there, on the scene, with the most information and experience. Friends and family members will turn to you for news and decisions. This is the reality you are in, and you come to accept it. This is how it is.

Before one brief vacation when Martha Jr and I were going to be gone we prepared a "Mom Operating Manual" for her sister – a complete itemized run-down of all the usual routines and procedures that Martha Sr was used to. About a year later we were going to be gone again for a few days, and thought that we should check the manual to see if anything needed to be changed – and almost everything in there was completely out of date.

Things had evolved slowly enough that we had lost track of how much change there had been.

This was educational for another reason – if all those routines in caring for Martha Sr had changed, how had we changed in response? As John says, both of us relied a great deal on being able to write and work through emotions as our own personal and cathartic coping mechanisms. We needed that time, that outlet. But when things with our patient were disrupted, we lost that opportunity. Both of us expressed, at one point or another, that this was "Frustrating, particularly in that it disrupts my ability to think and write further, meaning some of the stuff I wanted to get done today." Losing that helped contribute to a slow spiral down for us, as well as our respective mothers-in-law.

(Kathi's LiveJournal entry. 1/6/05)
Lawyers & Legalities

Meeting with the attorney was interesting. There's a murky part of my mom's assets I've only been dimly aware of – something to do with a real estate investment firm my dad had bought shares in before he died. The shares, of course, were passed to Mom *[Georgia]*. I have no recent paperwork, no canceled checks – nothing – to account for it, never mind any evidence that she still has or sold them. Grr.

The upside? We're getting her will, the Durable Power of Attorney (DPOA), and the health proxy redone. The house part is going to be tricky – it's a matter of discovering whether it'd be better to put it in an irrevocable trust (with me as the trustee) or to put it under the Medicaid "Caretaker Clause", meaning that if she needs long-term care, the state cannot take the house because it'd be a hardship on me.

She also had to name another executor should, god forbid, something happen to me. Of course I was asked to leave the room. I have no idea who she named.

(Email excerpt, Martha Jr to the family. 10/16/06)
Hospice consultation

Just want to let you know the latest with regard to doctors and hospice. When the hospice "released" Mom *[Martha Sr]* at the beginning of July, they made a point of telling us that they expected she would come back on to hospice at some point in time. She was just too stable then for them to keep her.

So several weeks ago we asked Dr. M what we should be looking for to know when it was time to call them back in. Turns out, he had not understood their releasing Mom in the first place. I explained that, based on their metrics she just didn't continue to qualify and he thought that very strange. Long story short, he called them up and said he thought she should be back on hospice.

So last week Nurse T, the other hospice nurse (whom we had met a couple times), called to say that they needed to come see Mom and talk to us to determine if she should, indeed, be re-admitted. We set yesterday morning as the time for that visit; it worked especially well for them because they have their big staff meeting where they evaluate cases, etc., on Wednesday afternoon.

In talking about it between us, Jim and I were concerned that they might re-admit her now only to release her again in another 90 days. That had caused such an emotional whiplash previously that we really didn't want to go through that again. So we intercepted Nurse T and the other staff member he brought with him on the front porch where we stood around and discussed Mom's current condition, what we see as the gradual arc of her decline, etc. We made it clear that, while we do want to see her re-admitted to hospice at an appropriate time, we are not at all sure that time is yet. If they thought it was appropriate, fine, as long as she wouldn't be discharged again after 90 days.

He had come prepared to visit with Mom and do a regular check-up on her, but as we talked, I think he got a clear picture of her current condition and what he needed to know to take her case back to his meeting. He promised to call me after the meeting to let me know.

When he called, he said that they could re-admit her now, but there would be no assurance that she would stay for the duration, so it was probably best to wait. We agreed. I asked what we should look for as markers that we should be calling them back in. He suggested a couple of possible milestones to watch for. One would be if she lost interest in food, or started forgetting to chew or swallow. We already have to remind her to eat when she's paying attention to something else, but this would be beyond that. The other would be if she stopped wanting to get up and around much, started sleeping a lot more, or just preferring to stay in bed.

So now we know what to look for, and we have some affirmation that we are doing a decent job taking care of her so far. As long as her routine isn't disrupted too much, she seems to get along just fine.

As an aside, we suspected this past weekend she had a bit of a UTI. We got some cran-raspberry juice for her to drink (she seems to like it) and it appears to have cleared right up. So we've added a couple small glasses of that to her regular diet each day.

So, that's where we stand vis-a-vis hospice, and other things. We'll keep on doing what we can, though I have to admit we're both getting pretty exhausted at times. Still, the reward is there in her eyes.

(Kathi's LiveJournal entry. 1/8/05)
Absence Makes The Mind Delusional

Mom *[Georgia]* has been delusional off and on lately. None last night, thank goodness, but for the past 3-4 nights she's been insisting that I have a small daughter and she can't figure out why my daughter won't speak. I've tried to get her to describe what my daughter looks like. Mom says she doesn't know because she never shows her face. John and I have been calling her "phantom daughter".

Okaaaaaaay.

Another night she was up until 2AM trying to pack every single item in her bedroom. Mind you, she could probably have 3 good yard sales with the crap she's been hoarding all these years and still have enough left over for another. She had stuff in bags, pillowcases, upside-down 70s-era dresses (including the one she wore to my dad's funeral – scary). The reason? She thinks she's visiting us and wants to go "home", meaning where she grew up. Sometimes she says we're sending her away. Um, no...not yet, in any case, and by then hopefully you won't know...

One thing we've noticed: She gets this way if John hasn't been around during the day. He had that out-of-town client earlier this week. The first full day he was home was Thursday, and that wasn't even by default because of the snowstorm. She's been perfectly fine since then.

(Jim's blog. 7/9/07)
Unbelievable

Here's a small insight into caring for someone with Alzheimer's/ Dementia: any change to routine will have repercussions for a day or more.

As mentioned previously, I attended the Heinlein Centennial this past weekend, while my wife was performing with the North American Welsh Choir. My wife's sister made arrangements to come and care for Martha Sr while we were to be gone. This is essentially what we have to do whenever we want to both be gone anywhere, and logistically it is problematic: my sister-in-law not only has her own life, but she lives on the west coast and has to fly in to be here. Given that she's a couple hours away from an airport on her end, and we're effectively the same here, it's more than a little bit of a hassle.

But even beyond that, our being gone presents other difficulties. Specifically, it throws Martha Sr 'off', compounding the problems presented by her disease. My sister-in-law is good about rolling with this over a short time period, but then it happens again when we get home – which tends to negate the psychological benefits of being able to get away for a short period of time. An example from this afternoon: Martha Sr had been napping after lunch, as is her custom. We have hospital rails on the sides of her bed, and a simple 'web' of 1" nylon straps over the top, from railing to railing, to prevent her from getting out of bed though she can move around freely in it. But she only sometimes remembers that she needs help getting out of bed, let alone standing or moving. As I told a friend in an email a bit ago:

Been unbelievable this afternoon.

About 2:45 I heard her moving around. Not usually a big deal, since she will shift position. But then I heard something concerning, so went to investigate.

She had managed to slide her legs up to mid-thigh out between the bars (which are horizontal), dangling them over the side of the bed. She'd then gotten tangled up in the webbing, trying to sit up. I asked her why she didn't just call if she wanted to get up, and I got a snarly response about her not needing any help, et cetera.

After sitting there and letting her try to untangle herself and get her legs back in bed, I got her sorted out. She was still snarly, said that I just wanted to keep her in bed for no reason, that she could do just fine, thank you very much, if I'd get 'that stuff' out of the way. Fine. I removed the webbing, put down the rail. Some minutes later, she finally admitted that yeah, maybe she did need some help to get up and onto the potty.

She's suitably chagrined now. That might last the rest of the day. Or maybe not.

That's just one example. The whole thing, from start to finish, took over an hour. And through it I had to explain repeatedly where she was, that her mother wasn't here, who I was, et cetera. Some of this is 'normal' (perhaps I should say 'typical') behavior – she'll fuss with the webbing or some such, rather than calling for help. But this is the first time that she's tried to slide between the bars of the railing, and it is rare for her to be hostile like that for any length of time. We've seen other examples of behavior that are somewhat extreme as well. I can't prove it, but I'm certain that this is all fallout from the change first of our being gone and my sister-in-law being here, and then her being gone and my wife and I being here.

Frustrating, particularly in that it disrupts my ability to think and write further, meaning some of the stuff I wanted to get done today (such as writing some additional posts about the Centennial) isn't going to get done. So it goes.

(John's diary. 2/7/05)
Kitchen Reorg, etc.

– Finian's

Kathi, Geogia and I came out to visit Marge. I begged off, asking them to convey my greetings, so that I could do some writing here prior to their arrival. I did, and feel better for it.

Kath & I reorganized a portion of the kitchen today. It was – like many things – long overdue. I'm glad we got it done, and I believe Kath is happy with it as well. I've been snippy/snipey with her, over items that I shouldn't be, that she had nothing to do with. I've gotta make that up to her.

(Kathi's LiveJournal entry. 7/8/04)
Mixed Up & Mischievous

She *[Georgia]* is suddenly having a difficult time choosing appropriate clothing to wear. Cleaning out all the closets in her room
and dressing room (the master bedroom suite takes up half of
upstairs addition – my dad detested small bedrooms) is a journey
in itself. Every day I push a bunch of out of season/old clothing
into a garbage bag and sock it away in the attic. I'm not even
halfway done, as she's got clothing around she hasn't worn in,
like, 20 years.

I don't have to physically help her dress, but I have to give her a
choice of outfits and lay everything out on the desk chair. I've
had to repeatedly tell her to wear an undershirt or camisole whenever she wears white/ivory because she refuses to wear a bra.
This is one of our biggest daily battles. She doesn't realize everyone can see her nipples if she doesn't wear something underneath.
One day it must've sunk in because she came out of the bathroom
wearing Kleenex over each (she'd taped it to her skin with
masking tape – don't ask). Of course she couldn't fathom why
the Kleenex was there when I asked her.

Her appetite's turned a 180. She no longer likes the foods she's
always eaten – cereal, bananas, beef, potatoes (except French fries),
most veggies...she's always been a fussier eater than me. If it doesn't
look "right" (i.e., like something served in a restaurant), she won't
touch it. All she'll eat is melon, Popsicles, chicken, anything fried,
eggs (bad for the cholestrol, but she's craving them), anything
chocolate, and corn off the cob. Oh, and muffins. Thing is, you
have to give her a teeny-tiny portion of whatever or she won't
touch it, claiming that you've given her too much. I'm talking
about how much a sparrow would eat. And it'd be one thing if
Mom were tiny and frail, but she isn't. She's got a pretty good
pot belly. She also can't tell if she's sated or not. That's disturbing.

If John doesn't watch her like a hawk, she gets into all sorts of
mischief. Once she tried taking both dogs on a walk around the

block. Ember nearly knocked her over while they were on the back stairs. She couldn't remember it happening even immediately after it did (everyone was OK, by the way). So...now she and John take the dogs 'round the block 3-4 times a day.

I could count the number of times she's messed up the laundry, the kitchen (especially after I rearranged everything – she put everything back the Way It Was, much to my consternation), etc., but I won't. It's difficult enough sitting here typing this without having to go there, if you know what I mean.

(Kathi's LiveJournal entry. 9/5/04)
Physical Deterioration & Instabilities

Spent the morning in ER because Mom *[Georgia]* nearly collapsed while trying to get out of bed. We didn't know about that until she attempted to come downstairs – she made it halfway until her legs suddenly gave out. She slid to the bottom step on her bum. Very shaky and crying. We got her into the kitchen, sat her down, calmed her, then called her doc.

We had her get dressed in the half-bath down here. John canceled meeting with a client while I tried to rearrange my schedule for the day (yes, I know – why am I making plans when I'm supposed to be off my foot? I have no idea.) We decided that John would drop Mom and I off at the ER while he went to my employer to deliver my doc's letter and run some errands.

The ER then. Well.

Her ankle's fine – just a simple twist – but there's something else going on that neither of us were aware of: The arthritis in her lower back is so bad that she's developing spinal stenosis. That's when the spinal cord cavity narrows. The narrowing impinges the spinal cord much like a herniated disk (of which she also has several, surprise surprise) impinges a nerve. In Mom's case, the referred pain is in and around her ankle. The X-rays confirmed all this.

What's baffling is that she's never, ever mentioned back pain. Not one bit. I'm sitting here wracking my brain, trying to think of any time she's ever mentioned it. I can't come up with anything.

They contacted her doctor, who in turn scheduled her for a MRI tomorrow morning. The MRI should show how bad the stenosis is. Treatment will depend on the severity, of course. The doc has already said that they won't operate on her because of her arthritis and age.

(Kathi's LiveJournal entry. 9/16/04)
Little White Lies

Just returned from Mom's *[Georgia]* MRI. The tech let me peek at the pictures as they came up on the monitor. All I could make out were 3 herniated discs, one of which looked quite prolapsed. *shudder*

We're due for lunch at the day center place John and I visited last week. The director advised us not to tell her about it so she wouldn't be upset beforehand. So we're going with "We're taking you out to lunch." It helps that the place looks like a big mansion rather than a nursing home or other health-type center.

I'm nervous as hell.

(Email excerpt, Jim to the family. 12/28/05)
Drug problems

I just wanted to update you guys on some aspects of Martha Sr's condition, particularly regarding something which happened tonight at dinner. We will be discussing this (and other matters) with her primary care physician (Dr. M) at a regularly scheduled appt. tomorrow, and so will probably have more information after.

In the last few weeks Martha Sr has been becoming increasingly hostile in her behavior towards me. This usually manifests anytime I ask her to use her walker correctly, to continue eating a meal when she's become distracted, or to use her hands to support herself while sitting down, or to call when she is ready to rise from the toilet or get up from bed, et cetera. (Please note, she doesn't always do this, but it is during these times that the hostility shows up.) At first, it was just a dismissive attitude, then it went to snide responses, then to challenges to my requests, and so forth. Initially I was able to just calmly explain that I'm asking her to do these things for her own safety, and that was that. But that became less likely to resolve her hostility as time went on. This evening, we had the first instance of actual combativeness, to the extent that she actually tried to bite me. I was, of course, in no danger, and didn't need to do anything other than move away from her. But the fact that she actually attempted this was significant.

This change in behavior, and increasing difficulties in our cajoling her to eat properly, seems to correspond to the time she started taking the Aricept (an Alzheimer's drug to reduce memory loss and maintain cognitive function). The two things may not be related, but the timing is a cause for concern in my mind. It may be best to take her off the drug, see if the behavior changes. We will discuss it with Dr. M. We also plan on discussing with him the advisability of discontinuing or at least scaling back our efforts to make sure Martha Sr eats properly at each and every meal. We've managed in the last year to help her gain a significant amount of weight, but our efforts have become increasingly difficult and, I fear, counter-productive. The real risk is that she will start losing weight, which is never a healthy thing for someone her age and frailty.

We'll keep you posted.

(Kathi's LiveJournal entry. 1/18/05)
Doctors

This afternoon is Mom's evaluation. When she *[Georgia]* realized
she had the appointment last night, she was furious:

"So what the hell do you want them to say? I'm old. You don't
let me do anything. I'm bored. That's why I get so confused. I
should be dead."

"See, that attitude is NOT
normal. You never think
of how your actions impact
those around you, namely
John and ME. And I don't
think you realize that all
the time. Plus I love how
you automatically snap to
attention whenever anyone
says the word 'doctor'.

"Maybe they'll give me a
pill so I can be over and done with all this. I'm tired."

"Uh, Ma, there's this thing called the Hippocratic oath that prevents
them from doing that..."

And on and on. Seriously, I wanted to pop her one so badly
during this exchange. Because – and I realize this is wishful thinking
on my part – if they don't find anything but "depression" in the
evaluation I'll very much want to pop her one in the jaw. For her
selfishness, her control issues, for doing anything in her power to
continue keeping me on a leash...

* * *

...because what I've been theorizing all along re Mom was exactly
correct, according to The Good Doctor™ at this afternoon's

assessment (I knew I said "evaluation" earlier – that's scheduled for 2 weeks from tomorrow.)

Ruling out the actual evaluation – the tests they give to see if you fall anywhere on the dementia/neurobiological scale – The Good Doctor™'s assessment? She has pseudodementia brought on by geriatric depression. In other words, her longstanding, very deep, very severe depression – the one she's been dragging around since I was a kid – has, in her old age, manifested itself as a type of dementia. That has no bearing if she actually does have any type of dementia – if anything, it'll compound it thousandfold. Heh.

She doesn't get it. The doctor and she spent a very pleasant-for-the-most-part 2 hours chatting about this and that. She broke down in tears 3 separate times, none of them long-lasting, but enough to alarm. Then there was the very long runaround about her longstanding perception that she does/thinks/acts the way she does because she THINKS I want her to do/think/act that particular way. Where the loving hell did she dig this up? The Good Doctor™ asked me several times if it was true. Um, no – all I want is for her to be happy and safe, but her actions forced me to act the way I do, as in I never asked to take over the house/finances/etc. She lost interest in everything. What was I supposed to do, watch her drown in bankruptcy?

...There's a lot to process. Then there's her utter denial that anything is wrong, why did I bring her there, everybody must think I'm nuts, right? Um no, quite the contrary. The Good Doctor™ praised her articulation, her repartee with me, and her overall manner to high heaven. Like a lot of people, he didn't believe how old she is at first.

It doesn't matter to her: she's OLD, and in her mind, OLD = SIX FEET UNDER. And don't try to change her mind because dammit, if I can't be the way I've always been, then I should be dead. My daughter says so (hello, I've never said that in my entire life!)

Anyway, her first therapy appointment is two weeks from today. They're going to tinker with her meds because it's obvious the Zoloft isn't doing much. The therapist is down the street from the store, so unless we can switch her to a later appointment, John's going to have to drive her there, and I'm going to have to drop her home during my lunch hour. She claims "nobody can fix me." We'll see about that.

(Email excerpt, Jim to the family. 12/29/05)
What the doctor said

Well, we did meet with Dr. M, Martha Sr's primary care doctor. After the check-up and discussion, he recommended that we drop the Aricept. The chances are that the drug has just messed with her neurotransmitter balance, and prompted the behavioral changes we've seen in recent weeks. So, effective immediately we'll drop that, and see if she returns to a more "normal" state in the coming weeks, as the drug purges from her system. Keep your fingers crossed.

In regards to her eating, Dr. M suggested that we just remove all distractions at mealtimes. We had been eating dinner with Martha Sr, trying to be more interactive with her, but she would become easily distracted by either what was on television or our conversation. He said that the best thing would be to just have her eat alone, maybe with some music playing, so that the only thing to get her attention would be her food. He did assure us that this was in no way being mean to her, and that it should prompt her to eat as much as she wants without additional encouragement or cajoling. So we'll do that, see how it goes.

Love to all...

(Email excerpt, Jim to the family. 1/3/06)
Dropping Aricept

Just a quick note I've been meaning to send about Martha Sr.

Dropping the Aricept has made a huge difference already. We saw a change in 24 hours. Still some obsessive behavior, and restlessness at bedtime, but she's no longer actively hostile. This is a good thing.

Love to all...

(Kathi's LiveJournal entry. 3/9/05)
Diagnosis: Almost

Speaking of appointments, we were supposed to get the results from her *[Georgia]* evaluation last month. Nope. The most her therapist could say was that "yes, there's a memory issue," but suggested I leave a voicemail for the doc who gave her the evaluation to set up an appointment with him. The rest of the time she (the therapist) tried to convince both of us that Mom definitely needs to go into a day program of some sort. The problem, however, is that Mom's too high-functioning for most programs around here (we went through this last year), so it's going to take a lot of diligence on my part trying to find a place we haven't contacted before that's nearby.

(Kathi's LiveJournal entry. 3/17/05)
Sleeping a lot

I'm still waiting for a call back from the doc who did Mom's *[Georgia]* evaluation. Seems that he's a consultant – Mom's therapist mentioned that he's only in the office once a week, and that he was going on vacation around this time. I left a message for the therapist, too. For the past few days Mom's been going to bed around 5PM and not emerging from her room until well into the following morning. She's not rummaging either – just sleeping.

I know her back's been bothering her a lot lately, so that probably has something to do with it.

Her therapist said that I definitely have to find a day center for her. The issue, once again, is that Mom's still too high-functioning for most of the places around here. Yes, she's faltering here and there, but it's not consistent. And I know a lot of this issue has to do with me, in that I'm still nervous about standing up to her and TELLING her she HAS to go there. I don't want her to be unhappy, nor do I want to start ordering her to do this and that because she'll turn around and raise holy hell. And I'm just not strong enough to stand up to her because, well...she's my mother. You just don't pull that stuff with her or you'll get it back thousandfold and be paying for it in some way for a long, long time. I know, I've tried, and she always bites me in the ass in some way. I've got enough on my plate without having to worry about that too.

(Email excerpt, Martha Jr to the family. 3/5/07)
Mom report

My turn to give you a little update on how things are going lately with Mom *[Martha Sr]*. Since Susan was here last month, Mom seems to have taken another step down in cognitive ability. At first we thought it might be a reaction to the extra stimulus of Susan's visit, and the extra appointments (dentist, nails) she had the day Susan left, but it seems to be continuing at the new, lower level. She's more confused more of the time, and remembers less. One day while Susan was here, Mom got up from her nap completely confused as to who she was, where she was, who her family were, etc. Susan sat with her for a long time looking through old photo albums of Mom's family, helping her get her bearings. We had another of those yesterday, and I did much the same thing. It helped some; though she still wasn't sure what place she was in, she could at least identify me as her daughter, Martha. It is really good that we have all these pictures of family ancestors, etc., because she really enjoys looking at them.

Other times she is not quite so confused, but clearly doesn't remember some of the main points. Where she is seems to be the hardest. She often seems to think she's in some sort of nursing home and asks about the others here, or says she doesn't want to wake anybody else up. When we assure her she's in the home she has lived in for more than 50 years, she often seems to grab on to some old memory of a house being moved from one place to another and thinks this is her old home that was moved from Boonville. We have to gently talk about when our house was built, which things were at her Mother's home in Boonville and which were not, and so forth.

Beyond that, she seems to be in fairly stable health. Her walking ability continues to weaken, mostly because she doesn't want to use it at all, and we don't force her. Just transferring from the wheelchair to her living room chair or back again is sometimes an adventure! I've found that it is actually easier for her (and me) to have her walk arm in arm with me (my arm around her waist to hold her up and hers around mine, holding each other's outside hands). She seems to feel more stable and can move more quickly than with the walker.

So, in general, we seem to have reached another level in the gradual slide. But she's mostly happy, and enjoys reading her books (she has zipped through the entire *"Church Choir Mysteries"* set, though I'm sure she doesn't remember the plot of any of them) and visiting with family. Do be aware, however, that visits tend to take a lot out of her, even if she won't say so at the time, and we often see repercussions (crankiness, more confusion) for a day or two after an extensive visit.

Just wanted to keep you informed. Do call or write if you have any questions, suggestions, or anything else.

Love to you all.

(Kathi's LiveJournal entry. 12/6/04)
Brain Farts

She *[Georgia]* doesn't believe I live here. She thinks I'm visiting. And she sometimes can't figure out why John is here ALL THE TIME (her emphasis) because she doesn't need a babysitter.

Today she asked me if Kathi has a daughter. Hmmm...well, I could've gone with the "I've got two fur daughters", but that would've complicated things. Instead I replied, "No, she doesn't. And I'm Kathi." I don't know if she believed me, but she obviously accepted it because she didn't ask again.

She keeps asking if John and I are married. She also keeps asking when we (John and I) are going home. Standard response: "We ARE home. We LIVE here with you." Then there's the issue that I obviously can't be living here because I'm never around. "I work, Mom. That's why you don't see me during the day."

Tonight Mom looked at me and asked how long I've been here. Standard reply: "Ma, you and I have shared this house for over 30 years." She denied it. I almost went the "I'm-going-to-convince-you-until-I-drop" route, but I held my tongue. Then she asked where her clothes are. I said, "Upstairs in your bedroom." "I sleep here?!?" (insert incredulous look)

I really should get a tape recorder, not to play back to her, but just for my own reference.

The ironic part? Mom will admit that her brain's rusty, that she cannot remember anything, she needs a keeper, and goddamn it, "I used to be SMART!" She always, always prided herself on her intelligence – hell, she's one of the smartest persons I've ever known. Sometimes it's painful to see her come to the realization that something is terribly wrong. But, like the trouper she is, she won't readily admit to it. At least not until dinnertime.

When she gets like that, John's the one to joke her out of it. He calls her faulty memory "brain farts." I call it a glitch. I'm very matter-of-fact about it to her face. She accepts it. Then John will crack some idiotic joke that'll make her giggle like a little kid. Sometimes she can't stop giggling.

One of the many aspects of dementia – particularly Alzheimer's – is that at some point the brain cannot process what the eyes see. I witnessed it with Stevie (my uncle) when we visited him earlier this year. In the dayroom my mother sat in front of him and kept repeating her name while pointing at herself. He cocked his head as if to say I know that name but he kept peering at her, squinting, turning his head from side to side, and I knew instantly he was trying to figure out how to match the name to her.

If it sounds like I'm treating it matter-of-factly, I am. On purpose. I can't afford to get melodramatic, or else I'll self-destruct.

(Jim's blog. 3/13/07)
Waiting game

I'm tired.

This stems in large part from the fact that the person for whom I am a care-giver has a bit of a cold/flu bug, and so needs more care and attention. As a result, I didn't get a lot of sleep last night, and I'm guessing that tonight won't be a lot better.

So I don't have a lot of energy. Not for blogging, not for writing, not for doing conservation work. Which creates a certain symmetry with the fact that right now I am largely just waiting for things to happen: waiting to hear back from any of the current crop of agents I've contacted, waiting to hear about that article in the newspaper, waiting to get feedback from anyone who is reading/ has read the novel. Hits to the site have slowed to just a hundred or so a day, and downloads of the full novel are slowly climbing towards 1900. Everything is on hold, waiting, waiting...

(Kathi's LiveJournal entry. 7/11/05)
OCD

Mom *[Georgia]* now has some sort of Alzheimer's-induced OCD:
She has lesions on her scalp that she cannot stop picking at. As
soon as they begin scabbing over, she picks at them again...and
again...and again. How she got the lesions in the first place is a
mystery. Her doctor thinks she might've originally scratched
herself while brushing her hair *shrug* or perhaps excessive dry
skin *shrug* or maybe she slipped, hit her head on the corner of
something, and as usual didn't mention it to anyone (my probable
scenario).

They're not very big – the largest is probably the size of a pinkie
fingernail – but they're red and raw like scrapes. I've been dabbing
Neosporin on them twice daily, but how much good it's done is
debatable since as soon as I stop dabbing them, up comes Mom's
hand again.

I've made a game of it. Whenever I notice Mom's hand heading
for any offending spot, I grab her wrist and hold her hand. Nine
times out of ten she'll giggle and reply in a mock petulant tone,
"It's MY head and I can do to it whatever I want!" I usually reply
that no, she can't because she'll only make it worse. Then up
comes the other hand...argh, what I wouldn't give for a pair of
toy handcuffs or something!

Her doctor's referred her to a geriatric neuro doc in Boston, but the
first available appointment isn't until the end of August. True to
form, my anxiety goes into hyper mode, so I call her caseworker/
counselor. C/C said she'll consult with their resident neuro doc
to see if there's any chance Mom could be seen sooner. I'm still
going to keep the Boston appointment, though, just in case.

I've been doing some research. Mom's already on 100mg of
Zoloft, but C/C thinks the neuro might up the dosage so the
Zoloft can work its magic on the OCD. The neuro might also
prescribe a low dose of Risperdal or some other anti-psychotic

med to take the "edge" off. OCD in Alzheimer's patients isn't unusual – once again it's the brain's wiring system shorting out, so to speak. Before Stevie (Mom's brother) passed into late-stage Alzheimer's, he manifested his OCD by continually wheeling himself around in his made-for-adults "toddler chair" at all hours, day or night. Twice he escaped from the ward, but that's another story . My cousin Gayle refused to have him medicated because she was afraid he'd turn into a vegetable. Sometimes I wonder if that would've been the case.

OCD aside, Mom's gait is worsening. She'll walk fine a bit, then suddenly she'll lurch to one side or the other for a split second, then continue walking normally. Then she'll either lurch again or stumble over her own feet. At times her balance suddenly shifts – we notice this the most whenever we take her on a walk with the dogs – if she wasn't hanging onto John's elbow, she'd probably go *splat* into a hedge or something. I think this alarmed her doc more than the OCD. C/C wonders if something else might be going that hasn't been diagnosed...Parkinson's? Lewy Body dementia? That's the dementia that closely mimics Parkinson's, except 1) it's relatively rare, and 2) most sufferers are male. MS? I refuse to get worked up over it...that is, unless she actually does go *splat* and winds up in the ER. *shudder*

Her body's changing, too. She's starting to get that gaunt-except-for-the-tummy look that Johnny (her older brother who lived with us) got a few months before he died. She's even got the same droops in her neck and through her cheeks. The skin on her upper arms and legs is flabby and slack, and her complexion is...well, gray. I can't think of another word to describe it. She's also squinting more, but that's because of the cataract. The only time she'll eat anything other than candy is whenever John or I are with her, and sometimes then she'll only play with her food. She says she has no appetite. I believe her – appetite loss is one of the major side effects of both Aricept and Namenda, but of course she can't tie the two together in her head. So we give her several snacks instead, like a bowl of fruit or half a sandwich, basically anything that won't overwhelm her.

(Jim's blog. 5/9/07)
Slice of life

"I need a toothpick."

"No, Mom *[Martha Sr]*, you had a toothpick after dinner. You picked your teeth for 40 minutes."

"I need a toothpick!"

"Why?"

"'Cause there's something stuck between these front teeth."

"You just brushed your teeth. There's nothing there."

"I can feel it."

"Let me look." (Looks. Nothing there.) "There's nothing there but your gum, swollen from picking at it so long earlier."

"I need a toothpick!!"

sigh Whisper, that only I hear. "Oh, not this again."

"I need a toothpick!!"

"Mom, there's nothing there. I just looked. Really."

"But I can feel it!!"

"No. You picked at it so long..."

"When?"

"After dinner. You had a toothpick for over 40 minutes."

"Really?"

"Yes, really."

"But there's something there! I know it."

"Mom, I just looked. THERE IS NOTHING THERE. You just brushed your teeth, and rinsed..."

"I did? When?"

"Just now. Just two minutes ago."

"But I know that there's something stuck there..."

(Kathi's LiveJournal entry. 9/1/05)
Emotional Hypersensitivity

I need to find an adult day center for Mom *[Georgia]*.

I hate that phrase, "adult daycare." Most of them around here say "Adult Day Health." but it's just the same beast, only camouflaged.

The thing I've discovered about them – and mind you, this is entirely based on the few centers John and I visited at the beginning of the year – is that they're essentially holding pens with some activities thrown in. I can't blame whoever runs them; it's the population. Most of the people we saw were one step away from the nursing home. Most of them were at a much later stage than Mom; indeed, at one place she was the only one who could participate in intelligent conversation.

I can't put her in a place like that, I just can't.

The only place I've been able to find, so far, where she might fit in is a day center for 1st stage Alzheimer's patients. It's in Jamaica Plain. I spoke to the director (who still calls me occasionally) a few months back – they specialize in "enhancing cultural opportunities," meaning that they go to the MFA, the symphony, the ballet, etc. They have art/music/dance therapists, along with the usual medical staff. Mom won't qualify for any aid because it's located in the Jamaica Plain part of Boston; therefore, another county. That means that after Medicare lops off the amount they'll pay, we'd be left with an over $100 weekly bill, not including transportation. *gulp*

She's been relatively well-behaved lately. A few outbursts here and there, mostly directed at John. I just wish she wasn't so hypersensitive to other people's expressions, vocal tone, etc., because it drives me batshit. For example, she'll automatically think I'm angry with her if I come home from work exhausted and bedraggled. I'll tell her I'm not angry, just tired. It doesn't matter how many times I repeat it, she'll keep thinking I'm angry. Then she'll start crying. Then yelling. Then she'll dash upstairs, lock herself in her room, and scream that she'll sell the house because she hates us.

I hate writing about all this because it seems to be the only thing I can write about at length.

I used to be an interesting person.

I used to be fun to be around – or I was always told I was.

I used to have a LIFE.

I know her dementia's not her fault, but I'm really beginning to wish she was already dead so neither of us have to go through this.

(John's diary. 6/12/05)
Hingham Bay Club

– Hingham Bay Club

Kathi, Georgia and I went here for a very nice dinner. It's on the water. Very windy when we went outside, but got some good pics of Georgia and Kathi together. I'd been big on getting pics of the two of them together during this period, partly because we didn't have a lot of the two of them together – and I didn't want Kathi to regret that later. Morbid thinking, with regrets and a sense of sadness and foreboding, but it's a path of potential future regrets I've been down before.

(Email excerpt, Martha Jr to her sister. 2/27/07)
Weird

I'm just a little bit weirded out and need to rattle a bit. Mom [*Martha Sr*] has been rather more out of kilter the last couple days and I'm not sure whether it is a new stage or just a brief phase. It is really disquieting to me.

Yesterday, when Jim went to get her up from her nap, she was really badly confused about whether it was 3 AM or 3 PM and about who and where she was. Apparently she said she needed to get up and get ready to go home. And she said something about wondering if any of her family was alive. Rather like the time early in your visit when she was so confused after she got up. But, though she got to feeling a little more comfortable in her surroundings, she never really seemed to be "back" all evening.

This evening, I had music. As has happened before (when I'm not there), Mom got testy with Jim about something, which led

to a long discussion about what she was doing and where she was
and so forth. (At one point, apparently, she said she wasn't going
to come here any more.) After I got home, I sat down to chat
with her and she mentioned the conversation with Jim. As we
talked about it, I asked her if she knew where she was. She said "I
know it is called my home" (as if to say, 'but it really isn't'). We
talked about when we moved in here, and she asked again if this
wasn't the house that was moved here from Boonville. I had to
explain that this house was built on this site in 1883 and that we
(and I had to explain who that meant) had moved in to it in 1954.

She was sure the paintings
on the walls in the living
room (where we were sitting)
had been in her mother's
house in Boonville (they
weren't). We talked about
the one over the fireplace,
painted by an old friend of
hers from the University of
Minnesota. (That fact I
knew, and she had sort of right.) When I pointed out that it is
dated 1962, she tried to figure out if that was while she was in
school there. The other two were paintings that Dad had gotten
and had had in the office for a time. One of them (the barn) she
thought looked like an old place she used to live. And she was
sure it was in the dining room at her mother's house. I pointed out
that it had hung in the dining room here for a long time before we
moved it into the living room.

I'm just not sure how to handle these conversations. I suppose it
isn't a problem if she wants to believe something that is totally
fictitious, but it can make for a lot of confusion if she starts
telling people these "facts" that have no basis in reality.

Oh well, I guess we just keep doing the best we can. Just thought
you'd be interested to hear this.

Love you -

(Kathi's LiveJournal entry. 7/17/04)
Dark Puddles

Mom *[Georgia]* is in yet another one of her what we call "dark puddles." When she gets like this, she verbally lashes out at everything, no holds barred. Doesn't matter if whatever she's angry about is based on truth or her imagination. Her hearing also gets super hypersensitive, more so than when she's OK. Just the barest hint of any sort of emotion in another's voice sets her off. When she's done, she sits and stews. Don't try to placate her, or she'll start up again. I just leave her be.

Her latest "thing" is the fact that John lost his job; therefore, I'm the only one (in her mind) doing anything around here, and, in her eyes, it isn't fair. Ergo, John's the bad guy, the bum, the one who keeps telling her to do stuff (huh?), and a boatload of other crap I won't get into here. John doesn't take it very well. On the one hand, he knows it's the "whatever" talking (I should say disease, but since we don't have a differential diagnosis, I hesitate to call it that). On the other, his automatic response is to fight. So is hers. The sparring began last night, and evidently hasn't let up. I got home from work with neither of them saying a word to each other, much less looking at each other.

I hate, hate, hate this. Whenever I come to John's defense, she refuses to believe me. Very paradoxical – 9 times out of 10 if she knows she's doing/saying something that bothers me, she'll cease.

Most of the time she gets herself so worked up that she'll start screaming that she wishes she was dead. If you try to make light, she'll tell you to shut up, then ask you if you know where she can get a pill or something.

My biggest fear?

That John won't be able to stand it much longer...

August
The hardest job you'll ever have

Things are still going more or less OK. The routines you've established still work, though they need to be tweaked from time to time.

But you're tired. So very, very tired. Because Alzheimer's doesn't only operate on a 9–5 schedule. People with the disease need help and monitoring around the clock. Their internal time sense goes completely haywire, and sleep cycles change almost randomly. All of which means that the care-giver suffers chronic sleep deprivation. The disruption to sleep patterns and utter exhaustion – as well as the toll it takes on the system – have a huge impact. You know this, and start trying to secure nap times whenever you can – if you have respite care, or your loved one goes off for some kind of Adult Day program, or you have a spouse with whom you are sharing care-giving responsibility. But doing that means that some things which need tending, don't get it. That can be paying bills, working, doing house cleaning. Whatever it is, you have to decide whether it is more important, or getting some sleep is.

People who have had children will have some idea what this is like. New parents are frequently in the same situation for weeks on end. That is well understood, and people make allowances for it. But with Alzheimer's, it just keeps going on and on and on. And it isn't well understood, so people don't make allowances for it: you're caring for an adult, so what's the problem?

Still, you consider it a moral duty to stick with the care-giving, no matter what. Because now, no one else could do the job you're doing – they just don't understand what would be needed. And you said you'd do this. To give up would be a breaking of sacred trust, would mean you were not true to your word, were somehow less of a man. You 'suck it up' and keep going.

One of the things I most enjoyed doing when I had a break – whether Martha Jr was taking over care for her mom for a few hours, or we had a respite care person in to sit with Martha Sr for an afternoon – was to go out target shooting. It may seem counter-intuitive, since I was usually so tired, but this would sometimes be much more beneficial than a couple of hours sleep. Why?

Well, because when you're handling firearms, you have to pay attention to what you are doing in order to be safe. You have to focus your mind on the task at hand – you can't be thinking about what is happening at home, or worried about this or that thing. So shooting would take me completely away from my situation as a care-giver for a few brief hours in a way nothing else, not even sleep, could. And while I would still be tired physically when I got home, I would nonetheless be much more mentally rested.

(Kathi's LiveJournal entry. 9/6/04)
Words of Advice

In the words of one of my co-workers, "You can't let yourself get sucked in by her behavior. Yes, she's your mother. But you need to take care of YOU first. You may not understand that now, but believe me, you will."

(Jim's blog. 4/3/07)
"The hardest job you'll ever have"

That's what the doctor said yesterday.

We took Martha Sr in for a check-up – first time she's seen the doctor in almost a year. Oh, he's been involved in her care all along, and will usually just prescribe meds or treatment without seeing her, based on our phone calls and stopping by his office, explaining what is going on, what we think she needs. That may seem unusual, but the truth is that it is easier and safer to do this – means that we don't have to get her up and off to his office when she is fighting the flu or has been hurt. My medical skills are very good, and generally we can cope with anything here at home so long as we get the support from him.

Anyway, it was time for him to actually see her, and since she was doing OK presently, we got her off to his office. Thorough examination, discussion of her condition, confirmation of what we had suspected: that she had a minor stroke three weeks ago which had led to more little complications to our lives, less comfort for her.

And he asked us how we were doing, as he usually does. Whether we were getting a break now and again, et cetera. He, perhaps of all people, understands what care-giving at this level demands. He confirmed that we're providing about the best care possible, based on what he can see, and made the comment at the head of this post. We came home.

And since then, we've been dealing with the 'fallout' of that visit. People who are living with many forms of dementia, and particularly with Alzheimer's-type dementia, are disrupted by any changes in their routine. We're lucky in that Martha Sr usually stays pleasant during such changes (visits from people, going out to someplace strange) – many Alzheimer's patients get very angry or combative during such occasions. But we always experience more problems in the 24 to 48 hours following. Last evening she was argumentative and hostile, and overnight she slept very poorly – changing position in her bed about every half hour after about midnight. And as a result, since I was 'on-call' and listening to the monitor to make sure she didn't need help, I basically didn't sleep during that whole time.

So this morning I'm exhausted, suffering a very nasty headache. And wondering just how the rest of the day is going to go wrong.

(Kathi's LiveJournal entry. 3/5/06)
Constraints

Well, of course I can't do anything I want, even if I wasn't exhausted, because of Mom *[Georgia]*. We can't leave her alone, lest she gets herself into mischief, like the time she tried throwing away her jewelry or shredded a pile of bills that I left on my desk. Or the time she started packing everything in her bedroom, including the curtains (that happens occasionally at night, btw). Or the time she tried to smash her dentures because she didn't recognize them for a moment. Oh, there's several more stories, as they say, in the naked city... *shakes head, rolls eyes*

The minute I have any free time, John dashes off, either sleeping (he's been having about as much trouble as I lately for some reason) or running multiple errands or taking pictures for an upcoming writing project. It ticks me off most of the time because 1) I have such little free time to begin with, and 2) what about ME, never mind Mom? I'm not saying that he doesn't deserve free time because he certainly does...for me, though, it's like I'm running from one job to another with no downtime until I go to bed.

There are those who make peace with a similar predicament – "Hey, this is the way life is right now, there's no use fighting it, and in a greater sense, what I'm doing is for the greater good." Some may not even question it. Obviously I'm not at that point yet. I don't know if I'll ever be.

I recall one Christmas a few years ago – way before Mom was diagnosed, way before

I knew John existed – where somebody remarked that, "If anything happens to Georgia, Kathi's going to be a basket case. If anything happens to Kathi, Georgia will be a basket case." There were a few tsk-tsks and shaking of heads in response. I think I just rolled my eyes. I can't recall Mom's reply, but she probably roared something to the effect of, "NOTHING is going to happen because I'll be DEAD before long!"

(Jim's blog. 3/23/07)
As John Lennon said...

I once had a boss who was one of those self-made millionaires, a real classic 'alpha' from circa 1965, complete with the mindset and abuse of employees, even though it was some twenty years later. Once, when something I did was screwed up, I went in to talk with him about it. All in a huff he told me "I don't want excuses." I looked him in the eye and said "I'm not here to give an excuse. I'm here to give an explanation, so we know what went wrong and can avoid having it happen again."

Eventually, I got him trained, and when it came time for me to move on we parted on good terms.

Nothing is screwed up, and I haven't made any big mistakes that I'm here to explain. However, I have commented several times about how tired I am, and how being a full-time (read "around the clock") care-provider for someone with Alzheimer's means that I don't ever get enough sleep. Basically, either my wife or I are always listening to a baby monitor at night, at most dozing lightly. We take turns doing this. The problem is, that even when you're not 'on-call' it is tough to sleep really soundly when your bedmate is dozing lightly. And while I am willing to make many sacrifices to care for my mother-in-law, giving up sleeping with my wife altogether isn't one of them.

Most parents know what this will do to you, since caring for an infant means this sort of interruption to your sleep cycle for weeks

on end. But for us, this has been going on for about three years –
it's been a full year since we had much of a real vacation from it.
It means that I operate at a chronic sleep deficit. I feel like I am
perpetually at about the third entry in this blog-post about sleep
deprivation, with a chronic low-grade headache, lack of focus,
shortened temper, forgetfulness, et cetera.

Anyway, there's an explanation for the next time I say that "I'm
so tired," echoing Lennon's song of the same title written after
three weeks of interrupted sleep cycle when off to Transcendental
Meditation camp. When I say I don't have the energy to do this
or that, or that it is difficult to get my focus for accomplishing
something, this is what I mean, not that I just didn't get a good
night's sleep the night before.

(Email excerpt, Martha Jr to the family. 5/2/07)
Anecdote

Just a regular update. Mom *[Martha Sr]* is holding her own. She's
still coughing and wheezing a lot, and having sporadic fevers (not
very high) but hasn't declined any further. Not an "amazing
recovery," but she's doing OK.

I do have to share one anecdote with you. Most of you know
that Mom sometimes loses track of where (and sometimes who)
she is, particularly right after her nap. Today's episode was just
classic. She had been napping about an hour and a half when I
heard her squirming around (apparently, I learned later, to be able
to see the clock – it was 2:35). Then she called, saying "Is it about
time for dinner?" I went to see about her, told her that it was still
the middle of the afternoon (pointed out the clock) and that, if
she wanted to rest some more, she certainly could. She allowed as
how that would be okay.

A few minutes later, I heard her squirming around again, so I went
to see what was up. She said maybe she ought to go ahead and get
up (she didn't want to miss dinner). "Are you sure that clock is

right?!" I assured her that it agreed with all the other clocks in the house and, if she wanted to rest, she could continue to do so. I got her repositioned comfortably on her back (the other thing she was trying to do) and she decided to rest some more, once I had assured her we would not let her sleep through dinner. She fell asleep in a little bit, and slept for another hour.

I was listening to the monitor and heard our dog doing something outside Mom's door. A moment later Mom called to ask if there was someone there, that she thought she'd like to get up now. I went to get her up and she asked "Were you up here?" (??) I said I had been listening to the other end of the monitor, and that I had heard the dog outside her door and then heard her call. That seemed to satisfy that question, but then she asked if everyone else was downstairs [our home has no basement, and Martha Sr's bedroom was on the first floor], and said she wanted to use the toilet and then she wanted to go downstairs, too. I said we'd get her on the potty, then we'd go get her snack. Well that was fine. She said something else about going downstairs, and I basically sidestepped that issue by just telling her that we would go have her snack then she could read for a while until it was time for dinner (without mentioning that it was all on the same floor). That satisfied her. After we left her room, she didn't make any more mention of going downstairs.

It is sometimes hard to figure out where she is, but I'm learning to roll with her 'reality' and gently help her find solid ground again.

Love to you all -

(Jim's blog. 7/10/07)
"Just" another TIA

I watched, one afternoon last week, while Martha Sr suffered a slight Transient Ischemic Attack. She was sitting in her wheel-chair, having just gotten up from her afternoon nap, and was finishing some yogurt. I was sitting and talking with her, when she just slowly sort of folded in on herself. While she is 90 and suffers from Alzheimer's, she is usually capable of responding to direct questions about immediate events (how she feels, if she likes her yogurt, et cetera), but she suddenly went quiet, almost insensate. I checked to see whether something like a heart attack was in process, and asked if she was hurting or if there was some other indicator of a serious emergency. Eventually I got enough information to conclude it was likely 'just' a TIA or some similar event, and got her back in bed. I monitored her, and all seemed to be well. She woke two hours later, with no evidence of damage. But it was an indication of her condition, and likely a hint at things to come.

(John's diary. 10/15/05)
Accidents

– Villa Rosa

Kathi & I, having some drinks. Georgia is in bed – hasn't felt great the past couple days, and has had a few "accidents" at night. This evening (afternoon), when Kathi suggested that she take a nap, she responded that if she went to sleep, she wouldn't wake up. She's made a lot of references to dying before winter/Christmas, esp. lately. It bothers Kathi a lot, and she's not showing half of how hard it's hitting her.

(Kathi's LiveJournal entry. 10/15/05)
Accidents, Chills and Shot Concentration

We can't figure out what's up with Mom *[Georgia]*. Alzheimer's is quite unpredictable, in that you can have one whole set of new symptoms show up without warning, only to have them disappear the next day. She's been freezing the last few days. I've got her bundled up in thermal undies, sweaters, sweatpants, two pairs of socks, and it's still not enough. It scares me to think how bad she'll be come January. She's also been having a few "accidents" here and there, and, at times, is truly out of it. All she wants to do is sleep. She doesn't feel like eating. Her concentration on anything is shot. We don't know what to do. *shaking head*

(Email excerpt, Martha Jr to the family. 7/24/07)
Decline

Just want to update you all on the latest with Mom *[Martha Sr]*. The last several days she has been markedly more confused more often, not just right after she wakes up. It has been harder to convince her that she's in her own home and that there aren't a bunch of other people there ("downstairs"). She has also some-times slept a lot longer in the afternoon – Sunday we went to wake her up at 5:30 to get ready for dinner. Yesterday she woke up after just an hour of her afternoon nap, and declared that she wanted to go home now. She wanted to know where the woman who had brought her here was. She was quite adamant. Jim had a very hard time convincing her that she was not at Stephens College (!) and that she had only been napping for a short time. She finally decided to nap a little more, and slept for another hour and a half. No hint of the previous episode when she woke up.

Just before dinner last night she got 'wheezy' again, and started coughing a lot. Through dinner and afterward she had additional coughing fits, and had become rather vague about what she was doing (or wanted to do). We got her in bed at her usual time. She woke about midnight with another coughing fit so Jim went to check on her. He got her up and on the potty at that time and back in bed, where she seemed to sleep pretty well for the rest of the night. But this morning when she got up she was, again, much more vague. She seemed to have little strength in her arms and legs (not able to stand very well at all). She took twice as long as usual eating her breakfast (at one point I asked her how she was doing and she said "just slow") and when we took her to get dressed she was even weaker at standing and seemed very tired. We got her dressed but asked her if she wanted to nap for a while.

Normally after breakfast she absolutely refuses a nap, even if she is showing every evidence of being tired. But today it was clear that this was a very inviting proposition for her. So, once she was dressed, we got her back in bed and she fell right asleep. I understand about 11:00 she woke up and when Jim checked on her she was ready to get up. He says she seems much more 'grounded' now.

Dunno what, if anything, all of this means. Just thought you'd like to know. Who knows, it could be like other times I've written that she's doing poorly, and she immediately gets better!

Take care, everyone.

(Kathi's LiveJournal entry. 10/16/05)
Bloody Hell

We've just been advised to take Mom *[Georgia]* to the ER.

This morning she woke up in a puddle of somewhat dried-out rank blood.

Hard to tell if she's still bleeding or not – she didn't even realize anything had happened until I showed it to her. She started crying. She wouldn't let me help her.

We've got her cleaned up and dressed. She's hungry, so we'll let her eat a little something. I know it's probably counterproductive, but she barely ate anything yesterday, and she's starting to whine about it.

They asked me if I was her proxy and if I wanted a DNR for her.

I said yes.

I want to cry and have a smoke. I didn't even mention it to John. One look at my expression and he nearly went off the deep end, saying that I'm just setting myself up for failure because I'm not actively doing anything about quelling the urge to smoke.

Later... They admitted Mom about 2 hours ago. They sent us home to get her stuff.

Her blood count's very low. She might have to have a transfusion. They'll be running tests on her tomorrow to see where the bleeding's coming from.

I signed the DNR papers.

Secretly I think she's relieved that somebody noticed. According to the ER doc, it's been going on for awhile. Mom's quite adept at hiding stuff. This is a woman who, because of the severity of her spinal stenosis, should be in a wheelchair. Her inner mantra? Nope, not gonna happen, pain doesn't exist. Meanwhile she's all hunched over and can barely move. *rolls eyes*

I've been sort of on automatic pilot all day. A few times John had to take over answering questions at the ER because I went into meltdown mode. I don't even want to begin to think how I'd be right now without him.

(Jim's blog. 7/27/07)
Death wins

This morning, when I went to check on her after hearing some stirring, Martha Sr looked at me and asked if I knew where her toothbrush was.

"Yes. I know where it is. When you get up, we'll be sure to use it."

This simple reassurance allowed her to get back to sleep, and when we got her up at her usual time about 45 minutes later, she had completely forgotten the whole thing. See, she is well into the arc of Alzheimer's, and has slipped to the point where she doesn't really know where she is or who is around her most of the time. But little things like knowing that she has her own toothbrush, and she can use it, seem to make her happy, give her a measure of security. I don't try to understand it. I am too exhausted for that. I just try to roll with it.

* * *

One day last week a steam pipe ruptured in New York City, killing one person and injuring many others. Each day in the US over 100 people are killed in vehicle accidents, and about half that number are murdered.

I was orphaned in early adolescence, one parent murdered and then the other dying about 18 months later in a car accident. I came to understand death much earlier than most people in our country do. I've had a few close calls myself, all of them stupid and unexpected things that had my luck gone just a little differently, I would have died. Now, at middle age, I've got the typical health risks for a man which could mean an early and unexpected death.

But I don't worry about that. Death wins. Every time. None of us gets out of here alive. We are all going to die, sooner or later. The only real thing that matters is that we live life as completely as possible, loving, creating, building the future. I like to think that my parents understood that. Martha Sr, who may not understand this on an intellectual level, still experiences life, still worries about her place in the world, still wants to make sure that she can brush her teeth.

(John's diary. 10/17/05)
More Accidents

Georgia went into the hospital yesterday morning; Kathi noticed that the "accident" was largely blood. Tests showed an extremely low blood count. They kept her over night. Kathi and I visited this morning, then left for a while. She looked weak, and was unsure of why she was there. She wanted to come home.

We visited Barb, then came back. Georgia didn't remember our earlier visit. She looked harried and angry, very unhappy with the staff, and wanted to leave. Her eyes lit up when she saw me – that was a good feeling – we helped her calm down. I left Kathi there and took the dogs home. Contacted Rick and Susie & Rich (spoke to Sandy & Susie) to let 'em know 'bout Georgia. When I got back, I found that Georgia had had another "accident," making a huge mess, and she almost passed out.

(John's diary. 10/18/05)
Pictures of health and happiness

Kathi & I created a single-sheet photo montage for Georgia, framed it, and brought it to her. She seemed more energetic, stronger, with better color and better humor.

(Jim's blog. 8/2/07)
Which reality?

We've recently had to make a change in strategy for dealing with Martha Sr's confusion (related to her Alzheimer's). Heretofore we've tried to keep her "grounded" in reality, through a series of questions about recognizing family member's pictures, asking if she knew where she was, and so forth. Generally, after a couple of minutes of this, she'd be pretty well settled about where we were, who was who, and so forth. It helped to keep her anchored in the real world.

But then last week I noticed that she was starting to become more anxious as a result of these questions. When she couldn't come up with a name, or wasn't sure whether we were in her parents home or someplace else, it just made her embarrassed and worried. She'd resort to trying to construct a reality that made sense of her mixed memories, and get hostile if you tried to challenge that reality.

The last thing we want is to have her upset. Not only does this make things more stressful and difficult in caring for her, but it sort of defeats the whole purpose of our caring for her here at home (her home of 53 years). Clearly, we had to change our strategy.

Now we don't try and 'lead' her to any particular view of the world, and rather concentrate on letting her know that she is loved and safe where she is (wherever she thinks that is). We'll answer her questions honestly, if she wants to know who is who in a photo, but we don't press her to come up with answers herself, or try and correct her if she volunteers an opinion. I mean, if she's wrong, so what? Nothing really hinges on whether she gets someone's name right, or if she thinks that we're in some other place.

But this is surprisingly difficult, if you don't make a conscious effort to allow her to be in her own little world. The tendency we all have is to try and coordinate on what reality is – to have a shared view of what the world is like. When confronted with someone who disagrees on something as fundamental as your location, it is easy to get your back up. You've probably experienced this with a friend or spouse when traveling, both of you looking at a map and drawing different conclusions about where you are – such disagreements become heated very easily, and can take on an importance beyond just a simple determination of location. We've now decided to let Martha Sr have her own little world, and accept that we're just visitors to it. It's her map, and she can read it however she wants.

(Kathi's LiveJournal entry. 10/17/05)
Hospital, Transfusions and Blood Count

She *[Georgia]* is there for another night. Even after a full transfusion this afternoon, she's still leaking somewhere in her G.I. tract – upper or lower, nobody knows. She's having the colonoscopy tomorrow morning. Whatever happens with that determines the next step. During one episode Mom passed out with the shakes and shudders. They gave her yet another series of blood tests, only to discover that her count's dropped past the danger zone for her age group. They had just ordered another transfusion as visiting hours ended.

I'd never seen Mom turn utterly white before.

I'd never seen her shake and shiver like she did right after she passed out.

We had trouble propping her into bed. Mom's not physically weak, but the culmination of nasty scenes must've left her too exhausted to prop herself. John and I would finally get her into a half-sitting position when she'd suddenly slouch and slide toward the middle of the bed. We finally managed to get her sitting upright enough so she wouldn't look like she was totally out of it.

(Jim's blog. 8/3/07)
The difficulty of accomplishing anything

One of the hallmarks of major depression is the energy-sucking nature of the disease. For someone in the throes of such a depression, it becomes almost impossible to even get out of bed, and regular correspondence, routine tasks, et cetera, all slide by the wayside, piling up and contributing to the downward spiral.

I suffer from a mild form of bipolar disorder – what is commonly called manic-depression. The arc of my mental state can be influenced by many things, but typically runs about 18 – 24 months through a full cycle. I have never suffered through a full major depression, but I've been down into it far enough to have glimpsed that hell, and know I want no part of it. I've learned to cope with my condition, and know full well that if I were ever to slip further I would want professional help to deal with it.

One thing I find in being a care-giver for someone with Alzheimer's is that as my charge slips further into dementia herself, the toll that it takes on me and my wife comes increasingly to resemble suffering a major depression. Basically, with the prolonged lack of sleep and growing effort to help her comes an increasing difficulty in having the energy to accomplish anything else. Last week I read the new Harry Potter book, and the effort left me completely exhausted and suffering a prolonged migraine. If I can get the focus to spend a few hours at the bench doing book conservation in a given week it is a minor miracle. Just contacting clients or suppliers becomes a task I cannot confront. I've promised someone an article on Pat Bahn of TGV Rockets, which I really want to write, but finding the energy to do so is another matter altogether.

And yes, my own mental health is stressed by all of this. I am constantly at risk of falling into the trap that I should be doing more, should be stronger. That's my image of myself. And when I put my mind to it, I really can accomplish some remarkable things. So the temptation is to push myself further, to goad more work out of myself, to criticize myself for being "weak" for not having the focus or the energy to do this or that. That is a dangerous path.

So, I do what I can, when I can, and try and cut myself some slack the rest of the time. And this afternoon, while Martha Sr naps, I think I will can some tomatoes. There is more conservation work waiting for me, and other writing I should do. But the tomatoes are ripe and ready, and it will be a nice change from the other tasks.

(John's diary. 10/21/05)
Balancing Acts

Georgia is back – Kathi brought her home this morning. Low-residue diet for 4 weeks, and a little weaker & rough-around-the-edges – taking some time to reacquaint herself with the home routine. We're out having a drink, now – the three of us. I put some significant time in with a client on behalf of another consulting firm – reports coming along nicely (I think, anyway). The funds earned working with them this month, ideally, will make up for fluctuations in payment from another consulting firm.

I'm hoping to ensure coverage of tax obligations and business expenses, including startup costs, without discrepancy. The balancing act is, at times, quite difficult.

(John's diary. 10/23/05)
Back in the saddle ... almost

– Ground Round, Quincy

Georgia & I came out for lunch; Kathi was working, first day back after being out due to the sprained ankle, and will join us shortly.

Georgia seemed quiet and –?– not sure of an apt descriptor. After I woke her around 9:30 and gave her breakfast, she washed the dishes and decided to go back to bed instead of getting dressed. She was awake but just staying in bed when I went in at 2:30 to rouse her. I have to wonder how much the recent hospital stay is influencing that behavior – she was essentially confined to bed, so had little stimulation. She appeared to want a reason to get up & out, and thought she had none.

Anywho, we're here...Kathi will be here soon, and I've ensured that we got to talk to Rick (a.k.a. Coni, her cousin in Florida). He and his family are prepping for Hurricane Wilma.

(Jim's blog. 8/9/07)
The *increasing* difficulty of accomplishing anything

A few days ago I wrote about the difficulty of accomplishing any-thing as Martha Sr slowly slips away due to Alzheimer's, and the impact that has on myself and my wife.

Well, it's taken a significant turn for the worse. For whatever reason, her condition has worsened substantially in the last few days, to the point where she now frequently asks to "go home," doesn't recognize me or my wife for who we are most of the time, and has long and elaborate "memories" of things which she thinks she has just done (going to see a movie, taken a trip with friends) earlier in the day. Her tenuous grip on reality has slipped to almost nothing.

I wind up spending long periods of time just talking with her, reassuring her that she's here at home, safe and we're taking care of her – we've long since given up trying to 'correct' her information or view of the world. This is very intense and demanding, and when coupled with increasing unpredictability in her sleep habits, means that I am increasingly low on sleep and energy and focus and initiative.

Still, I have a creative drive that wants outlet. Very frustrating.

(John's diary. 10/29/05)
Balancing Acts – Time triage

– Applebee's, Cleveland Circle

Georgia & I stopped in after visiting Rich at the Learning Express in Newton Center. I asked him to pick up the Lego Mindstorm robotics kit, and Georgia enjoyed seeing him.

It's snowing.

I saw the first tiny flakes when we left the driveway. While we visited Rich, the flakes became large and puffy. Not sticking yet, but...

Thursday, the 27th, I brought Georgia with me to pick up the family portrait reprints at Colortek on Atlantic Ave, then to attend Stevie's wake. (Her brother, Steven Rigas, died earlier in the week). Colortek had us come back at 3:00 for the prints, so we ended up arriving at the wake with only 5-10 minutes to spend there. It was sad, but I'm glad Georgia was able to go.

We didn't make it for the second viewing – Kathi worked late. We all attended the mass, funeral and reception together on Friday.

Kathi's working today. Georgia & I will be home soon, and hopefully get the house into suitable order. Kathi was a bit frustrated last night, and asked if I could try a bit harder to get some stuff done around the house. It's a fine line, at times, discerning tasks that supersede others, and she doesn't want to be a nag. Understandably. I've been working, plus taking care of family stuff, plus shuttling Georgia. Often, not accomplishing home goals and becoming equally frustrated.

(Kathi's LiveJournal entry. 11/5/05)
Spinal Stenosis: Risks of Operating v. Not Operating

Mom *[Georgia]* barely made it downstairs this morning. Right now she's sitting in what used to be my place at the table nursing a cup of coffee and sort of listening to the news. She's been sleeping a lot. We discussed the operation for the stenosis. The biggest issue with that is the anesthesia, in that "going under" tends to make someone who already has Alzheimer's decline much faster. But if one doesn't have the operation, they're basically sentenced to life in a wheelchair, which means if I did choose such for Mom, she could no longer live here. On the other hand, if she declined faster because of the anesthesia, she might be able to walk, yes, but I wouldn't be able to deal with her day-to-day if the decline were severe.

You know, I really wish I had something else to talk about other than Mom and the drama around here. I'm tired of it too.

(Email excerpt, Jim to the family. 8/10/07)
An excerpt

Our strategy of lessening Martha Sr's anxiety has been good, I think, though one possible result of not trying to "ground" her regularly is that she seems to be losing her grasp on reality more and more. She has good days and bad days, but I can usually count on needing to just sit and reassure her at least once each day, for 45 minutes to an hour. It has also become common for her to ask to "go home" when we get through watching some movie in the evening, or when she wakes up from a nap. When we explain that this is where she lives now, and that Martha Jr and I care for her and make sure she's safe, she'll get very happy (almost teary-eyed) and thank us. But that will usually only last for a few minutes, unless you get her attention focused on something else. Likewise, due to her inability to focus and her failing memory, she needs constant supervision and basic repeated instruction when doing anything such as brushing her teeth or bathing.

She often asserts that she came here with other people, and that she wants to call them to ask them to come get her. If queried on this, she'll frequently identify her mom and sister as the people involved (who died 38 and 16 years ago, respectively). Any effort to explain that they are no longer living is met with skepticism, no matter how phrased, and we'll need to redirect her attention to other topics in order to get her from dwelling on where "her family" is. It seems very much to be the case that she is regressing to those very early relationships as security, as her more recent memories become more confused and clouded. At night, when she wakes and needs to use the toilet, she'll usually ask whether Martha Jr or I are her parents when we come into the room. We no longer ask her if she knows who we are, but I get the sense that she's pretty much lost our names, just identifies us by sight.

(Kathi's LiveJournal entry. 11/15/05)
Calls and Options

[My mother had been born with Cooley's Anemia. It's endemic in those with either Mediterranean, Asian, or Native American background. I don't know the details, but I do know that it has something to do with platelet count and the inability to clot as quickly as compared to somebody who doesn't have it. You also tend to bleed out easier, even with the most minor injuries. I've never been diagnosed with it, although I also have a tendency to bleed out. My clotting's fine, though.

Another thing: Mom was "brittle" in terms of medications. She had many reactions to medications that most people don't have. I'm the same way.]

Fielded calls from both Mom's *[Georgia]* ortho doc and primary doc at work today.

Ortho doc's assistant needed to know if primary doc would OK Mom to have the surgery on her back. I explained what primary doc had said: No way, no how, six months minimum wait to see if Mom's blood levels stabilize. I then added that, considering the blood levels and her anemia, I wasn't sure if Mom should even consider it. On the other hand, she can barely walk right now. Walk's really a misnomer; it's more like peg-leg foot-slapping lunge-to-list let's-have-anything-hold-her-up. Of course she doesn't use a cane or a walker. Of course everything's OK! Meanwhile she starts to get up from a chair and nearly keels over.

I'm scared, I said to the assistant. What happens if she tries to get out of bed one morning and discovers that she literally can't stand up? Or what if the same thing happens when she's been sitting? If her doctor won't OK the surgery for the next six months, what do I do? I can't keep her at home if she can't walk. I can't afford to redo the house if she needs a wheelchair. Where would she go? And how the heck could I tell her all this and have her understand?

The poor assistant. I think I chewed her ear off for a good few minutes. The best empathetic solution she could give was to immediately let her know if such a scenario happens. Then ortho doc and primary doc will HAVE to put their heads together, they'd have to contact Social Services, etc.

You're truly stuck between a rock and a hard place, she said in closing. You must feel awful about it. I really don't know what else to tell you.

In other words, Mom's an accident waiting to happen. Great.

Call #2 with the Dr C (aka Mom's primary doc):

Her test results came in this morning. The good news is that there's no evidence of any internal bleeding. Her iron levels are still quite low, but they should come up to speed with the supplements you're giving her. However, we did discover two probable genetic issues with her blood – one is the anemia itself. The other is a clotting factor. Your mom bleeds very easily, and it takes longer than average for her to clot. Did you know that?"

Um, no, to be honest.

Are you anemic? Has anybody ever told you that you're missing a clotting factor?

No, I'm not, never have been. And no, although I do bruise quite easily. I've never noticed anything unusual about my blood clotting.

I know I initially said six months minimum for the surgery, but now I'm reconsidering whether I should OK her to have the surgery at all, given the findings. If something should happen to her on the table, her bleeding could easily become uncontrollable."

Well...what am I supposed to do? The PT isn't working, I just spoke with the assistant, I really don't know what to think.

"Call me immediately if she suddenly cannot get up and/or walk."

Yeah, I've been sort of shell-shocked all day. I still am. I'm really really really trying not to project upon it, but I'm finding it exceedingly difficult.

(John's diary. 12/4/05)
Stuff and such

Kathi & I switched (and are still switching) around some of the rooms. My office & our bedroom have been swapped. Much better space. And much to do to complete the swap. Trying to keep Kathi motivated on it; she's tired, but also dragging her feet because she feels it's like saying goodbye to her mom.

Anywho – got most of the "stuff" swapped: put the futon in the attic, setting up the other biz equipment, shelves, filing cabinets, table surfaces.

(John's diary. 12/6/05)
Triage – time and resources

Georgia, Kathi & I stopped in for a bite. Home stuff going very slowly. Kath's stressing, & part of the reason things are slowing down considerably. :(Office still in complete disarray. We need to work together – this can't continue. My business acct was nearly $300 negative...something which would not have happened if I'd had my workspace set back up. Already, I've given up (for now) on the painting / refinishing. I'll have to wait until she goes back to work. Hopefully, I'll be able to use this time effectively, but I'm not going to hold my breath.

Business development and research has, of course, now ground almost completely to a halt. At least I got some invoices out to the consulting company I did work for. Have to get out another company's invoices today, though they are still behind in payments.

Two new NASA challenges have been initiated; I'd like to get something going for each under RealmQuests, so need to pull a lot of things together fast.

(Kathi's LiveJournal entry. 12/17/05)
Falling apart

I have to enroll Mom *[Georgia]* in adult day care by the end of the month. I can no longer take care of her, especially the personal stuff. I am never here. John can't because he's male. It's also not fair to him to continue shouldering the burden (no matter how much he claims he's doing fine) considering that Mom's been more than out in left field lately for some odd reason. Nothing to do with anger or acting out...it's like she's a piece of seaweed attached to a rock and the seaweed's starting to lose its grip. She just goes wherever the current takes her.

I also have to get rid of her car by the end of the month...Mom's scheduled for cataract surgery on 19 Jan. Her ultrasound's on 4 Jan. In between she needs a pre-op physical. Surely they can operate on her eye, can't they? It's not like they'll be cutting her open like they would for the stenosis surgery. She had the other eye done back in 2000; she doesn't remember it, but I do. I watched the operation on closed-circuit TV. *shudder*

I can't continue working these back-to-back 10-hour swing shifts. I miss too much at home. John doesn't get a break. The house is filthy. I don't have time to cook anything. The dogs scold me.

But the most important: Mom sometimes doesn't remember who I am because I'm never around during the day.

(Kathi's LiveJournal entry. 12/31/05)
Frayed (more hammerhead)

I've been working. 10 hours one day, 10 hours the next, 4-6 hours sleep on average, haven't had an entire day off since early last week. I'm getting too old for this racket, but it's like I'm programmed.

When I'm not working I'm Mom-sitting. She *[Georgia]* has been sundowning something fierce the last few weeks. Risperdal isn't helping. To her 3AM = noontime, so the concept of being asleep in bed at that time, to her, is utterly ridiculous. It also doesn't help that she rummages through every single goddam thing. Hopefully everything will ease up once she starts the day program on Tuesday.

Anger's been my closest friend lately. You'd understand better how uncharacteristic this is of me if you knew me. I'm the goofy one, the sidekick who's there for comic relief. I play the part of the ditzy blonde very well. I'm the self-proclaimed "entertainment committee" at work in that I'm the one who always breaks the tension in some way. But that all dissolves the closer I get to home. Then all I want to do is smash everyone's head with a hammer. Except for the dogs, of course.

I'm afraid to talk because if I start, I won't stop unless someone shoots me point-blank with a tranquilizer dart. Or smashes me over the head with a hammer.

I'm also sick of venting about the same thing over and over. That's probably the real reason why I haven't been saying much lately.

(Kathi's LiveJournal entry. 1/10/06)
Smooth(-ish) Sailing

Right now Mom *[Georgia]* is at the day program. She LOVES it. Over the weekend she kept asking when she'd be returning there. She even asked the same thing while she and I ran around yesterday. Obviously I'm no longer scintillating company. Oh well...

John's upstairs asleep. He's been on downstairs nighttime duty the past couple of weeks, not only because of Missy not being able to negotiate stairs, but also because of Mom. He's paranoid that one night she'll wander out of her room and tumble like Winnie-the-Pooh, bump bump bump. She hasn't left her room once. Occasionally I'll hear her rummaging around in there around 3AM, but I soon fall back asleep because at least she's in there. What she does, though...ugh, don't get me started...

(Kathi's LiveJournal entry. 1/12/06)
Ill at ease

Respite is a funny thing. When you first hear that you're eligible for it, you're so thrilled that you FINALLY can do stuff for yourself and in the house without interference that you want to throw a party. FINALLY you'll have time to do the mundane stuff like clean; FINALLY you can pay bills in peace, start little house projects, go shopping, get a haircut, all the stuff most people take for granted. You can take the dogs on a nice long walk with no time limit. Heck, the possibilities are endless.

What have we been doing since Mom *[Georgia]* started the day program? Sleeping. Web-surfing. Taking the dogs on walks. Doing little errands here and there, but nothing out of the ordinary. Chores? What's that?

...I hate having unstructured free time because it makes me anxious. Nowadays I'm usually too tired to acknowledge the anxiousness, but every so often it still bursts forth. I feel like I should be doing something because this free time on my day off is a gift. I just cannot accept it as it is for some reason.

September
The crisis

You'll notice that this is one of the longer chapters in the book. Which is curious, because usually we think of a 'crisis' as a discrete moment or event, which happens suddenly.

But here is a deep truth to the care-giving experience: There comes a point where you enter into what feels like a perpetual crisis. And that period will last a long time – longer than you think possible.

The routines which you had carefully constructed to help your patient and yourself cope with the effects of the disease no longer need regular tweaking; they start to completely break down. You're no longer sure that you can cope with the situation. But you do. Mostly. Sometimes you do lose control. Sometimes you lash out. Relationships which were stressed before show signs of cracking. Things grind on and on, and the exhaustion which you were feeling before – which you were certain you could not continue with – becomes an unremitting, constant companion.

You start to become desperate for some kind of solution, some kind of help, some way to get out of this impossible situation. But your patient needs you more than ever, as the disease relentlessly progresses. You're caught in the perpetual crisis, and you will likely be there for months or even years.

> *The not knowing how long things would go on was in many ways the worst part of this phase. As I would at one point tell a hospice counselor "I can sleep on broken glass for six months, if I know that's the end of it."*

> *But I didn't know. Neither did Martha Jr. Neither did John and*

Kathi. And the experts you talk with can't really provide any answers. You ask, and they'll give you a range of times – "perhaps 6 to 8 months" or "about a year." But then they'll add "but that can vary greatly from individual to individual." At one point a doctor told us that Martha Sr had already lasted much longer than he would have expected.

When this sinks in – when you realize that there are no reliable answers – it feels like you have just been abandoned. Then all you can do is just get through it day by day. And some days are much worse than others.

(Kathi's LiveJournal entry. 2/26/06)
Financial Strains & Placement Facilities

...it's as though we're holding our breaths for that moment when something serious does happen to Mom *[Georgia]*. One of these days she's either going to fall and/or her stenosis will paralyze her and/or she'll have a heart attack or stroke and then something WILL have to be done. It's not that I'm wishing any of this on her. I've been told that any one of these will likely happen at some point.

The usual scenario is that the patient goes into the hospital, Medicare and the supplemental pays, etc. If rehab's needed, Medicare will pay for that, but only for a short period. After that, you're on your own.

The flip side? What if the care-taking takes too much of a toll? I'm pretty sure all of you must be sick of my whining. I'm sick of it too. John couldn't wait to get out of here Sunday night. It's not that taking care of Mom is impossible because 1) she's still "there" most of the time; 2) she doesn't have any chronic conditions; 3) she can still perform some self-care herself without help. But taking care of her has taken a huge toll on both John and me individually and as a couple.

We're not husband and wife – we're Mom-sitters. Plain and simple.

We have huge money issues. Mom's money's dwindling, thanks to property taxes, insurance, repairs, heat, anything house-related. John and I pay for everything else. Because John freelances, we cannot depend on his salary. I practically live at the store just to keep our heads above water...

Oh, I haven't told you about the visit to the assisted living facility yesterday. In the dining room without crystal and plaited napkins the director hands you the brochure, a list of activities, a price list, and asks if you have any questions. You can't reply because your eyes automatically dart to the monthly all-inclusive rate for that flat you just saw:

$5900. A month.

You vaguely remember hearing somewhere that this place, in particular, is one of the higher-end facilities. Well, OK, that means there must be cheaper places. You timidly ask if that's the average for the area.

"Well, it's close," the director replies. "Our competition charges roughly the same rates, give or take a thousand."

You gulp. "How do people pay for it? Seriously. I mean, I know some people sell their house..."

If the director's gobsmacked by my ignorance she doesn't show it. "That's usually what happens. By the time they've used the proceeds to pay for here, they're qualified for Medicaid. There's also reverse mortgages. Your mom's social security would automatically be sent to us, along with any VA benefits. But the rest, I'm afraid, is all private pay. That's the way these programs work."

"Oh." I didn't know what else to say.

She smiles at me. "Believe me, you're not the first to ask. What

I'd do is contact your mom's attorney and ask her opinion. What you want to do first is find a place, whether it's here or somewhere else, talk to their financial people, and together with the attorney you draw up a payment plan. It's a good thing you're thinking of this now. Most people wait until it's too late."

(Kathi's LiveJournal entry. 2/10/06)
Boiling points

How am I supposed to do everything? I feel compelled to keep apologizing for every single thing, even the things I know are either not my fault and/or out of my hands. I'm a horrible housekeeper. I'm a lousy wife. I'm even a lousier daughter. The only thing I'm remotely good at is being a 'Dog Mom.' Because, you see, they don't make any demands other than to be fed and/ or walked...

OK, OK, I can't ask John, seriously, to do much else because of Mom *[Georgia]*. I can't even pay him anything out of Mom's money because that's just like taking $ out of your right pocket only to put it back into your left. Besides, I don't want to complicate anything. I feel like dementia's beginning to eat my brain. Every time I have a brain fart I think, "Oh, don't tell me I'm going to have early-onset Alzheimer's", or something similar. They're becoming more frequent lately. *shudder*

We're fighting about the house, too. We really need to start thinking about putting Mom somewhere because, if we don't, John and I are either going to kill each other or we'll both kill her. Whenever she wobbles on the stairs I pray she'll fall. Maybe one day she'll wander out of the center and get struck by a car. Or, more likely, she'll suffer a sudden heart attack like everyone else in her family. But here's the thing: If we look for a place, we'd have to put the house up for sale, and if we do that, WHERE THE HELL DO WE GO????

(Jim's blog. 9/17/07)
Beats having a heart attack

This is pretty raw. I reserve the option to amend or delete it entirely
later. [9/18 7:15 AM: I've added a postscript – see below.]

I'm worn out. I'm emotionally and physically bankrupt. I'm
spent, empty. Just a dry husk.

It was a *very* long day. Started with the migraine I mentioned
in my previous post. Then care-giving was really rough. Worst
it's been, and that's saying something. I don't know whether
Martha Sr had another little stroke, or is fighting an infection, or
is approaching the end of her life, but damn – every fifteen to
twenty minutes today I had to go tend to her, see what she needed. It was always some variation on the theme of her "needing to
get ready to go home", or wanting to "look outside to see if her
ride is here," or "needing to call the people she usually lives with
in order to let them know that she was here." I tried everything I
know or could think of – distraction, answering questions, asking
questions, reassuring, re-directing, lying outright – and nothing,
nothing, would stick. Ten or fifteen minutes after I had gotten
her calmed down or focused on something else, or whatever, she'd
call again.

And this, of course, on a day when I was really trying to concentrate,
punch through the mild migraine, get some conservation work
done. Some rather delicate conservation work, at that. Work
which had been promised to a client two weeks ago.

And, of course, my wife had a thing this evening that she had to
go do (my suggestion that she do so – no fault to her). She got
home after I had Martha Sr tucked in to bed and was working on
the dishes.

And as I stood there at the sink, washing the dishes, thinking
favorably on the option of having a heart attack, it sunk in that I
was done. I mean, I'd been standing there, considering that a

heart attack might be the best solution to my problems. Yeah, a heart attack. Hell, at 49, I'd probably survive it. It'd come as no surprise to anyone, given the kind of physiological and psychological stress I'm under. No one could blame me for no longer being a care-provider for someone with Alzheimer's. Hey, it might even get someone to think about noticing my writing, since a tragic character (whether alive or dead) always gets more notice as an artist than does someone who has their life, and their shit, together.

So, that was that. I looked my own failure to continue right in the eye, and told my wife. I can't continue to do this. I can't deal with another day like this. Maybe later, but not now.

I thought earlier that I could do this indefinitely. But it has gotten so much harder in recent weeks. I don't like to fail at something. I don't like to set aside a job before it is done.

But it beats having a heart attack.

Postscript:
Like I said at the outset, that's pretty raw. And I'm going to leave it as is, though following 8+ hours of sleep I feel better and have a different perspective on things.

This is one of the functions that this blog serves for me: being a form of therapy, allowing me to express things in a way that allows me to vent and get some perspective. I get it off my chest, so to speak.

And it serves another, related purpose: to help others understand just how difficult and demanding it is being a care-provider for someone with dementia, to share with other care-providers my stories as a form of support. And here, I am talking about those who choose to be care-providers for friends and loved ones at home. Professionals who do this, God bless 'em, do not have the same perspective: they get to go home at the end of their shift (or even their double shift, in rare circumstances). Doing this at home means you never get to leave.

I am by no means a 'weak' person. Not physically, not intellectually, not emotionally. And yet you can see what effects the constant, unending wearing has on me. There's a good reason why care-providers suffer huge stress-related illness, including, yes, heart attacks.

As I said, this morning I feel a lot better. The migraine is just wisps and echoes, and I hope it remains that way. I have this trip to meet with my new client and pick up the first lot of books, which means a couple of hours road time to allow the worries and cares to unspool behind me a bit. Just getting out of the house for the bulk of the day will help.

I do not know where we go from here. My wife and I discussed my exhaustion last night, when I told her that I was "done." But since we were already going to change the care-giving package to allow me more time to concentrate on my conservation work in the coming months, it may be that we keep Martha Sr here at home and I just try and ride this out, knowing an end is in sight. (As I told the social worker for hospice when we first hooked up, "I can sleep on broken glass for six months, if I know that's the end of it.")

So, no fretting – I'm better this morning. And while I cannot control what might actually happen to me vis-a-vis my health (beyond doing what I can to stay healthy), I'm no longer even contemplating a heart attack as a good alternative strategy.

(Kathi's LiveJournal entry. 3/23/06)
A Day In The Life

It's impossible to do anything around here when it's only you taking care of Mom *[Georgia]*. Trust me.

It's like having a baby or a small child.

You cannot let her out of your sight for more than a minute.

You have to constantly entertain her or else she gets agitated and either starts throwing stuff around or unlocks the gate to let the dogs out into the world.

You have to gently take her wrist so she won't keep picking at her face or scalp. Right now it's the healing sore on her ear that's driving her nuts. She makes it bleed time and again.

You have to make her take your arm if the two of you are walking. If you don't, she'll either dawdle or wobble. If it's the latter be prepared to catch her when she lurches, especially going around a corner. If it's the former, you have to pull her along.

If you take her into a store you cannot look at anything unless she's right beside you. Otherwise you'll catch her putting a trinket or something in her coat pocket because "it's pretty." Forget about explaining about stealing – all you'll get is a blank stare.

Carefully enunciate your words and look straight at her as you're speaking. There's a chance she'll not only catch what you're say-ing, but might also understand what you're saying.

Sit-down family dinners do not exist. She eats when she feels like it, which isn't often. When she does feel like it, there's a 50-50 chance she'll change her mind once she looks at whatever you've made, so break out the blender, the protein powder, the frozen yogurt, and whatever else there is that'll make a smoothie. Sit with her until she finishes it – if you don't, she'll only take a sip and leave it.

Don't leave her alone with the dogs if at all possible. In general, this is a good idea for overall safety concerns. With regard to our dogs, it's because they're con artists. They know how to play her for

treats. Try to ignore the half-empty treat boxes lying around and
be happy you know enough to feed them a small dinner.

Once she's in bed, stay up for another hour or two in case you hear
shuffling or, heaven forbid, any crashes. Go upstairs to see if there's
light coming from the bottom of the door. If not, carefully open
the door and listen for her breathing. And do not wake her up or
else she'll be up for the rest of the night.

The awful truth I've learned this week thus far?

I'm not cut out for care-giving over the long term. I play the "What
If John Didn't Exist?" game in my head and shudder at the entire
life overhaul I'd have to make. Forget working full time, for one.
I'm not even sure I could stick it out part time for very long, only
because I'd get absolutely no respite since Mom would be at The
Club™ during those times. In other words, if I didn't work at all,
I'd have respite. I couldn't take care of the dogs the way they
should be taken care of. What if I get sick or something? Who'd
fill in for me? Forget about any kind of decent housecleaning
(haha, that's actually my respite time if I'm off). Forget about
venturing anywhere in the world unless it's via computer. You
get the idea.

First, I don't have the patience. I'm surprised I haven't chewed off
my lower lip yet for every time I've wanted to scream or figuratively
bang Mom's head against a wall. That's doubly scary – I mean, I
did special ed for a bit when I was teaching, and I never felt this
way with those kids. I'm pretty sure it's because it's MOM, and
MOM isn't supposed to be like this.

Second, I've discovered that I'm more selfish than I ever thought.
I'm praying it's coming out ONLY because of the care-giving. You
didn't know me before all this happened. Back then I was the
proverbial doormat sort of girl. Not anymore, no siree, if I have
an inkling that anything's mine, then dammit, it's going to be MINE
MINE MINE. Not a nice feeling. I don't like talking about it because
I'm utterly ashamed of it. But there you go. *shrug*

Third, I no longer have the stamina. What happens when Mom becomes bedridden or wheelchair-bound? My stamina goes into my work, and it stays there. That explains why I'm utterly drained the minute I get home, and yeah, I don't bounce back the way I used to. That's not fair to her.

(Kathi's LiveJournal entry. 3/27/06)
Rummaging about

This is why I want her *[Georgia]* out of here: I can't stand the rummaging. I can't stand her taking apart every single freaking thing in her bedroom, living room, kitchen, wherever and just leaving it heaped in a pile. God only knows what she's throwing around – is it some of her heirloom jewelry? Her clothes? Is she mangling all the old VCR tapes? Is she tearing up all her old quilting stuff? Let's not even get into her taking my work stuff and John's. Can't tell you how many times I've found my aprons, pens/markers, pay stubs, and who knows what else floating somewhere up there. Petty stuff, I know, but it irks me to no end.

And this "going home" crap. It's a universal Alzheimer's thing, I know, but what I wouldn't give to not have a conscience so I could just bash her head to make her understand that THIS IS HER HOME, not Somerville, not wherever else she's thinking of. She stuffs all her clothes and whatever else she can find in bags and pillow cases and sometimes within other clothing and leaves it scattered all over the place. I ask her how she's planning to carry all of it. She calls me a liar and that this isn't her house because she doesn't receive any bills. I tell her they all come in my name. That sets her off again, and who am I to pay her bills? It's too complicated to explain. I just walk out.

OK, the experts say to keep your Loved One entertained. You don't park them in front of the TV. You play games with them, you take them out, you do anything that'll keep them from descending into their own madness. That's all well and good, but it never lasts. People with Alzheimer's have extra short attention spans, so you have to literally be at their side almost every single minute.

There are some people who find much joy in this. I know a few of them from another message board. I don't want to say they're Pollyannas because of the unsavory side of that connotation, but are they truly genuine? Maybe they had loving relationships with their Loved Ones in their previous lives – I think of X's story about his birth mother and her husband, and how the husband took care of the mother well after she descended into Alzheimer's hell because he refused to put her in a nursing home. How could he have done that? How did he manage to push aside his ego to focus solely on her? How do the folks over at the other message board do it? Many of them are old enough to be my mother, so perhaps it's partly wisdom and reframing the situation in their minds. Oh sure, there are rants such as mine here and there, but far fewer than I ever imagined. Maybe they've gone past the ranting stage... I honestly don't know.

My mother and I have never had what I consider to be a close relationship. There were too many times while growing up that, for some reason, I could never conjure up a need to hug, kiss, or tell her I loved her, although she'd do it to me too many times to count. I felt as though I was her life raft, and I resented it. Oh sure, we did girlfriend-type things like shopping and whatnot, but there was always an unseen window between us. If I dared pass my hand through the window, would I be more scarred than I already was? I was too scared to find out, too afraid that she'd suddenly do one of her famous about-faces and once again declare me spoiled, selfish, and anything else that'd make me feel like the scum of the earth. Years later she was still stunned that I never once fought back.

She doesn't, of course, remember any of this. Perhaps deep inside her mind she doesn't wish to remember, a technique I didn't know until I was an adult that she used often to filter out anything that'd depress her. Early in her disease there was a time when she'd cry and ask me why I acted so cold toward her. How do you answer that? It's not that I never loved her – I do because she's my mother – but I've never felt any affection for her. I can't tell her that because, now more than ever, I am her life-raft. She deserves to be loved, just like everyone else on this planet. She was loved once. That love died back in '73 when my father passed. She never recovered from it. Now, to her, it never existed.

I don't know what the point of all this is. I keep thinking that if I write it, it'll click something deep inside and change me for the better. Instead of being just the dutiful daughter, I'll become the loving dutiful daughter who'll do ANYTHING without complaint. I'll become the loving wife John deserves instead of the screaming harpy I think I've evolved into. I'll stop thinking that what I do is never good enough.

Most of all, I'll stop everything and magically change into someone else. But that isn't likely to happen.

(Jim's blog. 10/26/07)
I am not a saint.

I just lost my temper. I just had a full-fledged screaming fit, eyes bulging, veins throbbing, face beet red. At a 90 year old woman who knows no better, who is confused by the world around her due to Alzheimer's, who is likely dying.

Why did I just do this reprehensible thing, and why on earth am I admitting to it in a public forum?

The first part of that question is the more difficult one to answer. I did it out of frustration, exhaustion, and fear. Frustration because Martha Sr has been exhibiting compulsive behaviors all morning which drive me nuts (tearing things out of magazines, wanting to write on the back of photos in the little album she has, 'cleaning' up some lunch mess with a Kleenex and in the process smearing stuff all over the table top and making more work for me). This sort of thing rapidly gets under my skin – it's like some small kid pestering you with a behavior that they know will drive you nuts. Except, of course, that in this case she doesn't really know what the hell she is doing.

Exhaustion is obvious. Though I have been getting a lot more sleep, this is the end of years of being a care-giver. I do not have 'reserves' to draw upon. I only have a worn and fragile veneer of sanity. I have had the discussions with her which tripped my outburst hundreds of times. Sometimes, like this one, I just snap.

Fear? Because she is dying. Because in some sense, while I know that we have done everything humanly possible to care for her, and extended her life by years . . . I will still feel a sense of failure as a care provider. I hate to fail at things. I fear that others will think less of me because of that failure.

So, why tell on myself, here, in this way? Because this is part of what it means to be a care provider. You lose your temper. You scream, you shout, you act in mean and petty ways. You will lose your temper, or your sanity, now and again. And if you are to be effective as a care giver, you then have to catch your breath, forgive yourself, and get on with the task at hand. None of us are saints. We're all frail, fallible human beings. You have to accept that, if you have any hope of getting through this. Because you can't just take the day off to go relax, or turn this project over to someone else. You have to deal with your own outburst, then get over it as best you can. You have to keep going, whether you want to or not, whether you feel fear, or exhaustion, or shame.

(Kathi's LiveJournal entry. 3/28/06)
Tensions

We just had an almost knock-down, drag-out fight with Mom *[Georgia]*. Things are still pretty tense around here.

John's deathly afraid of anyone shredding anything, particularly paper. Guess what Mom's favorite keep-busy pastime is?

She's shredded more bills than I care to count. It doesn't matter that we have a P.O. Box – the minute we bring anything home and hide it, she'll somehow find it.

She's shredded the last two checks he received from clients. That's what, more than 5-6K? I'm constantly late on payments – something which I've NEVER been in my entire life – because she shreds anything that's paper. Of course she denies doing any of this, so therefore it's our fault. The bills I've since put on automatic payments, but everything else, eh.

She's at the point now where Alzheimer's is highlighting the more unsavory aspects of her personality, namely the temper and stubbornness. Part of the aforementioned fight revolved around why John and I are here, and John must be a bum because he obviously can't afford to support me, and why hasn't she received any bills? Where's her checkbook? After several rounds of this John completely lost it and screamed bloody murder at her. That, of course, set her off. They both threw things. Nobody nor nothing was hurt.

Missy, our Alaskan Malamute, hates yelling. I let her outside. She shat all over the back porch and wouldn't come back in. I ran outside to find her. She was leaning against the bottom of the deck trembling.

Somehow all this morphed into the house and why we're here. Back and forth, back and forth – we're here because we don't want you to lose the house, Mom. We're here because the state mandated ME to remain here so you won't become a public charge. Believe us, we WANT TO MOVE OUT BUT WE CAN'T BECAUSE OF YOU. Yes Mom, we discussed all this with your lawyer. Yes, I know you don't remember. That's why I'm telling you.

"We pay all the bills and none of us can afford to do so much longer, including you, Mom."

"I never asked you to."

"I know, Mom, but it is the least we can do because we're living here."

"Well, you shouldn't."

"We do."

"I don't believe you."

Yadda yadda yadda.

"SO WHAT'S WRONG WITH ME? I CAN LIVE BY MYSELF."

"Um, no you can't, Mom."

"YES I CAN, DON'T TELL ME WHAT TO DO."

"If you did I could be arrested for elder abuse, Mom, do you know that?"

"I'M NOT ELDERLY." Then she looks around and wonders why the kitchen doesn't look like the one in Somerville. ARRRRRRRGH.

(Jim's blog. 8/19/07)
Are you *sure*?

I was still trying to get to the bottom of my first cup of coffee this morning, when Martha Sr called for the third time since I had come downstairs about thirty minutes previously.

I entered the dark bedroom (it was barely 7 AM), went over to her bed. I leaned over the railing. "What do you need, Martha?"

"Are we there yet?"

"Where?"

"Boonville." (A nearby town, and where she grew up.)

"We're in Columbia."

"Oh." Pause. "Well, how long will the train take to get to Boonville?"

"Train?"

"Yeah, we're on a train."

"Um, no. We're in your home." (The home where she's lived for 53 years.)

"Oh, no, we're on a train." She looked around the ample bedroom, complete with bookshelves, a desk, dressers, et cetera. "This is a train."

"Um, no, this is your bedroom. In your home. In Columbia."

"Are you sure?"

"Yup."

"How are you sure?"

* * *

After Martha Sr got up from her nap this afternoon, had a snack, and went in to sit in the front room, we had a storm roll through. Nothing serious, but there was a bit of lightning and thunder. I went to check on her, and it was clear that she was anxious about something. I asked her if she was worried.

"I'm worried about the people."

"Which people?"

"The people who I was talking with. Before."

"Maybe that was a dream, Martha. You've been here all day."

"Oh, no, I was up on a hill. Talking with people. They told me to come back here."

(We live on the highest hill around, and she'd been no where.) "Well, maybe that was in your dream."

"No, it was at a house, up on a hill over there," She gestured randomly. "Will you take me up there? I want to make sure the people are OK."

"I'm sure they're fine."

"But you have to take me to go see."

And thereafter followed 40 minutes of discussion about not needing to take her 'over there' in the car so she could check to make sure the people of her dream were OK.

(Kathi's LiveJournal entry. 4/7/06)
THEM

Evidently the paranoia stage crept in while nobody was looking.

"Come over here NOW, I have to tell you something so nobody else will hear."

"What? Why are you whispering?"

"So THEY won't hear us."

"Who's 'they'?"

"Oh, you know...THEM. They're watching us. They want the

house. They'll try to take it away from you. It's YOURS."

"Mom *[Georgia]*, there's nobody else but me and John. John has no claim on anything of yours."

"Yes, yes, but THEY'RE here. All those people. My family's relatives. They want everything after I go. It's all yours. You have to tell the lawyer that."

"What relatives? Who? Auntie Helen? Rick? Gayle? They're all that's left. They're not going to take anything."

"No, no, not them. The other ones. They keep looking at me. They're looking at us right now. They live here. I finally figured out why all these people keep coming in and out of here. You never told me about them."

"What other ones? There's nobody else here except you, me, John, and the dogs."

"Oh, never mind. I knew you wouldn't understand. You don't understand anything anymore."

Every night I help Mom get undressed and ready for bed. Mostly it's just giving her directions so she remembers to take off her glasses before pulling something over her head, no, put the dentures in the container, here, change your panties, put the undershirt on first then the PJ bottoms, and wash your face! We've made it into our own comedy routine, with Mom deadpanning "Yes, Maaaaaaaa" while rolling her eyes. She no longer remembers calling me "ma moutza vroma" a Greek endearment which translates into "dirty-faced girl", or the other assorted little good-night sayings we had. She curls up on her side, sighs heavily, and tells me she loves me. I kiss her goodnight and turn out the lights.

Nine times out of ten she's quite prompt getting into the routine. She sits on the bed while I stand in front of her in a mock MP stance, hands open, waiting.

Instead she wanders over to the big oak bureau and starts fiddling with whatever trinkets her fingers touch. I put her PJs on the bed and beckon to her. She doesn't look at me, fingers moving from an old brooch to a pile of rubber bands, oh look, a dime!

"Mama," I say, "it's time to get changed."

She looks over at the PJs, looks at me, looks back at the PJs, and asks, "Are you my Kathi? Did you come out of me?"

I nod.

"There's another girl here somewhere who looks more like her. You don't really look like her, you know. You sound like her, though, so maybe you are her. I don't know you anymore. How long have you lived here?"

"All my life, Mama," I automatically reply. "We've lived here together for over 35 years."

"No, no, I don't remember you ever coming over here. This isn't my house, you know. I have one exactly like it, but this isn't it."

She's been on this particular vein for the past few weeks. Are you SURE this is my house? Are you SURE this is the address? If it is, then why does it look so different? Is there somebody else living here? Who said John could live here? I never gave him my permission. You can't be married. You're my DAUGHTER. You're too young.

"Mama, please take off your glasses. It's time to go to bed."

She takes them off and places them on top of the clock radio on the nightstand. I hold out my hands. "I need your sweater."

"I'm not taking anything off. They're looking at me."

"Who's looking at you? Where are they? Can you describe them?"

She glances around. "You know. They're all here. They're wait-ing for me. They want everything I have, so I have to save every-thing so you can have it after I'm gone. There's so many people. They come in and out of here all the time." She looks up at me, then suddenly grabs my arm. "You know who they are. Don't tell me you don't."

"Ma, honestly, I don't. You know I'd tell you who they were if I KNEW who they were. Nobody's here in this room but you and me. John's downstairs. That's it. Just the three of us."

She starts to take off her sweater, but suddenly folds into herself as she's about to slip her arms from the sleeves. She's shaking.

"I can't get undressed. They're looking at me."

"Mama, nobody's looking at you but me. I promise. The shades are down. The door's shut. Nobody can get in without my knowing."

On and on this goes. She doesn't want to go into the bathroom alone, so I escort her, turning my back as she sits on the toilet. Her hands shake as she puts the dentures in the container; her eyes widen as I splash water over them so the tablet dissolves. Back by her bed she refuses to climb in unless I make absolutely sure nobody's peeking through the windows. She snuggles into the blankets, her eyes, forehead, and hair only visible on the pillow.

"Mama, are you going to be OK? Do you want me to stay in here with you?"

She looks up at me.

"I'm going to bed. Good night."

"Good night, Mama. Sweet dreams."

We haven't heard a footstep or peep since. I wonder if she'll remember if "they" were watching her tomorrow morning. They'll probably emerge tomorrow night because they're like that.

sigh

(Jim's blog. 10/17/07)
Unseen visitors

It was a half hour before lunch yesterday. I checked in on Martha Sr, who was sitting in the front room, reading. Doing this regularly helps her feel less anxious, gives her a chance to ask questions or if she needs something, since she doesn't always remember that she can just call for me.

"How're you doing?"

"I'd like to get up and look out that window."

This is unusual. "Um, why?"

"Because I want to see what's so interesting out there."

"???"

"There was a man here a few minutes ago, and he was looking out that window at something."

No, there wasn't – we'd been alone since my wife left for her office 90 minutes earlier. "A man?"

"Yes. There was a man there, looking out. He seemed to be very interested in something."

* * *

I was on-call last night. It's a lot easier to do this now that it's only a couple times a week. Martha Sr had been restless early on, so I went to check on her about 11:00.

"You OK?"

"Yes. But I need to get up."

"Do you need to use the toilet?"

"No. I need to make room for the other people."

"???"

"All the people who are here. I need to let them use the room."

"No, it's OK – this is your room, and they're happy to let you sleep here."

"Really?"

"Really."

* * *

At 5:30 this morning, she was stirring. I went downstairs to see what was going on. She was over at the edge of her bed, against the rails, trying to reach the lamp on her bedside table (which we keep out of range of her reach on purpose).

"Whatcha doing?"

"Trying to turn on that light."

"Why?"

"Well, so I can see the other people."

"???"

"The ones who are here for dinner. I want to go to dinner with them."

"It's 5:30 in the morning." There's a bright digital clock on the table, but she usually forgets to look at the indicator for AM/PM.

"Then why are the people here for dinner?"

"I'm not sure. I'll go ask them. But you can go back to sleep, and we'll be sure to get you up when it is time for breakfast at 8 o'clock."

"OK."

* * *

It was a little after 7:00, I was just sitting down with my second cup of coffee and catching up on the news online. I heard Martha Sr stirring again, went to investigate.

"Do you need something?"

"I'm trying to see if I can get my head through these bars." She means the bed rails.

"That's not a good idea. You could get hurt." She won't be able to, anyway, but still it's not a good idea for her to be trying it.

"Oh. OK. Well, I called my family in Boonville, and the oldest boy is going to come and get me." I think she's thinking of my wife's cousin Bob, who died earlier this year.

"Well, I'll be sure to come wake you when he gets here. But you can go back to sleep until then."

"You promise?"

"Yes, I promise."

Makes you wonder.

(Kathi's LiveJournal entry. 4/24/06)
Money can't buy love, but it could sure help with Mom

The geriatric care manager's assessment was interesting. Right off the bat she agreed that Mom *[Georgia]* is in no way ready for nursing home placement, but she would do wonderfully at an assisted living memory-impaired program IF she had the money. Money. She referred me back to The Good Attorney™ and to the county elder affairs office to speak with their Medicaid people because, certainly, Mom should be eligible for more services given her monthly SS pittance. She should already be eligible for Medicaid, but, yeah, we've got this joint account issue, and Massachusetts doesn't look too kindly on such if the co-signer isn't a spouse. I won't know for certain until I speak with the county Medicaid folks. The Good Attorney™ can't do anything until then because what she can do depends on what they say – no sense her going through the paperwork and charging me $ when the county people can do it for free. Legalities, legalities.

The house. Well, it really depends on me. I could have The Good Attorney™ put it under a trust and pray that Mom remains here for the next 7 years. I could have Mom sign it over to me and pray that she remains here for the next 10 years. If I wanted to go the low-income senior housing route I'd have to sell, but John and I wouldn't be allowed to move in with her – I'd have to hire help for her. If I wanted to stay here, I'd have no choice but to go through reams of paperwork to make sure Mom got every single service she'd require so she could also remain here – in other words, if Mom goes, so do we.

As A, my boss, says, "You'd be stupid to give up the house. You'd live nowhere cheaper than where you do right now because you don't have a mortgage. Try tacking that onto what you already have to pay for taxes."

Yeah, he's got a point. But wouldn't everything be less expensive if we moved somewhere less expensive? Hell, he's moving down to North Carolina within the year because it's cheaper. He already has his job transfer in process.

It really boils down to what is best for Mom.

That's the sticky point.

I was also told today – and I'm told frequently – that at this point in time, we're doing everything which needs to be done. There's nothing else we can do. Sustained limbo. It's unsettling because you keep thinking there's something else you're missing.

(Kathi's LiveJournal entry. 6/7/06)
Another stage

When I came home I found Mom *[Georgia]* holding a photo of her and Daddy taken when I was little.

She had no idea who he was.

Heh, she had no idea that was her in the photo.

I took us for a monthly pedicure at the spa up the street. We've been going there for years. One of the older women pulled me aside and said, "You know, dear, she isn't looking very good. We've been noticing."

They've been noticing, too, at The Club™. Ruth gives John and/ or I a report when either or both of us picks up Mom. No, she didn't eat. She cries a lot. She keeps picking at her scalp. We can engage her in spurts, but it doesn't last very long. It just means she's entering another stage.

Oh, the scalp. A few months ago Mom somehow picked up this nervous habit of scritching her scalp in different places. She'll scritch, then scratch. A scab forms. She plays with the scab and it tears. She doesn't know why it's all wet up there, so scratches some more. Another scab...you get the idea.

She has a red, raw, weeping spot a bit bigger than a half dollar on her left side, midway between the ear and top. She also has another one, probably quarter-sized, on the other side in the same position.

She also has smaller ones on her hairline and on the crown.

Last time this happened the dermatologist gave us three prescriptions, plus samples "just in case." We're on the last sample pack.

Unfortunately there isn't much else we can do. It's part of the Alzheimer's, he said. Almost everyone picks up certain quirks in the middle-late stages, be it toe-tapping, sighing, scalp-picking, whatever. She isn't conscious of doing it. She doesn't realize the damage until she says "My head hurts", but the minute you start explaining why it hurts, she's back Out There.

(Kathi's LiveJournal entry. 6/9/06)
Bloody OCD or Drugged and Dopey

Mom *[Georgia]* woke up this morning with parts of her scalp drenched in blood. For the past few weeks she's been pulling her hair, scratching imaginary itchy places on her head, and doing god knows what else...I can't even begin to tell you what her hair looked like. *shudder* We washed and dried it. We put on the prescription foam and hydrocortisone cream. She still complains it hurts.

I mentioned all this to the The Club™ people when I dropped off Mom this morning. The first thing they asked me was if her meds had been adjusted. Yeah, the neuro upped the Zoloft. The Club Nurse nodded – what Mom's doing is a very common dementia-related reaction. Usually what happens is that the neuro will prescribe an anti-psychotic like Seroquel or Risperdal to offset the agitation the Zoloft or other SSRI causes.

So I'm like, "Wouldn't it make more sense to just adjust the SSRI dosage? Putting her on yet another med's going to make her spaced out, especially if it's an anti-psychotic... I'd think."

Aye, but that's the rub. Mom's Zoloft has been adjusted no less than 4 times during the last year, and the neuro still hasn't hit on the correct dosage. Plus it doesn't help that Mom's system doesn't take to mind-altering drugs too well to begin with.

I wonder if this is the reason why most patient with dementia look more "out of it" than they naturally would. Nothing seems to control the destructive behavior, so you dope 'em up. They react to the doping up, so you add even more meds until they can't function independently anymore. Then they're whisked away to a nursing home if they're not already dead. Yeah, I'm being simplistic here, but that's the general scenario.

I don't know what else to do.

(Jim's blog. 8/14/07)
Dying at home

About 15 months ago, I wrote the following:

I sit, listening to the labored breathing coming from the next room. The end will come probably sometime this next week, likely as the result of a fever and while she is asleep. As deaths go, it'll be one of the best possible, with minimal pain, discomfort, and fear.

...because some short time ago, when it became clear that Martha Sr was not going to recover from her latest medical problems, my wife and I decided to enter her into hospice.

I knew of hospice as an medical movement designed to make the last weeks or months of life as comfortable as possible, with a primary emphasis on palliative care. And this it is. But I've discovered that it is so much more.

Our "hospice team" includes a nurse who comes by as often as we need her. If that's once a week, or twice a day, it doesn't matter. We have on call personal care aides, a chaplain, a social worker (to help me and my wife with any of the issues surrounding the imminent death of a loved one), as often as we need them. If we need any medical equipment, from a hospital bed to oxygen, it's arranged for. All prescribed meds for her condition are delivered to our door. Basically, anything we need or want which pertains to Martha Sr's health is provided. And it is all 100% covered by Medicare.

And it is a shame that you have to die to get this kind of medical care.

As is clear from my other posts, Martha Sr actually didn't die. Yeah, she's one of those rare people who "graduated" from hospice care. Basically, we were too good at providing care for her, and she just wasn't ready to go yet. So, after the initial 90 days of being enrolled, she was dropped from the hospice program administered by one of the local hospitals. I'm actually still a bit upset with the way that transition was handled – my wife and I very much felt like we were abandoned. The extensive network of support we'd had just disappeared, leaving us unsure how to proceed (because while Martha Sr wasn't ready to die, neither was she going to 'get well', and her care needs had increased significantly.)

Anyway, now we've noticed another downturn in her condition, and one of the significant markers of end-of-life has shown up: dramatic increase in how much time she spends sleeping, with no indication that she is suffering from any secondary illness or infection which would explain it. Her afternoon nap has gone from 90 minutes to typically three hours (or longer). And she now wants to nap in the morning after breakfast most mornings, for an hour and a half to two hours and a half. Noting this, my wife sent me this website: *Eldercare at Home: Chapter 28 – Dying at Home*,[4] which contains the following:

The end of life cannot be predicted for any of us. We do not know when it will happen, who will be with us, how it will occur, or what we will feel. However, we do know some useful things about how many people die and this can help put your situation in perspective.

Many misconceptions exist about what can happen during the final days and weeks of a person's life. One stubborn myth about dying is that the person will die from only one cause. In some cases this is true, but many older people do not die from one major event or for only one reason. Instead, they die because of many different factors that combine to slow down the body's important systems, such as the heart and lungs. In a sense, the physical body slowly "gives up."

* * *

Certain physical signs warn us that the end of life is growing close. Most people with an advanced, chronic illness spend more time in bed or on a couch or chair. People with any type of advanced disease eat less food, and drink fewer liquids. They also sleep more, lose weight, and become much weaker.

Not every warning sign is physical, however. People may talk about "leaving" or "having to go." Their dreams make them feel as if they want to "get going" or "go home." Although this does not occur in every situation, this language and the emotion behind it are ways of talking about dying. The person also may ask to see special friends or relatives, and some haziness or confusion can occur as each day blends into another. Keeping track of the day of the week becomes less important, as do other daily living details.

Martha Sr has been doing more of this, though it is difficult to really say whether it is pertinent, since she suffers from dementia. Still, it is good to see it described, to be able to point to this document to help friends and family understand a bit better where we are (the excerpts I cite are just one small bit of that chapter – and the whole thing is worth looking at).

And it helps some with my ambivalent feelings towards hospice, which, in spite of what happened to us, I know is a good program. I just wish I knew when to turn to them again – having the full support followed by being dropped like a hot potato isn't something I think I can take emotionally again. Not at this point, anyway.

(Kathi's LiveJournal entry. 6/26/06)
06/26/06 – Teh Suck

Something's got to give...I can't see any of this continuing without somebody's head blowing clean off. I haven't done anything because 1) I haven't had the time lately, and 2) I don't know what's best to do without bankrupting myself because, you see, that's what it all boils down to. I'm already financially screwed just by maintaining everything here, and it's making me into Very Bitchy Kathi. I don't know what to do without causing World War III. Or, conversely, anything I decide is going to cause World War III. Status quo is going to start World War III any minute. I other words, I'm royally fucked.

It's true. I DON'T HAVE THE TIME FOR ANY OF THIS. I have a job that sucks the ever-living life out of me, so much so that I'm basically Zombie Kathi the minute I emerge from there. All I want to do with my free time is sleep and make somebody else take care of stuff. Now, I suppose if I were anal and astute and all that OCD stuff, I would've financially planned to take FMLA and get everything squared away. But I'm not, and if I were, I'd be fighting against formidable opposition. See previous bullet re World War III.

The worst thing? Everyone close to me tells me to just suck it up, which yeah, I understand and in most cases I do, but you know what? Sometimes it just doesn't work.

Bottom line: I can't deal with anything anymore, and I don't know what to do.

(John's blog. 9/1/07)
Synchronicity

The 1983 album "Synchronicity"[5] by The Police featured two songs that, when combined, form an almost haunting description within my mind of one particularly interesting set of events that occurred during the later phase of our caregiving cycle: "Synchronicity I" and "Synchronicity II." The former set the underlying tone of the unrelated but curiously coincidental events, while the latter set the final mood – the darker, more foreboding hint of an ending yet to come. Playing "Synchronicity I" in the background as I write this, the initial lyrics flow over me: *"With one breath, with one flow / You will know / Synchronicity..."* And the memories of our curious encounters with one of Georgia's old friends began to flow, freed from the recesses of my memories.

When Kathi was fifteen, she and Georgia took a trip to Europe with Georgia's friend K and her daughter G. Georgia was very no-nonsense and very organized, but the nailbiting trips by bus were hard for her. Her friend K was good at keeping her calm and helping her through the challenges of high-speed, narrow-pass breakneck bus travel.

It was a reciprocal relationship.

K wanted to see everything all at once in the brief time they had at each stop. Normally quite capable and organized in her own right, the excitement of the vacation and the opportunity to see so many different sights had scattered her focus. Georgia came in handy here, having already organized and planned each and every detail of what they would do at each stop in order to maximize their time. K recounted her memories of that trip, now over thirty five years gone, when she and I had an opportunity to talk a few months ago.

A connecting principle,
Linked to the invisible

During the intervening time between then and now, the two families drifted apart, as friends and families often do. But, just as the moon in her phases will wax and wane, so too do the relationships of a lifetime. Some wax full and resplendent, blooming into fields of forever friendship and creating rock-solid extra-familial relationships, while others wane and fall by the wayside, relegated to the dusty back shelves of long-forgotten photo albums. Some, however, take the lunar or seasonal cycle: they burst forth into bloom in the springtime of life, maturing into solid relationships, then experience a colorful, reminiscent descent into dormancy as life winters different changes and challenges, only to bloom anew once again as the cycle repeats itself later in life.

Such was Georgia's relationship with K.

Fast-forward from the European trip of thirty-odd years ago to early 2007. Georgia had entered an adult day health facility – essentially, a form of adult day-care. Shortly afterward, K also began to attend the same facility, two and sometimes three days a week. K didn't suffer from Alzheimers' Disease, which was steadily progressing in Georgia, but her own medical issues left her needing the services offered at the facility.

Georgia had a little trouble placing K, that was OK. K reminisced and Georgia occasionally caught a stray spark of recognition and recollection – enough that they could both muddle through and share their mutual memories, rekindling the friendship of old almost as if it had never been on hiatus.

As the next few weeks and months passed, each woman's illness brought new complications and placed different demands on them. In Georgia's case, the progression of her Alzheimer's generated changes in her behaviour that made identification of new issues more difficult. It became harder to diagnose new issues and to distinguish between illness, injury and simple progression of the disease. In order to ensure that nothing more serious was overlooked, Georgia often had to go to the local ER in order to determine what had changed and whether it required treatment.

The last few times that Georgia had gone to the ER prior to her entry
into a nursing home in May, an interesting series of coincidences
began to occur. While I sat with Georgia in the ER on the first of
these occasions, I was surprised to see K wheeled in from the
ambulance entrance. She was overjoyed when she saw and
recognized Georgia and I; she didn't feel so alone in her experience.

We know you, they know me

The next two times I had to take Georgia to the ER, K was also
being taken in – they appeared to be on the same schedule. K
joked about it, saying that the adult day health facility would
begin to think that she and Georgia were starting their own club.
That was reference that got Georgia chuckling – she often ran
several clubs and organizations, like church groups and charities,
in her younger days.

Just before Georgia entered the nursing home, she had a week long
stay at a hospital for a series of tests when her condition changed
unexpectedly. On the first night, walking her along the hallway
to help her get some exercise, I noted a familiar face being wheeled
past on a stretcher...

K was admitted that evening, and also stayed for the better part of
the week for tests.

She and Georgia were glad to have each other, and took turns
wobbling over to each other's room in order to get both exercise
and a friendly visit as much as possible.

Fast forward again, now, to last week.

Georgia had recently been sent to another hospital for some tests
to determine whether her sudden deterioration was due to the
progression of her disease or to some other factor. It was a different
hospital than usual – her nursing home had a house doctor, and
the hospital was where he was based in order to ensure consistency
of care. Georgia'd been back at the nursing home for a couple

weeks by the time last week rolled around, and has been making good progress. She'll never get back to where she was before the drop that led her to the hospital, but she's doing surprisingly well considering the prognosis at the time.

We didn't have the heart to tell her that her friend died last week, and that Kathi and I attended the wake last Wednesday.

To be honest, it wasn't simply because we didn't want to upset Georgia.

We were a tad hesitant to trigger whatever it was that had appeared to keep them so closely synchronized over the past few months.

Did I mention that, at the wake, Kathi noticed that K was lying in state in the very same room where Kathi's dad had been waked when she was only 13?

Life – and death, and dying – are strange; an interwoven tapestry of events, causes and effects that may not directly impact each other in ways that we can readily identify, but affecting us all nonetheless.

I think it's worth keeping that in mind as we review the various events going on locally, nationally and globally in the world today.

And as finish typing, the last lines of "Synchronicity II" echo in the room: *"Many miles away / There's a shadow on the door..."*

(Kathi's LiveJournal entry. 8/6/06)
Synaptic Misfires and Worsening Wobbles

Speaking of synapses, Mom *[Georgia]* has been doing that with a lot of spoken words lately. You can tell if she doesn't understand something because she'll sweetly smile, nod, and say something like "Yes, dear" (something which she's never done before). Then if you repeat what you said another 10 times, she might get it, she

might not. Speaking louder only makes her upset because, as she
says, "I can hear PERFECTLY FINE, I DON'T UNDERSTAND
what you're saying!" The best thing to do is to let her nod and
drop whatever it was you were trying to say, unless if it's a life-
or-death situation.

A few days ago a friend pointed something I never knew: When
a Parkinson's or Alzheimer's patient starts wobbling, it's usually
the beginning of the end of remembering how to walk. First it's
the wobbles. Then it's the complaint of being too tired to walk
far (that's where Mom's at right now). Then it's more wobbles
until the patient basically doesn't feel like walking. Then one day
the patient will have forgotten how to walk.

When Mom reaches that, that's when I have to find her someplace.
I can't keep her here. I can't afford to modify the house. I don't
care what the state says.

It's the waiting game I hate more than anything. That's the most
frustrating thing about all this. You can't do X until Y happens;
Z can't happen until X and Y have been surpassed to the point of
no return. The interval between X and Y depends on a lot of factors.
If Mom was the frail type she would already be in Z. I suppose we
can thank Mom's innate stubbornness, but that'd be too easy.

If I sound disjointed it's because I don't know what to think. On
the one hand her innate stubbornness is a joy in this instance,
meaning that it's better for her to be as mobile, reasonably
productive and talkative as possible. In other words, she's not
totally out in left field. But it's also a liability because until she can
no longer do any of them, she's not eligible for more help, etc.

We hit a huge snag with getting VA benefits. The man who's
helping me secure Daddy's records needs his serial number and a
bunch of other stuff I've never seen in my entire life. The fucking
VA must HAVE those records SOMEWHERE because I never
would've gotten benefits as a kid. I still haven't heard anything
about their wedding license. I've finally spent down enough to

apply for Medicaid, but I haven't done so because I've got to search for past tax documents and all that nifty financial stuff that's god knows where. In short, I'm tired. I want SOMEBODY ELSE to do all this crap. And yes, this is where my spoiled 13-year old alter ego comes out of the woodwork, so deal with it.

(Kathi's LiveJournal entry. 8/28/06)
Mental Deterioration

We just got back from the neuro doc.

Mom *[Georgia]* scored a 12 on the Mini Mental Test. She'd scored a 20 back in early May.

Her comprehension's beginning to degenerate, both visual and oral.

So are her motor functions – not so much the wobbling as it is her hands. She's got the Parkinson's-type shakes, and they're much further along than I thought. When Neuro Doc asked her to write a copy of a simple sentence, Mom could barely hold the pencil.

Med change, of course. Neuro Doc wrote a scrip for Tradezone (sp?), only to be taken when Mom gets too agitated for her own good. It's an atypical anti-depressant as well as an anti-psychotic. It makes the patient very sleepy, which is why Neuro Doc doesn't want her taking it as a regular regimen. It'll also counteract the Risperdal and the Zoloft if the dosage is too high. The scrip's for a 30-day supply. I'm to call Neuro Doc after the first couple of times Mom takes it.

John and I got into a fight right before we took Mom over there. We always do. He was in the middle of a group write-up with some of his fellow online pundits when I reminded him we had to leave. He countered why he should have to go. I replied, "Because you're the primary care-giver! Neuro Doc's going to want to talk with you!" We haven't really spoken since we got out of there.

Mom's a bit woozy. I've got some errands to run, so I'm going to have to take her with me.

I hate this. It's not like I need to be officially reminded about what's going on with her. It just makes me even more helpless, as if I already didn't feel helpless enough already.

(Kathi's LiveJournal entry. 9/18/06)
Repeated and lingering UTIs

PART ONE

Mom *[Georgia]* has been having UTIs left and right for the past few months. It's common among elder folk; however, for the past couple of months I've noticed she's been straining whenever she has to pee. She has the urge, but when she gets down to business, 9 times out of 10 nothing comes out. Or, it anything does, it dribbles. Once in a great while, she might have a healthy-sounding whizzing. Otherwise, no.

Her belly's also distended. I know she's gained weight from the Risperdal, but nothing like this. I noticed it when I helped her change for bed last night. Her belly looks like one of those CARE starvation victims. Starvation doesn't apply to her because, if anything, her appetite's done a 180 recently. She now eats almost anything and everything.

She's also been complaining about her lower back and the sciatica shooting down both legs. I know part of that's from the stenosis, as she's also been having a horrible time wobbling lately. But there's now something in me that's questioning if it's just the stenosis or something else.

Anyway, I called her doc just to check. I hate calling her. She's nice and all that, but ever since she branded me as one of those "overly worried only children", I hesitate to call because I don't want to seem like I'm Chicken Little. Well, hell, she's my mother. *rolls eyes* I called. I told the nurse what I just wrote here.

"Go to ER as soon as you can," the nurse said.

Renal stuff. Kidney stuff. Kidney failure?!? AND WHY THE HELL DOES SHE KEEP CLAIMING EVERYTHING'S FINE WHEN SHE AND I BOTH KNOW EVERYTHING'S NOT?!?!?

PART TWO

We didn't get out of the ER until almost 7PM.
I've never seen so many ambulances in my life all at once. For a moment there I thought today had been named my town's "Day of Death" or something.
No deaths from what I could see, but a lot of frail elders.
Two hospitals in Boston turned down one patient, citing no room.
I thought one male patient was going to bitch slap the nursing supervisor, but they managed to get him under control.

ANYWAY.

Seems that Mom never got over her last UTI, so she's basically a walking infection.
They didn't need to cath her because she finally voided after a bit.
No kidney infection or stones.
Her distended belly might be the diverticulosis acting up again.
They were concerned about her leg pain, however, and weren't totally convinced it was from the stenosis.
They were thinking deep vein thrombosis (aka blood clot).
So off to the ultrasound suite we went.

I couldn't help thinking her leg tissue looked like a relief map of Mars or something.
The tech said it's because of all her varicose veins.
looks down at her own legs for a moment
The major vein is like a giant black hole.

The artery is a smaller black hole.
I thought they'd be opposite for some reason *shrugs*

Good news – no clot.
Bad news – it's probably the stenosis, but I already knew that.
When I check in with her doc in a couple of days, I need to ask for
a referral to the ortho doc
because "wheelchair time" is, according to the ER doc, just around
the corner.
I asked him how he was so sure about it.
He said,
"I've seen many similar situations. I could be wrong, but I don't
think I am."
(he's an older doc, btw, not some resident just out of med school)

I don't want to jump the gun, but I can understand his reasoning.

We got the scrip and the usual directives.
John and I took Mom out to dinner afterward.

When we got home she collapsed into her chair in the living room.
John and I had to practically drag her upstairs – not so much
because of her legs, but because she was utterly exhausted.
She's asleep now.

I don't know how I feel about all this.
On the one hand, I'm glad it's just a nasty UTI and nothing more
serious.
On the other, I sort of wish it was something more serious
because it'd end this waiting game we've been playing the last few
months.

(Kathi's LiveJournal entry. 1/7/07)
Further deterioration

It's time to place her *[Georgia]*. And for once I'm not teary-eyed
or wailing about it because there's nothing more we can do for

her except be her entertainment committee. She hardly recognizes me anymore. Of late I'm her girlfriend. She doesn't have a daughter.

John's fighting me tooth and nail on this. He doesn't want to spend money if we don't have to, even if it means continuing to live in a house that's slowly falling apart and needs updating badly in every way. I haven't told him that I've been looking for real estate investment companies who might be interested in flipping this house. Professionals, people – this house will NOT end up on "Property Ladder." A friend of a friend is definitely interested. The reason why I haven't told him? I don't have it in me to start yet another drawn-out bicker session. Besides it's MY MOTHER'S HOUSE and therefore MY HOUSE and I don't want to stay here any longer than necessary. I feckin' hate this house. He cannot, for the life of him, understand that.

(Kathi's LiveJournal entry. 2/3/07)
The Physical Toll

I've been refusing to mention how much I feckin' ACHE all over. Bone-crushing, bring-you-to-your-knees aching with no particular place aching more than the other. I especially feel it in my upper chest, arms, knees, and hands.

I have no symptoms of a cold/flu/pneumonia/Ebola. Not a trace of sniffling. If I did, then yeah, I could blame the achy-breakies on that. But I don't.

It's to the point that when I come home, all I want to do is go to bed or curl up somewhere. In either place the aching eases a bit, but not much. Walking Ember is agony. My hands and fingers stiffen whenever they feel like it. If I stand in one place long enough, my knees and calves scream for mercy, so I end up Kathi-dancing around to shake them out. You should see me at work.

Oh, and sleep? What's that? I'm a restless sleeper to begin with, so if you add the Achy-Breakies to it, I'm a mess of tangled sheets, stiff limbs, and deep chest aches when I actually awaken. Ember no longer jumps on the bed to sleep at my feet. John finds himself dangling on the edge because of my flailing.

ANYWAY, I haven't wanted to write/whine/whatever about this because I'm trying to get away from that mindset. But now that it's becoming commonplace, it's starting to worry me. No, I haven't made an appointment specifically about this either.

Instead I've got stuff running through my mind: Fibromygalia? Chronic fatigue? Arthritis spreading everywhere? MS? Some other disease I haven't thought of? Something related to my old arm injury or menopause?

(Kathi's LiveJournal entry. 2/17/07)
Foreshadowing

John told me when I got home from work that Mom *[Georgia]* stayed in bed all day. She didn't want to get up, she was too cold to get up, no she wasn't hungry/thirsty. "Please, just leave me in peace," she kept telling him. He didn't call me because he knew I'd be too worried.

He did manage to coax her downstairs when he told her I was home. He helped her to her kitchen chair. She sat down and looked right at me. I said hi and kissed her cheek. She said "Oh, it's you" after a second or two, then turned back to John, announcing, "I want to go back to bed."

His plan was to take her over to Ye Old Local Watering Hole/ Restaurant for a bite to eat, thinking that the activity there and seeing the staff would perk her up. First they couldn't find a parking space out front. When they finally found one and got inside, Mom begged him to take her back home so she could go to bed. They stopped at the local deli to pick up stuff John thought she'd like. They arrived home. Mom turned her nose up at everything John bought. She finally relented to let me make her some pasta and sauce. I'm waiting for the water to boil.

I think I'm correct in saying that she's entering the late stage. It's as though everything is beginning to shut down, whether naturally or, knowing Mom, by her own will. She knows she's having great difficulty walking. She's always said she'd rather be dead than depend on a wheelchair or a walker. She's always said she'd rather be dead than be put in a nursing home, and, somewhere in her mind, I truly believe she realizes she's hovering over that point. She says every so often, "I've lived my life. Why doesn't He take me NOW?" We always kid her that obviously He wants her to stick around for some reason. When she asks what the reason is, we tell her we don't know – it's yet another of of His mysteries. That doesn't sit well with her.

You know, I've always had this nagging feeling that I'm either going to find her dead in bed one of these mornings or John is going to call me at work saying the same thing. Or I'm going to get a call at work from The Club™. I don't have any vision of an ambulance. I think when she does go, it's going to be swift. She's never been one to linger.

(Kathi's LiveJournal entry. 1/29/07)
84 yrs plus a day

Yesterday was her 84th birthday. She *[Georgia]* didn't remember. I didn't expect her to. Nevertheless we had a nice time. We had lunch and cake on the house courtesy of Ye Old Local Watering Hole/Restaurant.

I don't know what else to say. I don't even know if there's anything else to say.

(Kathi's LiveJournal entry. 3/21/07)
Forgetting

Mom *[Georgia]* is beginning to forget who I am.

(Kathi's LiveJournal entry. 3/22/07)
Gobbledygook

Mom *[Georgia]* is quite weak and wobbly this morning. She's acting like she knows who I am, but when John asks her who I am, she doesn't know. So I'm figuring that either 1) her eyes are playing tricks on her, or 2) she's on the verge of the stage where one forgets how to speak. Maybe both, I don't know.

I'm leaning toward #2 because her everyday speech is beginning to garble. Instead of saying, say, "Please pass the potatoes," she'll substitute some sort of gobbedlygook for "potatoes." Or she'll say, "Oh, you know, that thing there – like what's on your plate." Then she'll point something that's not the potatoes because she doesn't recognize them in their cut form. John makes a game out of it – "No, that's the meat. Point to the potatoes. Nope, those are the carrots. Now, Georgia, you KNOW what potatoes look like. They're white. Tonight they're cut into cubes. Point to them." She replies by trying to tease him. He gently leads her back to the question. She'll finally point to them, but she then forgets what she's pointing at. Then she gets angry at herself.

I also think that more things are not making sense to her. Getting undressed for bed, for instance. I'm in charge of Mom Bedtime, so I sit her down on her bed and tell her to first take off her glasses. She does. Then I tell her that I need her sweater/top, can you take it off? She replies, "Cold." I reply, "The portable heater's right here. You're putting on something else that's really warm." She shakes her head as though she doesn't believe me. Now, understand that we do this same schtick for every item of her clothing, including shoes. Getting her undressed can take up to a half hour, depending on how cooperative and awake she is. Unfortunately "the sleepies" are now prominent for unknown reasons, so I have to keep nudging her so she won't fall asleep in the middle of doing something.

I'm also wondering if that partial obstruction she has/had is truly gone. Her belly doesn't feel as bloated as it did, so I know some of it is gone. She's not running a fever. She's a bit pale, though. No appetite. No interest in anything going on around her, especially here. She slept for most of Jean's visit yesterday. Jean ended up watching Oprah and preparing dinner for us *sigh*

(Kathi's LiveJournal entry. 3/29/07)
Stenosis

Mom *[Georgia]* woke up this morning complaining that her legs didn't "feel right".

I tried to have her explain. Could she feel them at all? Are they numb? Did she pull a muscle or two in her sleep? Do they hurt?

She couldn't articulate anything else except "not feeling right".

She stumbled a few times between her bed, the bathroom, and the upstairs hallway. I managed to get her downstairs without incident, except that she almost stumbled into her chair. I somehow got her into the Jeep so I could take her to The Club™. She almost went *splat* into the pavement when I helped her out.

About a year ago her primary doc and the resident orthopedist told me to call ASAP if she started doing all this. Their thought was/is that all the stumbling and the legs "feeling not right" is a sign that her spinal stenosis has grown to the more-than-advanced stage. I bounced this past Nurse Annmarie. She said that would explain all of Mom's voiding issues, because the stenosis must be affecting her nerve endings down there.

I called primary doc's office the minute I got home. Primary doc won't be in until noontime, but she'll call me as soon as she gets in.

I also went to the Nursing Home admissions office and had Mom put on the list for the Home that's close to my job. I'd forgotten they also have an Alzheimer's programme.

I'm on automatic pilot right now. I HAVE to be.

How am I feeling otherwise?

I don't know. I'm afraid if I let myself feel something, I'll be a basket case.

* * *

No stroke. But Mom does have fluid sloshing around in her cranium. The official term is hydro-somethingorother. It's causing the blood vessels up there to dilate. The worst of it is in the part of her brain that controls gross motor movement, hence the wobbling. The secondary item is the stenosis, which, according to the MRI, is more severe than originally thought. Add the two together and you get, well, a very wobbly, lurching Mom.

They admitted her right from ER. I was told to go home and

pack a few items. Visiting hours officially end at 8PM, but they're going to let us sneak in to say goodnight.

Mom slept the entire time we were in the ER. She didn't flinch when they took blood, which surprised me. I finished one of my library books.

Have no idea how long she'll be there. They're going to do a neuro workup tomorrow to ascertain exactly how much fluid, what else may be affected, and formulate a treatment plan. The ER doc told me that in most cases a shunt is inserted into the head to draw off the fluid. He didn't know if this would be true in Mom's case.

(Kathi's LiveJournal entry. 3/31/07)
Planning

Got out of work as soon as I could so I could meet up with John and go over to see Mom *[Georgia]*.

Ran into the resident physical therapist: Mom did "very well" on the initial assessment. I laughed. "Trust me, the minute you turn around she'll be lurching like a drunkard."

The therapist laughed. "I figured as much. She was trying so hard to walk that she nearly stumbled over her own feet. But she did very well, considering."

Gotta love Mom. More stubborn than the proverbial mule, refuses to admit that anything's wrong. Her silence speaks volumes.

Met up with the case manager, who asked us what plans we have for Mom. We told her about the 6 month wait for the nursing home, about how I'm afraid for her on the stairs, how she refuses to use a cane or walker. She applauded John's care of her, but added that even he cannot be 100% responsible for her safety. We discussed moving her downstairs into the den. "It's a mess," I said.

"We'd have to clear everything out before we could get her bed in there. Besides, she's very room-centric. I'm not sure how she'd take it."

"Well, we can't decide anything until we get the results back from the workup and talk to her primary doctor," Case Manager said. "But it's good you're thinking. She has more support than most of the elderly patients here. That's saying a lot for the both of you."

Mom was in a giggly mood. She kept playing with her pancakes while telling John how much she loved him. The two of them went into their little comedy routine. A couple of nurses and Mom's roomie nearly collapsed from laughter. She didn't even realize I was sitting at the foot of her bed. She suddenly realized where she was. "When am I going home?"

Meanwhile I ran across the building to the doc's office. Ran into the doc in the reception area. "I won't be seeing her until later this afternoon after I see the results. I can't put a timeline on it. You've just got to sit tight. I'm sorry."

John and I left and went out for breakfast. We got back about an hour ago. Fed the dogs. Ember's tummy is distended for some reason. John went up to take a nap.

I feel like the walking dead. I should be taking a nap. But it's too sunny and nice outside.

(Kathi's LiveJournal entry. 4/7/07)
She's Home

There is nothing more humbling than monitoring your mother in the intricacies of using a toilet. That's all I'll say.

* * *

She *[Georgia]* didn't recognize neither the house, nor the kitchen, nor living room once we got home. She sat in her corner chair petting her little stuffed dog while I did the dishes and John checked his messages on my computer. John made us dishes of chocolate chip ice cream with chocolate sauce. "Can I go to sleep?" she asked after a couple of bites.

This is ice cream with chocolate sauce, mind you. It's her very favorite dessert. She's a worse chocoholic than I, which is saying a lot.

John had to push her behind as she made her way upstairs. He says she doesn't recognize her bedroom, but that was OK because she saw the bed and crawled into it fully clothed.

Well, how do I feel about all this?

Other side first: John's tickled pink. I think he missed his daily routine with her more than he realized. "Oh, she'll be back in the swing of things come Monday when she goes back to The Club™," he said to me.

* * *

I honestly can't see her staying here much longer. Logistically, if she's having so much trouble walking, there's no way we can expect her to navigate the stairs, never mind going from room to room without one of us with her. Then there's the issue of what to do with her, especially on the weekends. I'm actually dreading taking her to the family Easter bash tomorrow, not just because she won't recognize anybody, but having to monitor her every single minute in what, to her, will be a strange house. John thinks I'm making too much out of it.

In the greater sense, we're approaching a wall where I know neither of us will budge on. He doesn't want her placed until she is utterly helpless. I, on the other hand, can't see why she should wait any longer. One thing her stay at the hospital proved is not only she felt safer there, but also she no longer sees this as her home. Although I'd love to see her in the Alzheimer's program at the nursing home attached to The Club, if she's having this much physical trouble (never mind the forthcoming shunt), then maybe we should seriously consider regular placement.

I realize I'm saying "we," but it is legally my call.

John thinks I'm "tossing her away", in that I don't want her in my everyday life, I don't want to spend time with her, I don't want the responsibility of caring for her. In a sense he's correct. It's a crapshoot now whether or not she recognizes me. In practical terms, there's my job with the wacky hours. I'm on a medication that hits me like a ton of bricks, in that it makes me sleep the sleep I desperately need to stay sane. We have the dogs who've been somewhat neglected these past couple of weeks. John will pay lip service in that he agrees with me on all these counts, but none of them should overshadow our responsibility of taking care of Mom.

I want a life. I want the life we're supposed to have. I do not feel guilty saying that. It is not my responsibility that a big chunk of his life will be taken away if she's placed, and he will not know what to do. I did not ask him to assume her day-to-day care. He volunteered.

She will be safer in a place where people will know how to manage her. She is past the difficult agitated stage and is now sweet and compliant, the total opposite of how she was for most of her life. John sees and understands this, but thinks he can still manage her.

Now I'm going to take a shower, get changed, and fall into bed for a bit. I can do this because both Mom and John are taking naps. If she were awake, I'd have to watch her until he wakes. What about me?

(Kathi's LiveJournal entry. 4/11/07)
Freakin' Bureaucratic Tangles

Got a call from Mom's new case manager. She *[Georgia]* has a new case manager because she's on Medicaid. Surprise!

She called to tell me that Mom's no longer eligible for her "spa day" at The Club™ because the Visiting Nurses Association (VNA) will be dropping in twice a week – one visit will be from the nurse; the other, from the physical therapist. They're both scheduled for the next 3 months.

Medicare pays for both 100%, so that's good. Medicaid pays for both The Club™ and the aide who does the spa days. They have nothing to do with the VNA. However, thanks to MA's wacky Medicaid rules, if a patient receives services from the VNA, s/he cannot receive what's called "personal services" at a Medicaid-certified facility that's not a nursing home. The Club™, although it's attached to a nursing home, is not considered a nursing home.

What this means is that Mom can no longer get her twice-weekly baths at The Club™. The VNA can provide an aide to give her baths here, but Mom cannot use the tub in our bathroom (her bathroom has a walk-in shower that is in dire need of a rehab, but that's beside the point). Our tub – hell, the entire bathroom – also needs a dire rehab. We've got one of those Bath Fitter-type jobs that's over 30 years old and is coming apart at the seams. I tried once to bathe Mom in it. It wasn't pretty.

The VNA aide, however, can give sponge baths. Ugh. While New Case Manager was telling me this, I'm thinking, Now where the hell would she get a sponge bath? In her bathroom? In ours? She's not going to like this one bit. WTF?!?

To add to the complication, Mom also now requires an afternoon companion who's certified to be "hands on", a sort of a quasi-aide. That means Jean's now out of the picture. Said aide would be able to do incontinence care (good thing, although Mom's not at that point yet), use a gait belt on Mom, navigate a wheelchair – basically anything in that gray area between strictly medical and non-medical. This person, however, would not be certified to give sponge baths. Medicaid can provide someone similar for the other three days, but only for an hour as opposed to the 2 hours Mom had before.

So, let me see if I've got this straight:

* VNA nurse and PT both twice weekly

* Home health aide from VNA to provide sponge baths only twice weekly

* Medicaid-certified aide to provide companionship 3x/week for only an hour at a time

* The VNA aide and Medicaid-certified aide cannot be the same person

* This is the scenario for the next 3 months

* head splat on desk *

(Kathi's LiveJournal entry. 4/19/07)
Waiting

The Good News: Mom's "spa day" at The Club™ has been reinstated, starting tomorrow. She [Georgia] will be getting baths 3 days a week instead of 2. I know this must sound icky, but she hasn't had a proper bath since being released from the hospital. On the other hand, she doesn't smell or anything like that. Honestly.

The Bad News: Her case manager is still looking for a trained hands-on afternoon companion. She's tried 3 different agencies so far. She had said initially it'd be difficult since this companion would be more than "just a companion" (like Jean), but less than a nurse, but not exactly a home health aide because Mom doesn't need the ADL services *points to self and John*. She said this 2-3 weeks ago, mind you. We're trying not to climb the walls.

She goes to the neuro doc next Tuesday afternoon, which means I've got to shuffle my schedule a bit. I can probably get out early that day, but I'm going to have to make up the lost hours on another. I've also got to get her cisternogram films from Radiology some-time this weekend.

Otherwise she seems OK. She's still wobbly, but she isn't lurching around quite as much as before. She's also suddenly a lot more talkative, and some of the memories she's coming up with have floored me – for instance, Alzheimer's patients usually don't remember the recent past, but Mom can tell you all about Missy-Woo and the first time she met John. This is, of course, when she isn't getting him mixed up with my father, but that's another story. Still, it's kind of spooky...obviously Missy must've made a greater impression on her than either he or I ever realized.

The case manager suggested we start looking at other nursing homes in the area. Even she said the 6-month wait at the nursing home attached to The Club is a bit much. If we found a place that'd take her sooner, there's no law stating we'd have to keep her there forever – we would have every right to move her when an opening comes up. It happens all the time.

Mind you, I'm not looking forward to going through the entire hunt again. *sigh*

October
Hospice, or placement?

After all you have been through, after all your care-giving, it has come to this: you need help. Not just a weekly break, not just someone coming in to help clean a bit, or check in on your loved one. No, you need some serious help. Because the Alzheimer's has progressed far enough that it is clear that the end is in sight – meaning more intense care needs, increased physical problems, actual medical attention required.

What are your choices? What are your options?

It isn't a simple matter of "do this," or "do that." Insurance coverage varies widely from place to place and plan to plan. Government programs at the local, state, and federal levels all have their own arcane rules. Visiting Nurses associations may be in your area, and able to help. Or not. Hospice programs may exist and be able to provide care. Or not.

It's a mess, frankly. And you're probably now so exhausted from the years of being a care-provider that you can't make sense of it. At all. Chances are you'll grab at whatever straw is first offered. Will it be the right choice?

There *is* no right choice. There is no wrong choice. Come to terms with that now, or you will beat yourself up for no reason. You can only do the best you are capable, at the time. It may be hospice, if one is available. It may be placement in a full-time nursing facility. It may be something else entirely. You may have little or no control over your choices, and the decision may be made for you by external factors.

Our nursing home decision was based on our hearing from the day care facility and doctors, both of whom told us hospice wasn't an option and that for Georgia's safety and well-being, she'd be better off at a care facility than at home. We got a runaround about whether Georgia even qualified for hospice and we were convinced that we didn't qualify, meaning that we were short at least one potential source of assistance that we should have had. The vehemence we got at the nursing home regarding hospice was soul-shaking.

And as noted elsewhere, every time we thought we qualified for a form of assistance, we either got wrong or inaccurate information, or could no longer find the documents that we needed. (Many of which may still exist, but we have no idea how much stuff Georgia discarded or destroyed.)

(Excerpt – John's blog "A Life's Worth of Memories" 03/11/08) Nobody Home

The lyrics were too close to what I imagined Georgia would have feared, and – as her situation changed – what she felt as she realized some of the changes were taking effect. It's a song that still brings those memories and the associated empathy/sympathetic responses into sharp focus. The way the song "Nobody Home" by Pink Floyd[6] starts is stark enough – *"I've got a little black book with my poems in / Got a bag with a toothbrush and a comb in."* – it seems so very familiar, so very resonant with our task of packing up things for Georgia to have when the day finally came where we were faced with the decision we had hoped to never make: the decision to place Georgia into a nursing home was upon us. We were fortunate that we located a highly rated one in the immediate vicinity, and were able to effect the transition smoothly. It was very strange, at first, not having Georgia here with us at the house. Not having her here to look in on, or to help as she'd wobble to and fro, or to engage in the occasional banter or snippets of song.

(Kathi's LiveJournal entry. 5/17/07)
What Do You Tell Her?

Here's a question: If you were to break the news about a nursing home to your loved one who has Alzheimer's, what would you say?

I'm torn between:

1. "Mom, you're going to be going to a new Club starting next week. It's a Greek Club, and people stay overnight! They do a lot of stuff! How does that sound?"

or

2. "Mom, I'm afraid it's become unsafe for you to stay here, with the way you're walking and all. You've been saying that you don't like going up and down the stairs, and I don't blame you because it IS dangerous for you. We found a really nice place for you to say where you don't have to worry about stairs and stuff like that. We're going to go there Monday."

#2 is, of course, the more truthful explanation. But given the Alzheimer's, I'm not convinced that she *[Georgia]* will understand it, never mind remembering it. #1 has the advantage of getting

her excited about another "club" because she does like to socialize and do things when she's not sleepy. Plus when I mentioned the other day that it's a "Greek Club," her eyes lit up.

John has no opinion either way. In fact, he's become very reticent about the whole thing. He finally filled out his portion of the personality assessment booklet this morning. There's one more page we need to discuss before filling it out – do we want to attend a support group? Talk to the care-giver counselor? Get involved in the care-giver council?

(Jim's blog. 8/27/07)
Another try at hospice

I'm tired. No, make that I'm weary – not just from lack of sleep, but that deep weariness of being on a long campaign of any sort, in this case three a half years as a full time care-giver.

I wrote a couple weeks ago about our previous experience with hospice for Martha Sr. Well, as reflected in that post, we'd seen a downturn in her condition, notably the tendency to sleep a lot more. Couple that with increasing comments from her, following naps, that she had been with her parents (who have been dead for decades) and that they "wanted her to come home," and we sensed that perhaps she was entering into the end of life. We contacted her doctor, discussed the matter with him last week. He agreed with us, prescribed hospice once again.

This morning we had a visit from the case manager (a nice woman named Jan) from a different health organization than the one we used previously. We went over Martha Sr's condition, expressed our concerns about what our experience had been last year, discussed options. According to her, Martha Sr fits well into the guidelines for hospice admittance under the 'debility' criteria, and there's little chance that she would 'graduate' from hospice care under those criteria.

So, we're giving this another try. My wife and I are good care-givers, and have done this job well for these past years. But now having the resources of hospice available is a comfort, so long as I feel that I can trust it. Knowing that we have someone to call who can advise and assist as needed comes as something of a relief, and I find myself a little overwhelmed.

And for some odd reason, more weary than when I got up from being on call this morning. Tension-release, I suspect.

(Kathi's LiveJournal entry. 5/20/07)
Tomorrow Is The Day

Yesterday I bought a small armchair for Mom *[Georgia]*. It's sleek gray microfiber. We pick it up from the warehouse tomorrow morning.

After work today I went on a small shopping spree at Wally World. Undies, sport bras, socks, toiletries. However, there wasn't anything on the clearance racks that was either her size or something she'd wear.

I need to get a couple more pairs of PJ bottoms. Here at home she wears various old mock turtleneck tops with the bottoms. If it's cold, she wears a sweatshirt. She also has an assortment of those screaming color fuzzy socks to wear to bed.

I'm in the middle of doing her wash. What to bring? What should be left behind? I always thought her wardrobe was small, but I nearly filled two trash bags with stuff, mostly cardigans. She's got elastic-waisted pants that aren't dowdy. I threw in a couple of pairs of my old sweatpants just in case. I still have to pack what's in the wash, her shoes, and slippers. Summer-type shirts? I honestly don't know. I threw in a couple anyway, even though I KNOW I could always bring some over when the weather gets warmer. It's not like she's moving 1000 miles away. I'm over-compensating, that's what.

I emptied the gray carry-on bag she's had forever. It was the bag I used to pack a change of clothes on her "spa" days at The Club™. I put the toiletries on the bottom, adding her 3 stuffed doggies (presents from John on various holidays – one of them is a dead ringer for Missy), a framed picture of the Greek flag, a framed picture of the Statue of Liberty, and the huge 'ol crucifix that was her mother's. Her framed painting of Dopey and the collage of Missy/Ember/John/me have to be carried separately.

I thought about a couple of books. There's the huge pictorial book about Broadway we got her the first Christmas John and I were married. It must weigh a good 10 lbs. I don't know...she no longer looks at it, but it could be a conversation starter between her and the staff.

Coordination...we can't physically move her in until the doc faxes back that 3-page medication form. The doc isn't in until noon-time. However, they did tell us to bring in all of her stuff before-hand so they can sew name labels on all her clothing while we arrange her side of the room. John figured he could go get the chair and bring that plus her clothing in the morning. While that's going on, I could take her out for breakfast or let her sleep in. Maybe I'll invent a few errands we can do so it won't look as though we're waiting for something.

Her roommate is named Greta. We met her briefly last week. Cognitive-wise she's probably the same as Mom, but the difference is that she doesn't wobble or need any type of assistance. She was a teacher. When we met her, she was cradling a bunch of text-books in her arms and told us she'd love to stay and chat, but she was going to be late for class. We watched her as she strode past us and into the corridor. She disappeared into the solarium. Later, as we were leaving, we noticed her sitting at one of the tables with the books open, reading aloud to herself.

John just told me that earlier today Mom was saying something about having to tell me something, something which I should know. When he asked her what it was, she started crying and said she couldn't remember.

I'm going to have a delayed reaction about all this. I KNOW it.

(John's blog. 5/22/07)
Georgia entered a nursing home today

Georgia was admitted to a nursing home with a special Alzheimers/ dementia wing today. She'd been getting more physically frail of late, so – with the added strong recommendation from the adult day health folks and an unexpected early opening at a facility we'd put Georgia on the waiting list for – Kathi and I thought it was the best move for her. An opening came up unexpectedly soon (about four and half months earlier than we thought) at one of the homes we'd checked out and liked, so we started the process that culminated today.

Below are my reflections on this momentous change; I thought I'd share them, for anyone who may have had to make similar decisions or who might yet face this difficult time of life with their own loved ones. It's weird, not having her here to watch over.

Karmically, I know we've worked hard over the past four years to keep her at home as long as possible; it was draining, but I honestly believe I was able to provide exemplary care as her primary care-provider, and Kathi worked her butt off to pick up the slack on the financial end as I had less opportunities for consulting over the past year and a half. Almost as if a switch was turned on, I received a call from a company I consult through: they had a client who was explicitly requesting my services for a three day training course out of state.

In addition, I've got several writing projects that I will now have time to properly pursue – two collaborations (one sci-fi, and one sci-fi/fantasy), plus a couple short stories and my own fiction writing. The two collaborations and one short story will take precedence over most other writing; they, too, coincidentally started just as we began to approach different nursing homes and realized that the time had come to put Georgia into a safer, 24-hour care-giving facility.

Life is changing, and my wife and I – married four years, and having spent all of that time watching over her mom – are finally beginning to emerge from the shell we've been in. Georgia had been functional, hiding her slowly accelerating illness fairly well until a few months before Kathi and I got married. Then, she suffered a precipitous drop in perception, cognition, memory and physical stamina and dexterity. Kathi and I put our plans to get a place to live nearby on hold, and I moved in with them.

Over the past few days, Georgia has struggled to remember something that she wanted to tell Kathi; she appeared to know that a change was coming, and has talked often about leaving us – sometimes, to go back to her mom, who she misses. She's made it an explicit point on many occasions to thank me for all I've done for her, even tho she can't remember a lot of it; heck, she probably can't remember any of it, other than the fact that I've been around nearly all the time lately for the past few years. I helped her get up in the morning, wash and dress, have breakfast and go to her "club" (adult daycare), meet her when she comes home and keep her busy until dinner. Kathi would generally take over for a little while then, and help Georgia to bed. I'd come in and check on her at least once in the middle of the night, every night, and pull her covers back up over her. If she'd gotten up and wandered out of her room, I'd be the one to catch her and put her to bed, sometimes after giving her a cup of tea and a cookie.

Tonight, there's nobody in her room for me to check upon.

The big dog, confused that Georgia isn't here, has examined her room multiple times; he's on the floor behind me now, wondering if I'll be heading out at 3 AM as has become habit – I've had virtual insomnia for the past couple months, unable to sleep because I always knew

when Georgia would be getting up and getting lost or that she'd need me to pull her blankets up for her. During those times, I'd be unable to get back to sleep without disturbing Kathi, who gets little enough sleep and has to be up by 2:30 some mornings, and 4:30 on others. To tire myself out, I'd either go for a walk or a drive. Jack – our new malamute – would usually accompany me.

Tonight, I'll be awake as usual when Kathi's up and getting ready; I'll join her for a cup of coffee, 'cuz caffeine only serves to calm me down and put me to sleep now. When she goes off to her bleary-eyed morning, I'll return to sleep, wrapped in fuzzy comfort by the two dogs, and I'll probably automatically awaken in time to wake Georgia...who is no longer here, and no longer in my charge. I'll know she's OK, and that she's in good hands; I'll probably putter a little to let the excess mental "wake up" processes calm, then – finally – get some sleep.

Tomorrow starts a new day.

I'll call to ensure that she had a good night and that the morning went OK, but won't visit until Kathi can accompany me in the afternoon. Hopefully, Georgia will begin to adjust smoothly, and all our lives will continue along their new paths, opening new vistas and providing interesting journeys.

Just thought I'd share that with you all.

Peace.

(Jim's blog. 8/28/07)
Daring to think

After she finished doing the nursing assessment of Martha Sr, I escorted Marcia from the hospice agency out to her car. We paused just outside the back door, and she looked at me. "You guys are really doing a great job as care-givers."

She probably tells that to all the people they work with. It's likely in the manual.

But you know, it was still good to hear.

* * *

Every one of the family and friends we've told have been very supportive. "Glad you're getting some help." "About time you were able to find a good hospice." "Good that you can have some support." "Maybe now you can get some regular assistance, even some more respite care in each week."

But you know, it somehow feels like failure. Like we're giving up, giving in, saying "we can't handle this any more."

I always knew this time would come. Just as I know that someday Martha Sr will die. Well, part of me knew these things. Part of me didn't. It'll take some time for the emotional reality to catch up with the intellectual.

* * *

I found myself while on my morning walk considering what it will be like. To be able to go visit friends without having to coordinate family coming in to stay with Martha Sr. To not have to listen to a baby monitor 24 hours a day. To get some real sleep night after night after night. Daring to think that I might once again have a life of my own.

Really, that's how it is. You develop such tunnel vision – everything has to be considered in terms of one objective: being a care-provider. Yes, you take breaks as you can, you try and get some exercise, some sleep, eat right. Maybe even do some writing or conservation work. But all of that is secondary. Distantly secondary. Because you have to be there for the person you are caring for. It is a sacred trust, perhaps the only thing I truly consider to be sacred.

But now I start to consider What Comes After.

And it frightens me.

* * *

Over 4,300 people have downloaded my novel. That's an average of 600 people a month. Pretty good for what is basically word-of-mouth. I have a lot of work ahead of me to turn this into landing an agent, getting a publishing contract. If not for this book, then for the next one, on the basis that I have at least that much name recognition, that much of an 'audience'.

I have the prequel to write. There's a couple chapters already done that will need to be revised. And outlines for the rest of the book to be reworked.

I have at least two patentable ideas – one firearms related, one a consumer electronics item – that I need to pursue, see what I can do to either formally file a patent, or convince the appropriate large corporation to buy the idea from me with something less formal.

I need to earn some money, pay off debt.

I need to lose a bunch of weight, get back into something resembling decent shape.

And I'm frightened. For the last four years, none of these goals has really been paramount. So it has been easy to not succeed at them, and not take it as a personal failure. Soon, I will no longer have that excuse.

Can I succeed? Can I accomplish something lasting with my life?

* * *

A friend sent me the "Quotes of the Day" this morning. It contained one of my long-time favorites:

There is no expedient to which a man will not go to avoid the labor of thinking.
- Thomas A. Edison

Certainly true. One only has to look around at the world to see that. So very few people are willing and able to actually think for themselves. Oh, they may believe this or that, and call it thinking. But to actually stop, and consider, and understand? That is a rare thing.

I have been chronically tired for years now. And my ability to think clearly, or for any length of time, has been correspondingly diminished. I can point to this or that instance recently when I was able to think and work for short periods, once I had a bit more sleep and time to decompress. But it is a fragile thing. And I worry that perhaps it has slipped away...

(Kathi's LiveJournal entry. 5/21/07)
Things To Know When You Place A Loved One

1. NEVER, EVER second guess yourself. You'll make yourself crazy. There IS a concrete reason why you're doing what you're doing. Keep telling yourself that, and the transition will be much easier.

2. However, don't let yourself be lulled into the idea that everything will be smooth. YOU, of all people, will be entering The Portent Of Mixed Feelings as soon as you physically place your loved one. Have I done everything I can possibly do? Could we have kept them longer? Am I just "giving up"? Everyone will have their own questions, of course. ALL OF THIS IS PAR FOR THE COURSE. However, keep in mind that if you keep ruminating over all the questions, you'll end up second guessing. Nope. Don't even go there.

3. Treat the day like any other. Follow your usual schedule. We twisted things somewhat in taking Mom *[Georgia]* to breakfast

then running a few errands. She was game.

4. Here's a sticky: Do I tell my loved one or not what exactly
I'm doing? It really depends on the person. If your loved one
just came out of the hospital, then yes, s/he should realize that
s/he is going into rehab for a bit. If not, it depends on their
cognitive level. We didn't breathe a word of it to Mom. We just
drove to The Greek House. She and John stayed in the truck
while I got a cart to roll all of her clothes and stuff up to the
Alzheimer's unit. When I returned, they were both asleep.
When we took Mom in, she was greeted by no less than 6 staff
members. They whisked her away to the activity going on at the
moment while I signed reams of paperwork in the admissions
office. When I went up to the unit, she was so engrossed in what
was going on that she barely recognized me.

5. Watch your loved one carefully. If there's any recognition as
to what exactly is going on, then yes, you're going to have to
explain. How you explain depends on your loved one and your
feelings about it. One thing, though – if placement is one of
those things you see as horrible but necessary, DON'T EVEN
LET YOUR FEELINGS SHOW. If you're upset/apprehensive/
whatever about the whole thing, your loved one will pick up on
it, and you really don't want a bout of agitation in addition to
everything else now, do you? MAKE EVERYTHING AS
UPBEAT AS POSSIBLE. Maybe your loved one will be like
Mom and will automatically introduce herself to everyone she
sees, Maybe she'll sing for them. Maybe she'll make the staff giggle
and innocently flirt with the doctor. Go with it.

6. Music is a key element in most Alzheimer's activities. As the
poet Anne Sexton once wrote, "The music remembers more than
I." There was a flute trio performing in the solarium when we
brought up Mom. She immediately headed for the nearest chair
and spent the next hour humming or singing along. One of the
staff members sat her with the "more with it" crowd. Within a few
minutes they were all giggling like schoolgirls.

7. The staff may tell you NOT to say goodbye. The concept of "goodbye", especially with a new placement, can cause extreme agitation because the loved one may take it to mean that you'll never return, and s/he will automatically start telling you that s/he wants to go home. THIS IS NORMAL. John was a bit put off, but once the reasoning was explained, he could understand it. I didn't even get a chance to see her because I was speaking with both the doctor and unit manager.

8. Speaking of wanting to go home, your loved one will probably say such every time you visit him/her, especially during the first few weeks. Again, IT'S NORMAL. Don't give in. Divert them so s/he won't be "stuck" like a scratch on a vinyl record.

9. Per #2, expect yourself to experience every emotion known to man. After keeping a nonjudgmental, matter-of-fact demeanor through most of the day, I broke down and cried over at Ye Olde Watering Hole afterward. I came to the realization that Mom must continue on her journey by herself, with little or no help from either John or I. That very thought unnerves me, as it should, but it's the truth. We've done everything we could. John still insists we could've continued as we have been for the next few months, but overall he FINALLY saw the light, so to speak.

As of right now, I'm indescribable. I'm not teary, but I'm expecting another breakdown at some point. I'm...well, blank. It's almost like being in shock where your psyche disassociates itself from you because ruminating about what just happened will make you into a basketcase. I think what's keeping me on a somewhat even keel is knowing that we did our best, and we did it longer than most people would've.

(Email excerpt, Martha Jr to the family. 9/1/07)
A parade of hospice people

So, we've had a parade of hospice people through here this week, or it sort of feels like it. As I told you before, we met with Jan on Monday, who admitted Mom *[Martha Sr]* to hospice. On Tuesday, Marcia, the nurse who does the initial assessments came, spoke with us for a bit (wrote down all her prescriptions, got a feel for what Mom is like, etc.) then went in and did a checkup on Mom. As Jim wrote in his blog later that day:

> *After she finished doing the nursing assessment of Martha Sr, I escorted Marcia from the hospice agency out to her car. We paused just outside the back door, and she looked at me. "You guys are really doing a great job as care-givers."*
>
> *She probably tells that to all the people they work with. It's likely in the manual.*
>
> *But you know, it was still good to hear.*

Anyway, apparently they have staff meetings all morning on Wednesdays, because then I started hearing from the other people that afternoon. On Thursday morning we had Lori, our social worker, come visit. We talked for a rather long time; she had some good suggestions and observations for us. She met Mom, too, briefly, before she left. I mentioned to Lori that we needed either to refill a few prescriptions before Friday night or get them from them (that is one thing hospice does, provides all the prescriptions), and that we hadn't heard from our regular nurse yet, who would be the one who brings medications as necessary.

Apparently she went back and contacted the nurse, so we heard from her later that day, and met with her Friday morning. (She brought a bag full of prescriptions, though several look different than what we have been getting so we have to re-learn what the various pills look like...) She talked with us for a bit and then went in and met with and examined Mom. This nurse will be our regular contact with the organization, coming at least once a week, providing anything we need, etc. She seems nice enough, though perhaps a bit more distant than everyone else had been. (Or maybe it was just my mood that day.)

At any rate, by lunchtime on Friday we had the whole thing in place, had met everyone and knew who to call, etc. Then after lunch, while Mom was sitting on the toilet before lying down for her nap, she apparently had another small TIA. Jim says she slumped over sideways and became very weak and shaky. She couldn't really stand, even with Jim holding her up; her legs were jerking around like they sometimes do when she is VERY tired. He managed to get her up, pull up her pants and get her in to bed to rest. She called only about an hour later DEMANDING to be 'let out' of the bed. When Jim went to check on her she seemed rather annoyed at the safety measures we have put in place and said she could very well get up on her own! So Jim undid the straps and put down the rails ... and of course she couldn't do anything by herself. She was even unable to pull herself over to the edge of the bed. Her legs were still jerking around and she seemed very weak. Jim convinced her that perhaps her body was telling her that she should rest for a little while longer, and got her situated comfortably back in bed, where she fell asleep fairly quickly and slept until about 3:40. When she woke up that time, it seemed someone had pressed the "reset" button – she was back to her normal self.

So that is where we are at the moment. Mom continues to be her usual, pleasant self most of the time, but there are hints of other things going on. As I mentioned in my last message to you all, Mom has been talking increasingly about "going home" and the like. One suggestion is to roll with that, to help her know that she is safe here but free to "go" when she is ready. After getting some good additional information from the hospice organization about recognizing and responding to 'near-death awareness,' I formulated a plan for the next time Mom mentioned that. Jim and I talked about what I had in mind, and he was good with it. I had hoped she would bring it up when she got up from her nap Wednesday, since I was home, but she did not. Then Jim sent me up for a nap before dinner, and he ended up fielding the conversation. Went something like this:

She was concerned about the "people" in the house in Boonville wondering where she was. He reassured her that everyone knew where she was. Then she asked about her parents. Jim told her they had left a message that she was to wait here, and we would take care of her, until they came to get her. She said something like "to go to heaven?" and he confirmed it. I expect we may have a similar conversation a few more times, but the subject has been broached.

I don't know if it is that, or the fact that we are connected with hospice again, but it feels like we're winding down. There is some un-definable quality difference in Mom's demeanor and attitude sometimes. It is possible that Mom could decide to go within a few weeks, or she could decide not to. We'll just have to wait and see.

Everyone take care of yourselves. Love to all.

(Excerpt – John's blog "A Life's Worth of Memories" 03/11/08)
"And that is how I know..."

> *And that is how I know*
> *When I try to get through*
> *On the telephone to you*
> *There'll be nobody home.*[7]

The first day after her first evening there, I came in early to visit her *[Georgia]*. As I came off the elevator, I heard her voice clearly telling the staff to call her son-in-law and he'd explain everything. I felt immediately as though I'd betrayed her trust – my heart fell. I walked right up, and she recognized me immediately. I explained to her that she lived here now; it wasn't easy, but she accepted that she wobbled too dangerously for us to be able to keep her safe at home.

I should say she outwardly accepted it; she saw no use to arguing, and swallowed a little bit of her pride. I was certain that I could see it in her eyes. She was stoic about it, however, and we had a good visit. I came back a few hours later with Kathi, and repeated the procedure.

There were some things that irked me about her new home. The nurses kept trying to put her into adult diapers – but she wasn't incontinent. They weren't prepared for that, and never did get over it. They had to assist her in pottying for safety concerns, and sometimes they had trouble communicating with her: several of the nurse aids had very thick accents. It was a little difficult to understand them, and they sometimes had difficulty understanding us.

I could imagine the level of additional complication involved in dealing with and understanding a dementia patient.

I felt a little more helpless and little more as though I'd let both Georgia and Kathi down by not finding a way for us to keep Georgia at home. There was an issue with Georgia's dentures, too. Caring for the dentures was a simple procedure. Simply get the denture container and put water in it along with a denture tablet. Georgia would rinse her dentures and then put them in – ta da! Georgia would then rinse her mouth with mouthwash and be ready to wash her face for bed. In the morning, the reverse: rinse the mouth, rinse the dentures, pop 'em into the mouth.

The nurse aids repeatedly didn't do that. They cut Georgia out of the "ready for bed" routine and treated her like their other residents; they'd take her dentures and take a toothbrush to them under the water, then drop 'em – dry – into the container. The dentures very quickly developed a plaque-like buildup on the inside gumline, becoming very uncomfortable for Georgia.

I raised hell repeatedly.

They occasionally got it right, vis-a-vis the denture tablet, but never brought Georgia back into her routine – the routine that she and I had successfully developed and used for years, which was automatic and fun for her.

(Kathi's LiveJournal entry. 5/27/07)
"She's One Of The Highest Functioning"

So far John has shown up nearly every day at different times, just like the books suggest. Yesterday he found out Mom *[Georgia]* had an accident trying to find the bathroom, and it hadn't been cleaned up. A couple of days before he discovered she was wearing Depends, which she doesn't need (she's the only continent "inmate" on the floor). Another time he nearly threw a fit when they left her by herself in front of the nurses' station during the before-dinner lull.

Overall, though, he's much happier with the weekday staff than the weekend. OK, anybody can flub something, which is OK in my book just as long as it's corrected ASAP. I think he's beginning to see what I mean, but he still bristles every so often.

She's with some real characters, people who deserve a separate post of their own. She, Greta (roommate), another woman (don't remember her name), and Uncle Panos (sweet grandfatherly type) are the 4 highest functioning. The nurses say that they all sing together every so often.

(Kathi's LiveJournal entry. 6/5/07)
"Easier To Handle"

All is not entirely well with Mom *[Georgia]* over at the nursing home. Got a message from one of the nurses about the doctor wanting to put Mom on Ativan, which is a mild sedative. They can give her a one-time dose with my verbal OK; I need to sign a form if I want her to continually take it.

John wasn't too pleased. We talked of maybe they want to drug her like everyone else there so she'd be easier to "handle." This goes against everything they've been telling us about how they can handle her, we have nothing to worry about, yadda-yadda. "They TOLD us they can handle high-functioning patients," John said. "So what's their problem other that she wants to come home?"

However, I'm the health proxy. He's not.

So I called and spoke to the charge nurse. It's not that Mom's hard to handle – meaning that she's not combative or anything like that, thank god – but when she gets agitated, she agitates like nobody's business. Plus her voice is LOUD. Always has been, always will be. She's no shrinking violet. She's been on this continual "going home" kick for the past week or so. I asked the nurse if perhaps she now realizes where exactly she is, and no, she's not coming home, despite the half-lie we're telling her about her needing anti-wobble therapy in the early morning, and that's why she has to stay overnight.

The nurse replied it's a possibility, but Mom hasn't come out and directly asked. She hasn't either with John or me.

I asked about re-upping her Risperdal. No, the doctor doesn't want to do that because it'll knock her out completely. The Ativan is fast-acting and doesn't last as long. Only use when needed.

I verbally OK'd a one-time dose for tonight just to see how she reacts to it. Unfortunately I'm not going over there tonight. John went over instead. I'm hoping he doesn't make a big stink about it.

To Mom's credit, she's otherwise getting along OK over there, even though most of her cohorts are either nonspeaking and/or non-ambulatory and/or continuously sleeping. We caught her last night singing to the aide who was helping her change for bed. The aide told us later that she and her coworkers are "thrilled" that they can actually converse with her.

Guilt? Nope. Worry? I wasn't until the whole Ativan thing came up. But I suppose worry is par for the course. We all know how good I am at worrying

(Jim's blog. 9/3/07)
"When does this plane land?"

"When does this plane land?"

"Mom, this is your home. Not an airplane."

"Well, I don't want to lose my glasses. I'll need them."

"I'll make sure you have them."

* * *

My wife and I have both noticed a lot more "journeying" reference
from Martha Sr in the past few days. From such things as above,
to stories of people waiting for her to return, to news that she is
going "on a trip."

Yeah, that's probably right.

* * *

There's a phenomenon familiar to those who deal with Alzheimer's.
It's called "sundowning." There are a lot of theories about why it
happens, my own pet one is that someone with this disease works
damned hard all day long to try and make sense of the world
around them (which is scrambled to their perceptions and understanding), and by late in the afternoon or early evening, they're
just worn out. You know how you feel at the end of a long day
at work? Same thing.

So we usually don't worry about it when Martha Sr gets hit by
this. Still, it'll catch you completely off guard if you let it.

* * *

We're not yet into our first full week of being back on hospice.
And I think that it didn't come a moment too soon. Martha Sr is

exhibiting more and more of the common signs of an approaching death. Her incontinence (and general body awareness) has gotten a lot worse in recent days. She's shown signs of restlessness at odd times. There are other physiological cues.

But most notably, there has been talk of seeing her long-dead parents, and a sense that they are waiting for her to "go on a trip" with them.

I'm an atheist. I also have no belief in any kind of soul or 'life after death.' I try and be completely honest, yet not obnoxious about my beliefs. Yet when the other day Martha Sr looked at me and said that she was worried about her parents missing her, I told her that they left a message for us to care for her until they came to get her.

"To take me with them?"

"That's right."

"Up to heaven?"

"Yes."

Why did I say this? Because she smiled happily at me when I did.

* * *

I think we're all getting ready. Ready for her to die. And I will be relieved.

No, I'm not being morbid. Or cold. Or selfish. I'm being honest.

Yes, this has been a long and difficult journey, and as I've said, I will be glad to be on the other side of it. I'm deep-bones weary. But that is not really why I will be relieved at her passing.

No, I will be glad to see her freed from the pain. Not just the physical pain she suffers from her various health issues (though we do a pretty good job of palliative care, thanks to her doctors and our attentiveness). But rather the pain of confusion, and loss, and fear she suffers due to the dementia. There is only so much we can do to allay that particular pain, and with each passing day it gets a little bit worse, eclipsing her ability to cope while leaving her with a very fundamental fear.

'When does this plane land?' Soon, I hope – soon.

(Kathi's LiveJournal entry. 6/7/07)
Sundowning

Seems that Mom's *[Georgia]* sundowning has suddenly gone off the charts, according to the nurses and the doc. It roughly starts around 1PM, and doesn't let up until she gets her bedtime meds. She gets "stuck" on whatever's fueling the agitation, be it wanting to go home or wanting to kill herself or telling herself she's stupid because she forgot to do/say something earlier. She starts pulling her hair. She wrings her hands. She chants. The aides will try redirecting her. Sometimes it works, sometimes it doesn't. Hence, the Ativan.

I told them the period of sundowning is par for the course because it's the same time she started doing it while she was at The Club™. I don't know if she was as bad there as she is now. We circumvented it by taking her to Ye Olde Watering Hole or running errands. John also had a large part in redirecting her. She usually responded wonderfully to his verbal redirection. Me? 50-50. It's a mother/ daughter thing, I'm told.

After I OK'd the one-time dose, they gave it to her the next morning. It worked like a charm – no agitation, nothing. Plus she ate like a horse.

I told them I'd sign the release form on the condition that 1) they'll only give it as needed, and 2) I'm informed whenever they give it to her. They said fine. I signed.

As I said in my last entry, Mom's suddenly come down with a bad cold that's thrown her for a loop. I'll be going over there later to see how she is. I'm just hoping it's not going to suddenly morph into pneumonia. *shudder*

(Jim's blog. 10/1/07)
Another day, another T.I.A.

I got back from my morning walk with the dog to find my wife helping Martha Sr take her after-breakfast pills. Not just encouraging her, but actually placing the pills in her mouth for her, helping her hold up and drink from the glass of juice.

I changed the dog's collar, put away his leash. Took off my knee braces and the little belly pouch I wear for walking the dog which contains some treats, a small bottle of water, plastic bags for droppings. Removed my light jacket and MP3 player. Went back into the kitchen and leaned against the counter opposite where my wife and Martha Sr were sitting. My wife looked up.

"Another T.I.A.?"

She nodded.

* * *

From MedlinePlus:[8]

Transient Ischemic Attack
Also called: Mini-stroke, TIA

A transient ischemic attack (TIA) is a stroke that comes and goes quickly. It happens when a blood clot blocks a blood vessel in your brain. This causes the blood supply to the brain to stop briefly. Symptoms of a TIA are like other stroke symptoms, but do not last as long. They happen suddenly, and include:

- *Numbness or weakness, especially on one side of the body*
- *Confusion or trouble speaking or understanding speech*
- *Trouble seeing in one or both eyes*
- *Loss of balance or coordination*

Most symptoms of a TIA disappear within an hour, although they may last for up to 24 hours. Because you cannot tell if these symptoms are from a TIA or a stroke, you should get to the hospital quickly.

TIAs are often a warning sign for future strokes. Taking medicine, such as blood thinners, may reduce your risk of a stroke. Your doctor might also recommend surgery.
– National Institute of Neurological Disorders and Stroke

* * *

They're coming more frequently now. We saw the first (that we noticed) early this year. I was helping Martha Sr out to the car for a hair appointment, and all of a sudden she just slumped, slipping straight down, knees buckling to the pavement before I caught her.

The first time you see a T.I.A. hit someone, you're completely bewildered by it. Well, at least I was. Martha Sr, who was capable of standing and stepping with care and help, and who is usually somewhat plugged into her immediate surroundings, just seemed to "shut down." I got her in her chair, but she slumped over. She seemed unaware of anything around her, barely responsive to my questions and prodding. It was early in the day, but she was acting like it was the very end of the evening, when she would usually be deep into 'sundowning', exhausted and ready for bed. So, I put her to bed.

Then I called my wife, did some research. I had thought it was likely a T.I.A., and brushing up on the available info confirmed it. So did Martha Sr's doctor, who my wife called.

What to do? With someone of her age, and with her other medical issues? Nothing really to be done. Bed rest, note it. Roll with it.

* * *

When we'd had a couple more T.I.A.s this summer, and with the other indications we'd seen (some of which I've mentioned), we decided the time was here to again seek hospice. In the month since, Martha Sr has had several more T.I.A.s, about one a week. Each time, the treatment is the same: get her into bed, let her sleep it off. After a couple of hours she's back to what passes for normal. We note it, and are sure to tell the hospice nurse when she comes for her weekly visit.

A T.I.A. itself isn't really that big a deal, as noted in the information cited above. It is, however, something of a warning. As the Wiki page on T.I.A. states under "Prognosis":

> *Patients diagnosed with a TIA are sometimes said to have had a warning for an approaching cerebrovascular accident. If the time period of blood supply impairment lasts more than a few minutes, the nerve cells of that area of the brain die and cause permanent neurologic deficit. One third of the people with TIA later have recurrent TIAs and one third have a stroke due to permanent nerve cell loss.*

* * *

So, we wait. For either another T.I.A., or a full-fledged stroke. And we try to make her days as comfortable and enjoyable as we can, within the constraints of our own exhaustion and need to pace ourselves for what could yet be a long haul.

And in the meantime, tomorrow is our 20th wedding anniversary. For the most part, observation of same is postponed until later by tacit agreement between my wife and I, though we will make a favorite meal and bake a cake. We have one another, the details will sort themselves out later.

(Kathi's LiveJournal entry. 7/5/07)
A Fascination With Butts

Spent most of my visit with Mom *[Georgia]* this evening trying to
piece together her confabulation of three separate events. I managed
to make sense of the time where, as a girl, she was waiting on a
table at her parents' restaurant and, for some reason, the cook
refused to honor the order because the dishes were from the old
menu that was no longer used. She kept trying to say that her
mother saw what happened, but may or may not had done anything about it, and that "I was stupid because I didn't know what
to do." This led into a stilted description of "some man who
carried big books but never let me look at them", which suddenly
morphed into something about hair being cut and not having any
money to pay for it. The last one is understandable, as the hairdresser at the nursing home did cut Mom's hair a week or so ago,
and Mom never has to pay for anything because I arranged a
standing account which takes care not only of her hair, but also
anything else she needs.

Anyway, I tried not to look too shocked at the way she talked. She'll
start a sentence all well and good, and suddenly in the middle of it
she'll grope for words. A particular object becomes "this...this
THING" punctuated by low grumbles, a lot of "aaaah"s, and a bit
of stuttering, as though her mind is racing faster than her vocal
mechanics. When I asked Nurse Andrea about it, she confirmed
one of the worse realities of Alzheimer's – that, in most cases, the
word groping is as precursor of one eventually losing the gift of
sensible speech. "It doesn't come right away, though," she hastened
to add. "A lot of people continue on like your mom for a bit,
then little by little fall silent. Others grunt, groan – well, you
know what happens around here."

However, that wasn't as alarming as The Sex Thing.

Seems that Mom's agitation as of late is taking on sexual overtones,
something which isn't unusual in the dementia realm. I personally
haven't seen any of it in general, but I've heard and read stories of

people walking around buck naked, openly masturbating, fondling, groping, etc.

Mom has a fascination with buttocks, I was told. She always wants to pat them and doesn't care if the owner is male or female. A couple of nights ago she grabbed an aide's butt and demanded that the aide pull down her pants so Mom could see it. She did the same thing to another aide yesterday and ended up scaring off a visitor. When she thinks nobody's looking, she'll somehow unhook herself from the wander alarm on her chair and follow whoever's walking down the hallway, asking if she can please squeeze/touch/fondle. Up until now the staff has been able to redirect her, but after the scaring-off-the-visitor incident, the resident neurologist suggested that Mom be given a daily dose of Ativan to alleviate the agitation. I'm not really happy going the med route, but if it HAS to be done, so be it.

Butts. My mom. Butts. WTF?!?

(Jim's blog. 10/6/07)
Fever

We found out yesterday that starting Monday, we're supposed to finally have someone providing respite care for us overnight three nights a week (Monday, Wednesday, Friday). More on how that came about later.

But I wonder whether we'll actually get there. Or, if we get there, whether we'll be taking advantage of this service for more than a brief period. See, I think that there's a good chance that Martha Sr may be coming to the end of her life.

For the last couple of weeks she's had a sporadic fever of indeterminate origin. Not a lot, just a degree or so over her normal temp. And it would come and go. The hospice nurse has noted some congestion in her lungs, but nothing else which would account for it. But in the last couple of days it has trended higher, and been more consistent. Today it has steadily crept higher each time we've taken it, and doesn't seem to be responding to any of the usual meds which will combat fever. It's still fairly mild, just about two and a half degrees more than normal, but something is going on.

And in the last few days she's talked more and more about being concerned that her family knows where she is so they can come get her. More than once she's indicated that her mother "just left" and would be returning soon. When we tell her that everyone in the family knows where to find her, she's happy. It's as if she were a little girl, excited about getting to go on a trip, waiting for something to happen.

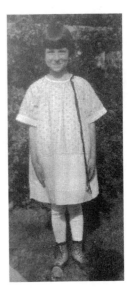

And we're waiting with her, unsure how to proceed, wanting only to have her happy and knowing she is loved.

(Kathi's LiveJournal entry. 6/18/07)
"If I Didn't Have You I'd Kill Myself"

Yesterday we went to my sister-in-law's for the annual Father's Day cookout. I didn't know until the night before that Mom *[Georgia]* would even be coming with us – John decided to invite her on the spur of the moment, saying that "she needs to get out of there" and other words to the effect that if she didn't come with us, she'd end up as vacant as most of her cohorts on the Alzheimer's wing. An exaggeration, to be sure, but his heart was in the right place, my sister-in-law and mother-in-law and all the others said sure, so off we went.

Most of the time when Mom attends a family event she's the picture of the perfect guest as much as the Alzheimer's will allow. She'll talk some, but most of the time she loves watching John's younger nieces and nephews. She might nap if the surroundings overstimulate her, but otherwise she keeps to herself as we tend to her food, her toileting, and chat with her. We've basically gotten it down to a science, and except for moments of sundowning here and there, Mom's OK.

Yesterday, though...I don't know if it was the heat, the kids splashing and yelling in the pool, the general hustle-and-bustle, or a combination of all three, but Mom suddenly morphed into The Woman Who Has No Freaking Idea Of What's What. She first kept asking where I was ("I'm right here, Ma, right in front of you!") If I wasn't directly in front of her or sitting next to her, she'd start a litany of "Where's Kathi? I want my Kathi. She's the love of my life," to whoever was in the area. She started crying when I'd excused myself to go to the bathroom. When I returned, she started in on "Oh, I thought you had left me all alone," When the food was ready, we brought her into the dining room (everyone else ate outside). She sat between John and I. She'd take a bite of her burger, turn to John, and ask, "Where's Kathi? I haven't seen her for so long! I want my baby girl!" John told her to turn to her right. She did. She then asked me, "Who are you?" "Maaaaaa..."

At one point she went into a variation: "If I didn't have you, I'd kill myself." Or, "I love her very much and I don't know why she never talks to me." (For the record, the only times I left her side was to either use the bathroom or go out for a smoke, the latter of which I did twice).

John couldn't calm her down. Usually he can joke her back into a more pleasant frame of mind, but for some reason she kept resisting. At some point during this my frustration escalated and I snapped at her. Unfortunately it was loud enough for my mother-in-law and a couple of the younger nieces to hear. My mother-in-law, being the embodiment of propriety, shot me a look that made me promptly shut up.

I won't go into the ride back to the nursing home. Suffice to say that Mom went into "I may be dead tomorrow" mode and it was all I could do to keep from throttling her. John kept shooting me looks so much like his mom's that I wanted to throttle him, too.

(Jim's blog. 10/8/07)
Thanks, Lori

As I mentioned previously, we now have someone coming in to stay overnight three nights a week. Seems like a nice woman, but it will still be a little weird to have a stranger here on Mondays, Wednesdays, and Fridays – and there's a chance that it won't work out with Martha Sr, if she freaks out over having this strange person help her in the middle of the night.

That was one of the main reasons we'd held off on taking this step earlier: we weren't sure whether the trade-off of getting a night's undisturbed sleep would be worth whatever disruption it caused Martha Sr that we'd have to deal with the rest of the time. But when we met with the Social Worker from hospice, a nice woman by the name of Lori, she was fairly assertive that we needed to take this step, just for our own health and sanity. Getting an outside professional's perspective helped, and affirmed what friends and family had been suggesting for some time.

The other main reason we'd held off in doing this was insurance. Now, let me get my biases right out in front: I think that most insurance is a scam, designed to scare people and sell them policies which provide little coverage and plenty of loopholes for the company to escape payment. I know that this isn't always the case, and yes I have always had plenty of insurance – I just accept it as a necessary and unpleasant part of life. Our experience in this case proved not to be an exception.

See, Martha Sr has a long-term care policy which carried an option for an 'alternative care plan', meaning something other than a nursing home, which could be set up with the agreement of the company (and would save the company money, since it was a lot less than what a nursing home would cost). She's had this policy for decades. Under the provisions of the plan, the company would pay up to $xx.xx dollars per day for in-home care assistance. We wanted to have them help pay for having a home-health aide in overnight a couple of times a week. Except that the cost of doing so was a little less than twice what the per diem specified in the policy. But hey, no problem – since it is overnight, the billing could be broken into two days, and fall under the specified coverage. Logical, right?

Um, no. Not as far as the insurance company was concerned. At least that was the position they took when they denied our request. My wife argued with them. For a while. Not long enough. Because honestly, we didn't have the energy to fight with them over the long haul, given that we're exhausted from being care-providers. It was easier to just curse the bastards and drop the matter – what the insurance company counts on, no doubt.

Except then we talked with Lori, and she made her point about us needing more rest. Further, she asked about any insurance policies that might allow for some in-home care. We explained the situation we'd gone through with the insurance company earlier this year. She nodded, asked to see the policy. Looked it over. Looked at us, said, "Let me handle it. The sad fact is, I have a lot more success than our hospice clients do with these things – the insurance companies know that they can't just wait me out."

Three weeks later, we had a tentative agreement in place. A week after that, the paperwork was all signed. The company will indeed pay for someone being here three nights a week, billed under the per diem for six days. Starting tonight.

Thanks, Lori.

(Kathi's LiveJournal entry. 7/16/07)
Basil

Mom *[Georgia]* has been quite chipper the last couple of times we've visited. We discovered she can still somewhat read if the print is big enough. Out past the patio is a raised-bed garden full of herbs and flowers. Everything has a sign printed in huge lettering, laminated, and stuck in the soil. John wheeled Mom close to the bed as I pulled up a sign at a time and asked her to read what it says. If she couldn't make out the word right off the bat we sounded out each syllable, like "Bay...sil...Mom, can you say that?" Mom would parrot it back, then repeat it a couple of times. "Basil. Basil. OH, BASIL!" Trying to convince her that it really was a basil plant was another story, though (she kept thinking it was mint for some reason).

And I really wish she'd stop obsessing over Why-Don't-You-Have-Children? thing. It's funny that she can come up with a zillion different ways of asking the same question. If I ask her why she keeps asking it, she replies that she's always been worried that nobody would be around to take care of me when I'm her age, and that I can't depend on John because it's a fact that men die sooner than women (Gee, thanks for reminding me.) I tell her I'll cross that bridge when I come to it.

(Jim's blog. 10/11/07)
Some updates

I thought I would post some updates on recent events...

Martha Sr is still doing pretty well, in spite of my concerns. Her fever did abate for a while, but yesterday it was back up, and higher than previously. We still cannot identify the source for it, but the hospice nurse will be here today to do a check-up, and we'll see if she has any ideas.

I've slept every night this week! Amazing what a difference it is making already, even if I haven't fully settled back into sleeping deeply on the nights when the respite person is here. Normally, my wife and I will split the other four nights a week, but she helped me out by taking the Tuesday night shift so I could be well rested for doing my conservation work. I will probably still need months of regular rest to be fully restored, but at least now I no longer feel like I am constantly dragging. Remarkable.

(Kathi's LiveJournal entry. 7/20/07)
I Don't Have A Real Mother Anymore

Mom *[Georgia]* is...eh. The night before last when I visited, she was too tired/out of it to realize it was ME, not John, Sophia or Andrea or Marie or whoever the nurse was on duty said that she hasn't been taking her afternoon naps because there's a daily musical activity in the commons room downstairs. I guess Mom's one of the biggest supporters because she does nearly everything except get up and dance (and if she does get up, she does her "wiggle" thing). They made her stop getting up when she nearly tipped over a couple of times.

The other thing I didn't know is that they've been giving her more Ativan, especially around dinnertime because she suddenly goes off the wall and refuses to sit and eat. Now there's 2 or 3 other "inmates" who do the same thing, but the difference is that they either don't talk or talk gibberish. Mom stammers and stutters trying to find the right word, but her voice, as always, CARRIES ALL THE WAY DOWN THE HALLWAY whether she's yelling or not. They haven't been able to redirect her; hence, the Ativan. John hit the roof when I told him and went into a diatribe about how they're drugging her when all she needs is interaction and, worse of all, "They're ruining all the work I did with her!" I started to reply with "Well, that's the trade-off you have to consider when you consider institutionalized care," but he kept ranting and raving so much that I thought my head was going to explode. You just don't interject when he's ranting. You just don't.

Anyway we took her out to Ye Old Watering Hole last night for dinner. We couldn't get our usual parking place by the door because the gas company has been repairing lines, so the closest I could get was around the corner, 4 storefronts away. It was pouring rain. I had to park across the street at the 7-11. When I finally crossed the street, I found John balancing Mom on bended knee because she nearly collapsed going from the corner and past one storefront. After we yelled at each other, we linked arms with Mom and dragged her into Ye Olde Watering Hole (OK, not literally drag, but it felt like it because she no longer walks, she shuffles). She now definitely needs the wheelchair, raining or not (I'll spare you John's rant about that).

She did eat most of her chicken salad sandwich. We had to remind her to swallow her 7-UP, not hold it in her mouth and swish it around like mouthwash. Everyone came up to say hi to her, and of course Mom was gracious, but she had no idea who anyone was except for a couple of the waitresses. If neither John nor I were talking directly to her, she'd doze off (typical Alzheimer's behavior, btw).

I don't have a real mother anymore. This – this woman looks and sounds like my mother, but she comprehends very little what anyone says and has eyes only for anyone male. She thinks I'm a boy half the time because of my latest haircut. Oh, and Kathi is now supposedly 6 or 7, never mind 12. Trying to explain to her that I'm Kathi and I'm sorry, I'm 46, not 6 is an exercise in futility much of the time. I'm over the anger. It's the emptiness that engulfs me and makes me speechless.

(Kathi's LiveJournal entry. 7/24/07)
She Thinks I'm Male

Mom *[Georgia]* thinks I'm male. I think it's because my hair is short. John thinks it's because she's getting him and I mixed up, even though there's a marked difference in height, weight, and hair. After she introduced me to the nurses as "my son" for the

100th time last night, I finally thrust my chest and replied, "Look, Ma, boobs!"

She contemplated me for a good minute then replied, "Ohhh, you've got a lot [trust me, I really don't]. Tell me, do the boys chase you because of them?"

I really tried not to laugh out loud, but I did so and was joined in by 2-3 of the other inmates.

A few minutes later down in the commons room she turned to me and said, "You're such a handsome boy. Do the girls chase after you?"

"Ma, I'm your daughter. Look at me. No, not there, here!"

"But you didn't answer my question."

"Ma, I have no idea if girls lust after me. But they don't chase me. Besides, I think John would be a bit put out if they did."

Then I thrust my chest again. "Look, Ma, I'm a girl!"

She looked around. "Where's Kathi?"

GAH!

I told John all this when I came home. He thinks she's starting to get him and I mixed up. I think the eye/brain connection is starting to wonk out. He then launched into a whole "Well, she's so used to ME being there that she got the two of us mixed up." I didn't have the heart to tell him that NO, IT'S PROBABLY MY HAIR that caused the whole thing.

(Jim's blog. 10/20/07)
Confirmation

Thursday morning the hospice nurse, Lisa, came for her weekly check-up for Martha Sr. She went through, did the usual stats, talked with Martha Sr about how she was feeling, whether she had any pain, et cetera. I like Lisa, she has a quiet and caring way I've found typical of hospice nurses.

After she was done, Martha Sr wanted to lie down and rest a bit, so I helped her with that while Martha Jr went out to chat with Lisa. Once I had her settled and secure, I joined them. It was the usual conversation, filling her in on our observations of how Martha Sr had been doing the past week, letting her know of any TIA episodes and whatnot, discussing any additional scheduling and so forth for the coming week. Lisa had been unable to bring some of Martha Sr's meds with her, since the pharmacy at the hospice hadn't had a chance to get them filled. She said that she'd drop them by late in the afternoon.

The rest of the morning was routine, and we had our regularly-scheduled respite care that afternoon from 2 – 6. My wife wanted to work, and I had errands I needed to run, so we agreed to meet at 4:30 for an early dinner at the brewpub near her office.

Over sandwiches and a good dark ale, sitting out on the patio of the brewpub, enjoying a lovely warm autumn afternoon, we talked about Martha Sr's health. No, not so much exactly how she was doing (we compare notes on that regularly), but of the likelihood that the end is near, and what that would mean for us and the other family members. Even with a fair amount of chatter around us from other patrons, it was a quiet and relaxed conversation, exploring the emotional landscape of an upcoming death. Both my wife and I have lost other family members often enough that we know this terrain. And we know that while we will grieve, and need to learn to re-integrate ourselves back into regular society, there will also be a sense of relief that this long and difficult time is over.

And that evening, when Lisa dropped off the ziplock with the pill containers from the pharmacy, she also left a handful of different publications from the hospice, all of them variations on the theme of 'how to prepare for approaching death.' Yeah, we'd seen most of this material previously in one place or another, but it was evident that she felt we needed to review it now. Getting that was an outside confirmation of what my wife and I had discussed previously, and a lot of what I've written about in recent weeks. I suppose we really are getting close.

November
Endgame

The dementia has won.

You have failed.

But you knew you would. You knew that it would come to this point. And still, you fought the hard fight, doing more...and doing it longer...than you ever dreamed possible. There is nothing that you have ever done before which had ever prepared you to think you could do this.

And even now, your loved one still has those rare lucid moments, those brief flashes of light in their eyes. This gives you strength to make the final few miles of this ultra-marathon, accepting all that comes along the way, just so you can let them know that they are still loved. It is perhaps the most precious gift you have ever given. Or ever received.

In the last year or so of care-giving for Martha Sr, I got sick and tired of hearing some variation of the comment "You're a saint for doing this."

Oh, those friends and acquaintances meant well, when they said it. So I didn't respond except to thank them for their kind words.

But I knew I was not a saint. I did not do this out of some kind of religious belief. I did it out of simple, intense love and respect – both for my wife, and for her mother. And in doing it, I became a better person.

(Jim's blog. 12/18/07)
"My name is Lisa"

Yesterday was dreadful.

I don't know what happened to trigger it, but it was one of the worst days that Martha Sr has had in a while. And this time it manifested itself as a constant need for reassurance.

I literally spent at least half the day just sitting and talking with her, doing my best to help her remain calm and not obsess over contacting her parents or going "back to school." Even with all my experience and what I've learned about distracting her and redirecting her attention, it was an almost constant battle.

And in the middle of it, I got an email from a friend with a YouTube link to the video "My name is Lisa" by SheltonFilms. Search on YouTube for it and watch.

That's basically the last six years of my life compressed into six minutes. You want to have some idea what it is like to be a care-provider for someone with Alzheimer's or other age-related dementia? Watch it.

(Kathi's LiveJournal entry. 8/8/07)
Maybe She's Giving Up

Haven't heard anything yet. The results were supposed to come back yesterday, but for some reason they didn't. Ditto the doctor. I must've been on the phone 6-7 times asking, "Did you hear anything? Did you? Did you? Please call me when the results come in."

Meanwhile John visited her *[Georgia]* at lunchtime. She wasn't wearing her dentures. They were still sitting happily in the solution and somebody had tried to scrape off the detritus. Mom pitched a fit whenever anybody tried to put them in her mouth. She slapped

John when he tried. She also hasn't been eating nor drinking. Nope, no way, no how. She made him spill a cup of water he tried giving her. The staff hasn't had much luck either. At this point they're loathe to say what they think is wrong. Right now the choices are: nasty UTI, minor stroke, and/or sudden slide into the next Alzheimer's stage. Nobody's talking. I can't really blame them.

Coincidentally I got a letter from the nursing home yesterday saying that Mom's next care plan meeting is in two weeks. Her last one was back in June. Normally care plan meetings are 3-4 months apart. I wonder if they upped this one because of her behavior.

Conversation with L and her husband R over at Ye Olde Watering Hole last night:

> L: *She's not eating nor drinking? Wonder what brought that on?*

> ME (shrugging): *Maybe her dentures are really bothering her, so that's why she pitches a fit when somebody tries to put 'em back in.*

> L: *Can she be fitted for another pair?*

> ME: *I suppose so, but Medicaid doesn't pay for dentures. There are also very few dentists who take Medicaid. I only know of one, and her waiting list's 6 months long.* [Jean, the old afternoon Mom-sitter, tried to hook me up with this particular dentist. 6 MONTHS?!? She's the only Medicaid dentist within a 10-mile radius.]

> R: *Maybe she's giving up.*

> L *and* ME (together): *Huh?!?*

> R: *Well, think about it. She's making a decision that only SHE can make right now, and it's probably the only decision she*

CAN make. Didn't you tell us about her saying she wanted to end it all?

ME: Well, yeah...she used to say that whenever she got frustrated with something...but we never took her seriously.

R (gently): *Think about it. I'm not trying to be mean. God love her, but she's basically in a prison right now, a prison that treats her well, but a prison nevertheless. She still has something up there [taps head]. If somebody's imprisoned, what's the one choice they can make?*

(silence)

ME (small voice): *Whether to live or die.*

R: I'm sorry, honey.

R might've been half in the bag when he said this, but he's got a point.

(Jim's blog. 10/25/07)
Take everything you think you know...

...about care-giving and throw it out the window.

At least that is somewhat what it feels like as we're entering what is likely the final phase of Martha Sr's life. The routines we'd established previously (Alzheimer's patients typically like routines – it helps keep their world a little more ordered, a little more secure and predictable in amongst all the other changes they are experiencing) are starting to break down. Martha Sr is becoming somewhat less predictable, her sleep/awake cycles disrupted, et cetera. What were simple things she could do for herself now require greater supervision and instruction. She tires more easily, and the "sundowning" effect I'd mentioned previously tends to occur earlier in the day.

And there are the medical indicators, as well. Lisa, the hospice nurse, was here this morning for her weekly check-up. Following that, we chatted for a bit outside. As I wrote a week ago, she also sees the signs of end of life approaching. Drop in blood pressure. Decreased heart rate. Congestion in her lungs. It probably won't be long, and Lisa wanted to make sure we have what is necessary to keep Martha Sr comfortable through it.

She also told us that we're doing a marvelous job in providing care. Bittersweet, but as I said back when we started this round of hospice, good to hear.

Anyway, as we enter into these final weeks, the routines to which we've all become accustomed are starting to dissolve. To use a musical analogy, we're shifting from playing well-known and rehearsed classical pieces to playing something which requires more improvisation – it's not 'free jazz' yet, but that's where we're likely headed. As the end grows closer, we'll likely need to discard the sheet music altogether. This will be difficult, but will likely only last for a limited amount of time. I'm comfortable with predictable routine, and largely prefer to have some order to my life, but know full well that I am capable of dealing with uncertainty for at least a while.

At least that's been my experience so far. I guess we'll see how it goes this time.

(Kathi's LiveJournal entry. 8/8/07)
Willing Herself To Die?

Just got off the phone with the nursing home. Mom's lab work was normal – no UTI, no low blood counts, nothing. Dr P, the neuro doc, suggested Mom [Georgia] probably had a TIA. Unfortunately, for the most part, TIAs aren't a one-shot deal – if you get one, chances are you'll have a bunch of them.

The only way to check if Mom did indeed have one is to have her sent over to Dr P's attending hospital for a neuro workup – CAT scan, MRI, etc. There are some Catch-22s, though. One is that Mom would have to be admitted overnight because she's at the point where she'll have to be sedated in order to have the testing. Sedation, unfortunately, can wreak havoc on the testing, as can the radiation, so if she did get the workup, it'll be anyone's guess as to how much good it'd do.

The other is her refusal to eat/drink anything. I don't remember the time frame, but if she doesn't do either within X days and if I haven't given them the OK to put her on a feeding tube, they'll do so without my permission. Feeding tubes can be nasty. People on them tend to become infected easily, and each subsequent infection weakens them more.

Andrea, the charge nurse, went on to say that in similar situations some families choose not to do anything. The reasoning is basically "Why put Mom/Dad/whoever through all that stress when basically it doesn't do anything except give you a general idea of where s/he's at?"

The dentures: It could be that they're really bothering Mom. Medicaid doesn't pay for them, so I'd have to take Mom to my dentist and pay out of pocket. That's $800-900 I don't have. A lot of families have the nursing home switch their loved one to a soft diet when this happens, which can, again, wreak havoc on the digestive system. ✓

Andrea continued – Mom's relatively happy right now. She's still babbling and still refuses to eat/drink, but today she's not being nasty about it. "This is something you have to think about because you're her health proxy. Do you want her tested after knowing the pros and cons? The feeding tube? Her dentures? Only YOU can make those decisions. I'm sorry."

I'm really beginning to wonder if Mom's willing herself to die. I didn't mention this to Andrea, but I might.

(Jim's blog. 11/4/07)
Ethical considerations

When the hospice nurse was here the week before last, she clearly saw a decline in Martha Sr, as I noted then. What I didn't mention in that post was that one of the things she suggested we consider was to move to a transdermal patch to help alleviate some of the pain associated with the breathing difficulty Martha Sr is starting to develop. (When people start to develop pulmonary aspiration problems, the coughing and gagging can be quite painful and cause a great deal of distress for both the patient and care providers. Trust me on this.) Pain relief and comfort are our primary concerns with Martha Sr, but choosing to go to a derm patch of a powerful drug could well contribute to hastening her death – a common concern about all opioid-class drugs with the elderly. My wife and I discussed the matter, agreed that it was an option we should consider if conditions worsened.

Well, when Lisa (the hospice nurse) came this week, it was clear that Martha Sr had continued to develop aspiration congestion in her lungs. And we'd seen several instances of very painful and frightening coughing fits, usually late in the day when she was tired. She was exhibiting additional effort at breathing even when just sitting at rest. We talked it over again with Lisa, and decided to give the derm patch with the lowest dosage a try, in spite of the potential problems.

Lisa also recommended using an oxygen supplement for Martha Sr, to ease her breathing problems. We discussed it, and agreed to give it a try. Lisa left, saying she'd make the arrangements for getting the derm patches to us, and would have an oxygen set-up delivered to the home, both that afternoon (this was Friday).

The guy from the medical supply place called, then came over to deliver the oxygen machine. We got a back-up tank of compressed oxygen as well. He walked us through the operation of this machine, which concentrates O2 from the air and delivers it in a regulated flow at whatever volume you need. It's about the size of a kitchen trash can and sounds just like the food cooker 'Aunt Beru' was using in the original Star Wars movie.

When Martha Sr got up from her afternoon nap, we got her settled in her chair in the front room, where she usually looks at magazines and whatnot. And we showed her the new oxy set-up, explained that it would help her breathe when she was sitting up. To say that she looked on it with a dubious eye would be an understatement. I've mentioned before that Alzheimer's patients don't respond well to change, and as far as she was concerned, this new-fangled thing with the tubes coming up to her nose was just more than a little weird. But we convinced her to give it a try.

A short while later Lisa came by with the derm patches. We got one on Martha Sr, and discussed with Lisa how we should change the mix of her other pain meds once the new drugs got into her system (a derm patch takes 12 -18 hours to saturate the system, then delivers a constant dosage for a period thereafter, in this case about 60 hours). Lisa also checked to make sure we had the oxy set-up correctly, just to be sure. Everything was fine.

So, results since then? The new pain meds have definitely helped Martha Sr. She has been sleeping better at night, and seems more free of pain. But she has also been inclined to just stay in bed more, particularly the last two mornings. The oxygen has also been a clear help, and she is working less hard to breathe when she is sitting in her chair.

The difficulty is that she pretty clearly doesn't like the oxygen delivery system. The tubing coming up to a simple cannula is strange and distracting, and she wants to fuss with it or just take it off altogether. We told her that we wanted her to try it through this weekend, to see if she could get used to it, but that if she still didn't like it, we wouldn't force her to wear it.

Because while this would probably lengthen her life, if it is decreasing her 'quality of life', it isn't worth it. It is the exact flip side of the ethical considerations of whether or not to use the transdermal patch, where quality of life is improved but there is a risk of shortening her life. And that's not a neat and easy calculation to make. We know that she is entering the final weeks of life, but there are no clear mile-markers indicating just exactly where we are on this journey. We want her to enjoy as much life as she can, but that is a judgement call as to whether it is better to go for a longer period, or for more comfort.

And no matter what choices we make, we can never be entirely sure that they were the right ones.

(Kathi's LiveJournal entry. 8/8/07)
The Late-Stage Portal

Finally got a hold of neuro doc who said that he doesn't think Mom *[Georgia]* had a TIA because she's showing absolutely no physical signs nor weakness. What he does think, though, is that she's passing through the portal to late-stage Alzheimer's. Every patient is different. Late stage is when everything basically goes to pot – speech, appetite, sphincter control, what-have-you – but it's random as to when each happens. Uncle Stevie, for instance, lost his speech first, although he could understand for a time what you were saying. His appetite was the last to go. Seems that Mom's appetite/thirst has gone first. Her speech – judging by her babbling – will probably be next.

Speaking of appetite, one of the nurses told us that she got Mom to eat half of a half of a PB&J sandwich. First food she's had since this whole thing started. Another nurse let us give Mom a bit of Ensure. She had maybe two sips by herself, then motioned that she didn't know how to take another sip. When I held the cup to her lips, she took a sip but didn't swallow. She finally did, though. Maybe it's the fact that people now have to feed her, that's causing the hunger strike?

We made phone calls to our extended family (Daddy's business partner's daughter & husband, aka S and R) as well to Cousin Rick down in Florida. S and her daughter are going to try to stop by tomorrow. I told S not to be shocked if Mom doesn't recognize her, and for her not to be shocked that Mom's no longer wearing her dentures. Haven't heard anything from Rick yet. I'm not surprised. He doesn't deal well with stuff like this.

Got some more info about the Feeding Tube Scenario: By law, it's implemented if the patient loses 5% of his/her body weight. 5% isn't much, which is why nursing homes try to fatten up everyone. If there's no directive, by law the home has to admit the patient to a hospital, the tube is inserted, the patient is put "on watch" for a couple of days, then is sent back to the nursing home. The quality of life usually takes a nosedive. The tube opens the body to all sorts of infections, which, in turn, weakens an already-weak immune system. Some patients pull it out, which causes a whole other set of issues. The patient eventually ends up bedridden.

If there's a directive for no feeding tube, hospice is called in. The patient is moved to another floor in the nursing home, the hospice people provide palliative care, and everyone lets Nature take its course. A woman who lived kitty-corner to Mom when Mom first moved in is currently in the hospice wing. We chatted with her daughters a few times. The mom, Bridget, has early-onset Alzheimer's (she's in her early 60s) and was paralyzed and in one of those Barcalounger-type wheeled chairs. She'd stopped eating about a month ago. I have no idea how she's doing.

I know Mom wouldn't want a feeding tube. I also know she's never wanted artificial life support. There's already a DNR in her health proxy.

It's one thing to plan stuff like this out in advance. It's another thing when it hits you straight in the face in that yes – YES – this is REAL, and once the decision's made, there's no turning back.

So far I've been managing pretty well.

I know I'm also due for a major delayed reaction at any time now.

(Email excerpt, Martha Jr to her sister. 11/6/07)
Every day brings something new

Every day brings something new. Mom *[Martha Sr]* has told us innumerable times that she has had a nice time here but she thinks she should be getting home. And variations on that theme. Sometimes I can't figure out how to respond to her.

A week ago last Sunday we went for a drive to Boonville. It was a gorgeous day, and we were looking at pretty trees all along the way. On the way there, I went by old Highway 40, thinking Mom might recognize it. (I hadn't really said we were going to Boonville, just out for a drive.) She never mentioned it if she did, but as we crossed the (new) bridge into town, I asked her if she knew where we were and she said Boonville! We just drove around some – there were two absolutely magnificent flaming maple trees in the park above the river – and eventually made it to her parents' house. Which she only sort-of recognized. We drove to the end of Shamrock so we could look down on the parade ground (which had a gorgeous tree) and she made no comment. We went around another block and came back to look at the house from a slightly different direction – so we were looking right at the front. She said something about it not looking like she remembered it. (It did to me, for the most part.) Then we made our way out of town and headed home. On the way out of town she started telling me about this little house she and another woman (whose name she could not remember) had built somewhere there in Boonville and lived in for a while. Totally out of left field.

She does seem to be fading somewhat. Last week when Lisa, the nurse, came we decided to start Mom on a duragesic patch and cut back on the vicodin. She has done well with that. But at the same time, Lisa recommended that we try giving her oxygen to help her breathing (which has often become more difficult, especially in the afternoons/evenings). We decided to try it for a few days, at least. They delivered the concentrator on Friday afternoon and, when she got up from her nap and had had her snack, we got her settled in the living room chair and hooked her up to it. You could tell she was very skeptical. We convinced her to try it out for the weekend and then we would decide whether to keep using it. She never did warm up to it at all. She used it for the afternoon and evening (until bedtime) Friday, Saturday and Sunday but indicated she really didn't want to use it again. A couple of times Jim has noticed her having difficulty breathing and asked her if she'd like to use that for a while and she was pretty adamant that she would not. So we may keep it for a while in case she starts needing it more, or we may not. She hasn't used it since Sunday.

(Excerpt – John's blog "A Life's Worth of Memories" 03/11/08) Ice Cream

> *Your love*
> *is better than ice cream*
> – **Ice Cream** by Sarah McLachlan[9]

Georgia loved candy and ice cream; she was well known for her confectionery affection her entire life. While she was still mobile in her wheelchair, we'd take her out to a homemade ice cream shop at a local dairy near the nursing home – she loved those road trips. Other times, when the whether wasn't permitting, we'd try to bring in a special ice cream; other times, we'd try out several of the small ice cream cups that the nursing home had for residents. The consistency and variety left a lot to be desired, but we were able to punctuate several visits with ice cream cups from whatever the source, and Georgia appreciated that. The nursing staff did, too – particularly when Georgia went on her "not eating this food" binges.

Georgia had, in past times, often told me that she'd always been a finicky eater. "My parents owned a restaurant, and I ate whatever I wanted," she'd say, but invariably describe how very little that was – a corner of toast dipped into the yolk of a runny egg, as she remembered it. And she was fiercely proud of that fact.

(Kathi's LiveJournal entry. 8/11/07)
"Go Away!"

Alzheimer's is unpredictable from one day to the next. You might have thought the disease robbed your loved one of this or that ability to do something, but then, in a flash, they'll show you that yes, dammit, I CAN DO THIS or I CAN TALK LIKE THAT, only to retreat into murmuring blithering and then, silence. That's what happened to Mom *[Georgia]* last night.

She was still sleeping when we came in. She twitched while mumbling something about "No, they're not doing their jobs." That's what I thought she was mumbling. Anyway, John stayed by her while the weekend charge nurse and I stood at the foot of her bed and discussed the papers I had to sign. I signed no to everything except antibiotics. I asked him what would happen if she didn't start eating/drinking. He said that in most cases the patient isn't starving to death because of the ketones already in the body. Feeding tubes and IVs can lead to infection, and when that happens, it's a mess and not a very pleasant way to spend one's last days.

Anyway, our voices must've carried because in the middle of our conversation Mom suddenly sat straight up, eyes wide, and hollered, "Be quiet! Go away!" She then slid back down. John then called her name, asking if anybody was home, where is she, hello? Are you there? He bent over and cranked her bed so she was sitting up. She opened her eyes again and said, "They're stupid, they don't know their jobs." Who doesn't know their jobs? "They just don't. They're going to blame me. I ALWAYS DO MY JOB!" John broke the train of thought by asking her if she wanted some ice cream. "Ice cream? MMMMMM, oh boy oh boy oh boy!"

The nursing home offers small cups of Lactaid frozen ice cream product in the communal freezer over by the elevators. While he was gone Mom turned to me and said, "Who is he? Where did he go? He talks too much! They don't do their jobs because they're stupid! Don't you be like that! Where's the money? Don't spend all your money!" I gave up trying to follow her line of thought, so I just kept nodding and agreeing with her. Her eyes got wider and more wild-looking as she kept talking.

John returned with the fake ice cream, scooped out a spoonful, and put it to Mom's lips. She took it. She swallowed. "MMMM-MMMMMMMMMMMMM!" He gave her another spoonful. She then suddenly grabbed the cup and spoon from him, swallowed what was in her mouth, then carefully dug the spoon into the cup, eyes lighting up while she mmmmmm'd in ecstasy. After feeding herself the next few bites, I asked her how it tasted. "Eh," she replied. "Not great. But it's ICE CREAM!" [The nurse told me later that, in late stage Alzheimer's, one's taste for sweet is the last taste ability to go. Stevie had the same penchant for ice cream. Must be genetic.]

When John tried to give her some water, though...he held the cup to her lips to give her a sip. She took the first sip, then made a face (Mom the ice-cold water lover?!?) He tried again. She pushed him away. He tried again. This time she held up her arms and screamed "NO NO NO NO NO!" I honestly thought she was going to smack him. He wanted me to try. I said, "She obviously don't want it, so why would I try giving it to her?" He started to reply, then stopped because right then Mom flopped back into her pillow and groaned.

A few minutes later she opened her eyes and said, "Go away. Bye."

"Are we being dismissed?" John asked.

"Go away."

"Evidently," I said.

Later on at Ye Olde Watering Hole you could tell John was so happy and excited that Mom finally responded to something and ATE. Obviously there's no swallowing issue. I reminded him about Mom's innate stubbornness and somewhere in there she knows that SHE ultimately makes decisions, not the docs, not the nurses, not us. Taste buds out of whack? Then don't eat. Certain sensations now bothering you? Stay away from them. If all else fails, then sleep. Can't say if all this is permanent or a one-night deal. Who knows how she'll be today? We'll see.

(Excerpt – John's blog "A Life's Worth of Memories" 03/11/08)
Ice Cream Memories

> *Everyone here knows how to fight*

Georgia's family was Greek – traditional in some ways, and very competitive. Kathi recalls watching them playing cards together, "fighting" in her words, but not in theirs:

> *They'd be sitting around the kitchen table, the condiments and napkins up on the counter behind Rigas's chair because, of course, you had to have space for the dummy. Mama would sit across from Rigas. Stevie would sit in my seat, back to the fridge. Johnny would be in his seat against the wall. I never really understood bridge, even though I'd watch them numerous times. You had to have a partner, and usually Mom would get either Stevie or Rigas. She couldn't stand having Johnny the life master as a partner because his quiet scrutiny of the board would drive her nuts – "JUST PLAY THE DAMN CARD!" she'd holler at him as he silently plotted his next move.*

> *The hollering.*

> *It's not yelling or shouting. IT'S TALKING IN A LOUD VOICE THAT SOUNDS LIKE YELLING. Most Mediterranean-based families have a version of it; whether it's the legendary "hot blooded-ness" of the Italian/Greek/Near East peoples or something just simply genetic, I have no idea. It was also the cards, too.*

I remember Mama telling me that Greeks take card-playing and gambling very seriously; therefore, the air of Damocles with the sword dangling over his head hung over every bridge game. And woe was the sibling who bid wrong or played a lousy card.

Somewhere deep in their souls, I believe that the ice cream sessions we had with Georgia helped to call up and surround them with these memories, allowing both Kathi and her mother to re-experience the shared memories of their lives and add an unseen depth to the quality of the visits we had together.

Everyone here knows how to cry

The ice cream sessions occasionally brought up references to Georgia's husband, who had sometimes told her "If only you'd look at me with the same look in your eyes that you get when you're eating chocolate." Those conversations invariably led

to memories of how Georgia's husband got along with her mother – a very good relationship, full of mutual love and respect, almost like he had become a surrogate son. I like to think that my relationship with Georgia achieved that. She often went out of her way, both when she lived with us at home and after she'd been moved into the nursing home, to look me right in the eyes and thank me for everything I'd done for her. She didn't want to forget to do that, so she took care to ensure that she thanked me often.

(Jim's blog. 11/9/07)
"Thank you, son"

It has been a difficult week in caring for Martha Sr. As noted previously, we went to a three-day transdermal patch to help with the pain associated with her aspiration and breathing difficulties. And that has worked pretty well. But as I suspected would happen, after her trial period with the oxygen she didn't want to use it any longer – even when she was laboring to breathe and I offered it to her, she declined. Only once, when she was having a coughing spasm, did she consent to put up with it again. This means that she has continued her slide, probably at a faster pace than were she using the oxygen. It is a tough thing to watch.

* * *

After a particularly rough patch of it yesterday morning, I was helping her from the toilet to her usual seat in the front room, where she likes to sit and look at magazines. As we transitioned from the wheelchair to her comfy chair, and I got her settled safely there, she looked up at me, her frail thin arms still around my neck, her light brown eyes clear for a moment, and said "thank you, son."

In the more than twenty years I've known her, in the twenty years I have been married to her daughter, she has never once before called me "son." In fact, since my own parents died almost 40 years ago, no one has called me that. It was a strange word to hear directed my way. And it touched me like no other thanks she has ever offered.

* * *

She had a restless night last night. I was 'on call', and consequently didn't get a lot of solid sleep. After I had been downstairs early this morning, trying to get her to settle down through one of her (fairly rare) combative fits, it hit me: we'd screwed up and not replaced her duragesic patch late afternoon, like we should have.

Meaning that the opioid in her system had been tapering off for about 12 hours, with nothing else to mitigate the effects of pain. And with all the other difficulties her brain faces, that extra pain causes unpredictable effects.

I mentioned this to my wife, who woke somewhat as I came back to bed. Shortly thereafter, we were back downstairs, getting a new patch on Martha Sr, and getting her something else to relieve her pain more quickly than the patch would kick in. As we were getting her tucked back in, she whispered to my wife, asking: "who is that strange man?"

* * *

Lisa, our hospice nurse, did her routine check of vitals, asked the usual questions about changes we'd noticed. After spending an extra long time with the stethoscope, she looked over to me and my wife, an honest but pained look in her eyes.

Later, after all the rest was done, she chatted with us on the front porch, Martha Sr again sitting in her comfy chair in the living room. "Yeah, there's a lot more crackling all over her lungs."

This came as no surprise. I'd been able to hear it myself, just in her routine breathing. But it was a substantial change from the aspiration congestion being confined to just one part of one or another lung.

Then she added: "And her heartbeat is much more irregular."

Ah. I asked, already knowing the answer: "Is that ... significant?"

"Yes."

* * *

My wife's older sister is coming to visit from California beginning Thanksgiving weekend. Last week I was worried that Martha Sr might not last that long, given how things had been going. The beginning of this week I had changed my mind, since the duragesic patch seemed to help so much.

Now I'm not sure again, even though we are a week closer to Thanksgiving.

That may be the toughest thing about this, the not knowing. I mean, there are few of us who know in advance the how and when of our deaths – I've long accepted that, having lost both parents suddenly (and separately) just as I was on the verge of adolescence. But when you are dealing with a terminal illness, such as hospice usually aids with, you usually have some kind of time-frame that everyone understands. This is different – this isn't cancer, or a fever, or some other relatively simple cause & effect. This is a general debility, prolonged by our caring and care-giving in a way that both breaks your heart and makes you proud.

(Kathi's LiveJournal entry. 8/10/07)
Funeral Plans

Today is going to be hairy. I can just feel it. First it's raining, and being the somewhat superstitious sort, raining + somebody not well = possibility of the "d" word. It happened with Daddy, with Mom's *[Georgia]* mom, and Uncle Stevie. Uncle John died the day after a snowstorm. Daddy was buried in a torrential downpour.

To that end, and also being somebody who liked to be prepared because of delayed reactions, I talked with Al, the funeral director at the other end of the street, before we went to see Mom. He buried Uncle John. Before that, he and his then-business partner buried Daddy. So it's like I've known him since I was a kid. His secretary and Mom were both members of the church guild and the town women's club. When she first saw me, her mouth fell open. "You're Georgia's daughter, aren't you?" she asked. "You looked more like her when you were younger." For some reason that comforted me.

I won't go into the details re Al right now. I've got an itemized bill. The least I can put down on it is $1K. The total bill is, of course, much more than that, but it's also considerably less because we already have the plot and stone. Cremation is just not done around here. Besides, Mom once told be she hated the idea. Death notices in the two major papers cost more than $500 for a 2-day run! The obits are free, as well as the thank-you cards, the registry book, and the prayer cards you send with the thank-yous.

I gave Al and his secretary all of Mom's information off the top of my head. It completely filled both sides of the sheet of paper that starts her file there. Excluding vital statistics/next of kin/ other family, I told them her schooling, where she worked, all of her past president-of-such-and-such-town/church-group, her interests, etc. When I finished, the secretary – wish I could remember her name – gazed at me and said, "You know, what you did is amazing. We get families in here who argue about every single detail, and others who don't know the decedent's background. I've never seen such a comprehensive bio before. You should be proud."

(I can't imagine that. How could you NOT know the basics of your parent/parents unless you've distanced yourself from them or something? And even if you did, they raised you, so wouldn't you remember at least where they were born and on what date?)

* * *

There was a 2-3 hour turnaround between when John and I left Mom around dinnertime and returned. During that time they knocked Mom out with Haldol so she'd stop playing with the IV and agitating about anything and everything. She refused to use the bedpan, kicked off the diapers they'd put on her (I swear, she'll be damned if she ever HAS to use them...as long as she can still make you understand that she needs to go, she's gonna tell you in some way and will expect you to walk her to the ladies'). They finally found a bed for her up on the 4th floor around 10PM. We went up with transport. Mom stirred, but never woke up, not even when they moved her from the Stryker to the bed. She winced when they took her vitals. We left shortly thereafter.

John's going to do this morning's "Mom watch" shift as he's got to take his friend B to physical therapy this afternoon. I'll then go to take his place. I'm sure the docs are going to want to talk with me. I've also got to go get my paycheck and I probably should tell them about Mom. I'm due to return to work Sunday, but depending on how Mom is and whether or not she returns to the nursing home, I may tell them no, I can't work that day. .

I'm tired.

It's raining.

I had two more crying jags last night. I wish I could just get everything out in one fell swoop and be done with it, but unfortunately it never works that way.

* * *

At this very moment Mom is in an ambulance heading back to the nursing home. There was nothing the hospital could do for her except to either give her a MRI and/or a feeding tube. I said no to both. The MRI could possibly show a clearer picture as to whether she had a stroke, but the process itself, to a dementia patient, is excruciating with all the thumps, noises, and the notion of being able to lie perfectly still in an enclosed area. I can't put her through that. No way. Ditto with the feeding tube. I asked the attending doc what's the worse that can happen. "Hard to say," he replied. "She'll go back to the nursing home, and you're going to have to talk with them. I know you'll have to sign some forms. You're going to have the option of a 'DNH', which means do not hospitalize. Her comfort comes first. You've got some serious thinking to do."

Today's been one of those "Am I dreaming?" type days, the days where you're walking around in a mental fog because everything seems so unreal. The drizzle outside adds to it.

I had a major crying jag when I went to pick up my check. John had called M ahead of time to tell her I was coming in, and she might want to talk with me in a more private place than the back room. First thing after getting my check was telling 3/4th of the department. Everyone hugged me. I burst into tears the minute I went upstairs and saw M. She gave me Sunday off. The rest of the week is up to me, she said – she'll do anything to rearrange my schedule, whatever. I told her I'd call when I got a clearer picture.

Mom was totally out of it when we got to the hospital. They couldn't do the swallow/gag reflex test on her because she physically refused everything. All the nutritionist could ascertain was that so far Mom's within her ideal weight range, but whether Mom stays there is another story. They must've given her another Haldol before we got there. Never opened her eyes, never acknowledged we were there. She didn't twitch when I played with her hair, kissed her forehead, and held her hand. She was still curled up sleeping when we left.

We're going over in a little bit to see how she's doing. Have no idea if I'll have to sign papers tonight or whether it's going to have to wait until the doc is there. I keep thinking, though, of how they're going to feed her if she's refusing to be fed. What about water? Are they going to hook her to an IV and send her to another floor? I honestly don't know.

(Jim's blog. 11/25/07)
Close to the veil, but fighting with everything she's got

It was the second time I'd been in this morning, checking to see what the sounds I'd heard coming over the monitor were all about. Martha Sr was over next to the side of the bed, almost up against the safety rail. "Are you OK?"

"Yes. I was just trying to turn on the lamp."

The lamp is deliberately out of her reach, otherwise in her confusion she'd turn it on in the middle of the night. "Why did you want the lamp on?"

"So that they could find me."

"Who?"

"The people who are coming for me."

Ah. "Well, until they come, is there anything I can get you?"

"Do you know where my toothbrush is? And toothpaste?"

"Yes. They're in the bathroom."

"You're sure?"

"Yes."

"Well, I don't want to forget them."

"We won't forget them. And we won't let anyone else use them."

"You promise?"

"Yes, I promise. Now, see if you can go back to sleep. It's still early."

"OK."

* * *

After my last post, and other conversations, my wife's sister decided to come in a week early, rather than wait until her scheduled visit starting the day after Thanksgiving. She didn't want to miss seeing her mom one last time before the end, since it seemed so sure that the end was close.

She got in late, and we chatted a bit before she retired. She asked how her mom was doing.

"Not bad. Of course, now that you've rearranged your schedule to be here I'm sure she'll live until January or something."

"Yeah, but had I not come early, she would have died this week. That's the way of it."

"True enough."

* * *

There's a common phenomenon with Alzheimer's patients which has been known to drive care-givers nuts: that for short periods, they can rise to a level of lucidity which makes it almost impossible to tell that they are suffering from the disease. This usually

happens in response to the visit of company, particularly family members, whom they don't get to see often. As a result those family members will have a decidedly mistaken impression of how their loved one is doing, and will wonder whether the care-provider has been over-dramatizing things, or what. It is insidious, in that it undermines the support the day-to-day care-provider gets from the rest of the family, who think that things really can't be as bad as they say. And it leads to a lot of tension between the care-giver and the patient, since the care-giver will sometimes resent the 'performance' put on for other family members but not them.

The solution to this is to have a family member stick around long enough that the facade fails and the true condition of the patient is shown. Since my sister-in-law usually comes to visit for a week or more, this always happens with her mom, and she has come to expect it. This time, however, the period of performance was extremely short, reflecting Martha Sr's deteriorating condition. I think that, as much as anything else which has happened in the last ten days, told my SIL that she was right in coming early.

* * *

It was the third time I came into the bedroom. "What are you doing, Martha?"

"I want to get up."

"Well, it's early still. You don't get up until 8:00. See, the clock says that it is only 6:50."

"But I have to get up early to get to school!"

"Don't worry, today is Saturday. There's no school on Saturday."

"Oh, OK."

* * *

I was napping when the hospice nurse came to visit this past week. Because of the holiday the schedule was rearranged, and she came in the middle of the afternoon rather than first thing in the morning. I'm trying to do a lot of sleeping now, banking it while my SIL is here to help out, because the coming weeks are likely to be even more demanding. So I didn't get to hear what the nurse had to say. It sounds like it was the usual routine – slow decline, we're doing all that can be done, let her know if there's a problem.

* * *

Martha Sr started choking and coughing at the dinner table, disconcerting the other family members who were over for the big Thanksgiving meal. As she coughed spasmodically, her face turning red, my wife and I looked at her, and in unison called out loudly "Take a deep breath. Real deep. Hold it. Now cough real hard." She did, and it cleared the blockage caused by aspirating some of her food. In a moment she was back to eating, her attention focused on the food before her, mostly oblivious to the reaction around the table.

"That's the best way to clear it – she just had a bit of something go down the wrong way," I said to the others. And from the look on their faces I realized that my wife and I must've appeared unconcerned and relaxed in the face of what seemed to be a sudden crisis. My SIL nodded.

* * *

I came down from a nap this afternoon, came into the kitchen where my wife was doing some baking. The monitor to her mom's room there on the counter, the sound of my Martha Sr snoring emanating from it.

"Good nap?"

"Yeah." I nodded at the monitor. "How's she doing?"

"Pretty well. We got her up from her morning nap, and she wanted to know where her mom was. Said that she had been in bed with her just a little bit earlier."

"That's becoming pretty common." It has – she has said some variation on this almost every day for the last week.

"Yeah. She's close to the veil, but fighting with everything she's got."

(Kathi's LiveJournal entry. 9/25/07)
Deterioration

She *[Georgia]* is deteriorating. There's no use beating around the bush. On an intellectual level it's expected. And I'm fine with the medical aspect of her care, although I still bristle about the Ativan, which she now gets twice a day. But if it's for both her comfort and the safety of the staff and other residents, there's really no other choice.

The combination of the Ativan loopiness and the Alzheimer's does a number on Mom. She perks up from around mid-morning through lunch – activity time – then automatically goes into sleepy mode. Nurse Andrea tells me that if they don't put Mom down for a nap after lunch, Mom's sundowning becomes severe later on. She'll scream, try to walk unaided, throw things, start to take off her clothes...I don't know what else, but then again I really don't want to know. Sometimes she'll become agitated around nap time, so she's given another Ativan. When John and/or I visit her around dinnertime, she either is in head-almost-falling-in-food mode or she's babbling. Sometimes she recognizes us. Sometimes not.

The babbling. Every so often Mom will say something completely coherent, like the other day when she greeted us with "I'M GOING TO DIE!" Um, thanks for reminding me. You can't right now because I haven't done the pre-pay yet! There's still the X number of disconnected stories all running together, although she hasn't done that lately. And the counting! After dinner she lolls in bed like a little kid, staring at the ceiling and counting random series of numbers from 1-30. She never goes beyond 30, even if we prompt her. Once in awhile she'll recite part of the alphabet. Sometimes it's random Greek phrases I've never heard her say before.

She no longer likes to go outside to the patio. The last time I tried, she became extremely anxious, so much so that she didn't want her beloved cup of ice cream, courtesy of the nursing home (each floor's fridge has a stash of 'em).

Mom no longer remembers how to use utensils. She gets some kind of sandwich for both lunch and dinner. She's OK with that. We feed her the ice cream. It's a bit unnerving playing "here goes the airplane into the hangar" with an 84-year old woman, no matter how used to it I am.

She's also got what I call "That Alzheimer's Look." Stevie, my uncle, had it too. It's an unfocused, faraway look, the kind of look that registers that the person isn't really there. If you're at her side and call her name, she doesn't turn. Ditto if you tap her arm. Sometimes she'll briefly look up if I kiss her forehead, but if I kiss her on the cheek, no response.

If I say "Mama", she looks at me and replies, "Mama?" I've learned not to go into the "Do you know who I am?" realm. If she recognizes me, great. If she doesn't, I'll try not to show it and pretend that I'm a very nice woman without a name who visits her.

So yeah, right now I've got my crazy work schedule as an excuse not to visit. It won't last though. Nothing ever does.

(Jim's blog. 11/7/07)
Deteriorating

> *Those who dream by day are cognizant of many things which escape those who dream only by night.*
> – "Eleonora" by Edgar Allan Poe

A friend passed that along, from today's 'Quote of the Day.' It is very appropriate. Howso? Well, because for the last 24 hours or so we've seen a rapid deterioration of Martha Sr's mental condition, including a lot of her seeing people and things which are not there (at least in my perception). Further, she's been holding conversations with these people and things, as though they are responding to her. And when you come into the room, genteel and considerate woman that she is, she wants to include you in the conversation, or explains what has been going on so that you don't feel left out, and expects you to understand and participate. It is very disorienting, because there really is no logic or coherence to these visions, and the conversations are little more than word salad.

Further, her sleep habits have changed as well. She had been sleeping more and more, but all of a sudden yesterday afternoon she didn't really nap, and last night she was awake more than she was asleep. My poor lady wife, who was on-call, had a very rough night of it (and I've sent her up to nap for as much of the day as she can).

We don't know what is going on, and all my experience and speculation has been useless. I have a call in to our hospice nurse, and will discuss the situation with her, see if she has any thoughts on the matter. It could be as simple as a urinary tract infection, which is a common problem with dementia patients, and known to cause such symptoms. But we take prophylactic measures to limit the chance of a UTI, so I would be surprised if that were the source.

Clearly, something is going on. Whether or not it is something we can or should try and correct, we'll see.

(Kathi's LiveJournal entry. 10/5/07)
The Eye

Mom *[Georgia]* has done something to her left eye. It's puffy, half shut, bloodshot, and very glassy from what I could make of it.

At first everyone thought it was conjunctivitis, but there was no discharge nor crusting. One of the aides figured out that when Mom assumes her dozing-in-the-wheelchair position, she leans the left side of her face against her hand, and her fingers start digging around. She used to do something similar with her scalp a few months ago.

It's not only that. Tonight I cleaned out her fingernails with an orange stick. I've never seen so much crud in my entire life. Who knows what kind of germs were in there – never mind regular skin-sloughing crud, but there were also traces of zinc oxide from when she was bed bound (meaning that she was digging at her bum), perhaps some food...GROSS! Don't they ever clean her finger-nails?

There's no infection, thank goodness. Right now they're irrigating the eye 2x/day with a saline solution. If it doesn't clear up by Monday, the house doc will prescribe something. I'm trying not to picture her yelping if they end up squeezing an ointment in there. *shudder*

Otherwise she was quite chirpy. When I didn't morph into Grandma or a work associate, she kept telling me she loved me in an Gregorian chant-like monotone. Then she said she wanted to take me away somewhere. When I asked "Where?" she asked me what she should do about "that old file cabinet" (read nightstand). I told her she didn't have to move it until tomorrow.

I'm at the point where I really don't want to see her anymore. I can't do that. So I'll persevere.

(Jim's blog. 12/5/07)
A bit messed up

We're back to the train metaphor. Martha Sr has either been traveling via train, or is waiting for someone to arrive on a train, or is going to catch a train, or just thinks that she is presently on a train (this last happens when she's in bed, with the bed safety rails up). I cannot help but think that this is her subconscious' way of understanding that she is in transition from this life to whatever comes after. Why a train? Because when she was a young woman, that's how she traveled, to St. Louis for shopping, back and forth to college.

* * *

But she doesn't stop there. Yesterday morning I went to get her up from her morning nap, and she asked: "Is there a job or something I can do to earn some money?"

"Money? Why do you need money?"

"Well, to call my mother."

"???"

"I came over here to play, and have been out playing on the grounds. Now I'd like to go home, so need to call my mother. But I was laying here thinking, and realized I don't have any money!"

"Ah. Well, that's OK. You can use the phone here – you don't need any money."

* * *

As I walked with the dog in the cold, stiff wind this morning, little pellets of spitting snow falling around me, I realized something I should have noticed a week or two ago: I'm a bit messed up. Lethargic, unmotivated, finding it difficult to concentrate even enough to write short entries for my blog. But I haven't been sleeping well, either. I've been grumpy and short tempered, impatient and always feeling slightly annoyed. In other words, my mild bipolar condition has crept into darkness, a slight depression.

Part of it is just the ongoing effort of being a care-provider, of course. Part of it is seasonal, with the grey clouds that settle in this time of year. And part of it is just personal, as we approach December 12th, the anniversary of my father's murder. I've learned to expect something of a downturn this time of year, but it always seems to catch me off guard at first. You'd think after almost 40 years, it wouldn't come as a surprise.

It's not the vicious blackness of a full depression, and for that I am thankful. But still, it needs some tending – awareness, being a little more lenient with myself, a little more indulgent. Try to nap when I can. Worry less about my weight, enjoy some favorite foods in moderation. Work when I can, hope that my clients and readers will understand. Be as gentle with myself as I am with Martha Sr, at least for a while.

* * *

I was on-call last night. I first heard Martha Sr stirring around 1:00, but she settled back down again until a little after 2:00. The second time I got up, dressed, went downstairs to check on her.

I put down the safety rails, helped her sit on the side of the bed. At first touch I knew she was running a fever. I got some slippers on her feet, helped her onto the commode that sits beside the bed. Her eyes were watery, uncertain. Her temperature was 2.5 degrees above normal.

"Here, Martha, you need to take these pills," I said, dropping her usual nighttime meds into the palm of her hand.

She looked at the pills, then at me, then back at the pills. "No."

"???"

"I've already taken my pills. That woman was in here a few minutes ago, and I took them then."

"Um, no, no one else has been here tonight. Maybe that was just
a dream. These are your pills – you need to take them."

"No!"

This was a completely new one – she'd never refused to take her
meds before. "Um, yeah. You need to take those. Now. Here's
some water..."

"NO!"

It took me over 10 minutes of cajoling and commanding and
pleading to get her to take the medications. She was adamant that
she had taken them already, some memory fragment or bit of
dream stuck in her head.

And it was almost two hours before I was able to get back to sleep.

* * *

She's been cranky today. Stubborn, demanding, a bit petulant.

But also so very weak and confused. Perhaps another TIA. Or
perhaps just another step down in her overall condition.

We'll know more when the hospice nurse comes tomorrow. Or
not. You learn to live with that ambiguity, that uncertainty. As
best you can.

(Jim's blog. 12/8/07)
Follow-up

I wanted to follow-up to yesterday's post, for anyone interested.

It seems likely that Martha Sr has had one or more T.I.A.s or
possibly even a small full-blown stroke. This would explain her
marked shift in sleep habits, increased confusion and much greater

aphasia – and is really about the best explanation we can come up with, since there haven't been any other changes in her diet or condition which would account for the rapid deterioration.

It is frightening, for both us and her. Clearly, she is confused and unable to explain herself and her worries to us, and frustrated by trying. She is completely lost in time and location, not aware of being at home, constantly fixated on "going home" and seeing her parents. But we know she still loves us – every chance she gets when my wife is close to her, helping her stand or dress, she will kiss her, holding on tightly for a moment, letting that touch express her feelings.

I never did hear back from our hospice nurse, which is both disconcerting and disappointing, but since there didn't seem to be a medical emergency to deal with, I didn't want to keep calling her. This morning we will contact the hospice agency and see if they can help us out with some additional anti-anxiety meds, since that seems to be the best thing for her at this time. Otherwise, we will do what we can to continue to make sure she feels comfortable, and safe.

(Kathi's LiveJournal entry. 10/3/07)
Wan As A Dead Lily

Yesterday was Mom's [Georgia] first day up and about since the weekend. Nurse Marie told us that the sores and rash both look much better. They've padded Mom's wheelchair seat with several folded pads-used-when-you-wet-the-bed with flannel covering everything. I sat on it while Aide Maggie helped Mom in the bathroom. Nice and comfy.

However Mom's as wan as a dead lily. At first I thought I was seeing things, but John agreed with me. Was she running a temp? Mom did seem a bit warm. Her appetite was good – she downed 2 cups of ice cream in record time – and until she went out of it she sang, smiled, and babbled happily. Nurse Marie said that sometimes their temp can spike even from a rash, and that it was nothing to worry about since she still has an appetite.

The humming. I don't think I've mentioned that yet. In the later stages Alzheimer's patients tend to pick up a plethora of habits out of the blue. Some, like the ever-wandering Susie, rub their hands together constantly. Some, like Demetra or Georgia or Joanne, have imaginary conversations with the wall or ceiling. Aphrodite mutters to herself in Greek-English creole. Helen constantly wipes her brow.

When Mom isn't counting or reciting pieces of the alphabet, she hums. Loudly. One note like a cicada but without that annoying sharpness. She'll stop most of the time when you give her food, but sometimes she'll manage to hum while she's eating. If you sing to her, she'll keep humming the same note unless she realizes that you're singing, then she'll hum along with you for a bit. If you talk directly to her, she hums louder. Sometimes she'll stop and babble, but automatically returns to humming.

The other night we caught her having a three-way imaginary conversation. Most of her words were clear. She was telling who-ever was at the near wall something about Form Whatever (I figured she must've been reliving her days with the Feds because of all the form numbers she recited) while being interrupted by who-ever was at the foot of her bed. Then somebody from the ceiling came in and told her something that made her eyes big. Then the two-way conversations started up again. We tried to follow, but gave up when her words drifted into humming.

She did recognize me for a minute and said my name. Then she turned toward John and disavowed any knowledge of my presence, even though both of us kept telling her that I was still there. ✕

Our extended family visited her the other day. We didn't know it until Susie called that evening. Ann, Susie's mom and Mom's best friend, left in tears. And of course Mom had no idea they'd been there.

(Excerpt – John's blog "A Life's Worth of Memories" 03/11/08)
"I got fading roots"

> *I've got wild staring eyes.*
> – **Wish You Were Here** by Pink Floyd[10]

Toward the end, Georgia had not only lost most of her ability to communicate, she was also becoming less and less responsive to outside stimuli. She would talk to herself, and sometimes recognize and talk to me, telling me how her mother or our dog Missy – both dead – were visiting her; sometimes, she talked of how her husband was standing by her bedside. More often than not now, however, there's nobody home.

> *I've got a pair of Gohills boots and I got fading roots.*

Kathi burst into tears more than once. "I'm the last one," she'd cry. How do you console someone at such times? I did what I could.

(Jim's blog. 12/16/07)
Forgetting

"Well, I've enjoyed my time here, but I really should go."

I sat on the couch next to her chair. The slight hiss of the oxygen cannula under her nose could still be heard over the sound of the concentrator in the other room. Her hands picked absently at the shawl we had over her lap and legs. "Well, we'll be having supper in about an hour."

"We will?"

My wife entered the room, sat on the floor by her mother's feet. "What's up, Mom?"

"Well, I was just saying that I thought I should be getting home, but he tells me that we're going to have dinner soon. I don't have any money for dinner."

"It's OK, you don't need any money," said my wife.

"Oh." Pause. Look at me. "But I should still tell my mother. She's been on a long journey, and just got back. She'll want to know where I am."

This has become routine. I answer, "She knows. Everyone in the family knows where you are. They know that you live here and we take care of you."

"Are you sure?"

"Yes, here," my wife grabs a nearby phone book, turns to the page we've marked during this exact same conversation previously. "See, right here is your name, and the address, and the phone number. Anyone who wants to find you can, right here in the phone book."

"Oh." Still dubious. "But does my mother know?"

"Martha," I say, "she asked us to look after you, until she comes for you."

"Really?"

"Yup. And you can stay for as long as you want, until she comes. And then you can go with her." I'm impressed by the certainty and reassurance in my wife's voice.

"Oh, thank you dear, that

would be lovely. This is a very nice place you have."

Indeed it is. It's been her home for 53 years, and is just the way she wanted it.

* * *

She seems to be stable again. Following the events mentioned in my post a week ago, we weren't sure which way things were going to go. But after talking with the hospice people, tweaking her meds some, a few days of increased sleep, and with long talks with her to help settle things when she got anxious, she settled back more-or-less into the most recent patterns we've seen. There's little doubt that she suffered one or more TIAs, or a small scale hemorrhagic stroke.

But she has once again proven to be surprisingly resilient. I'm fairly confident that she'll make it at least to Christmas, probably to the new year. But as in all things, nothing is certain.

(Jim's blog. 12/21/07)
"I hope I've made the right decision."

I walked into the dark room, stepped up to the bed. Martha Sr looked up at me, and said "I don't like these rails and straps."

There are the standard 'hospital rails' on the side of her bed. And since she's attempted to climb over them several times (and broken bones in the subsequent fall), we put some nylon straps across from one rail to the other in a sort-of cargo net arrangement. It allows her to move freely in bed, but stops her from trying to climb out on her own. "Well, I'm sorry, but they need to stay on."

She smiled. "Doesn't matter – I've decided that I'm going to leave today, go back home to Missouri."

We live in Missouri. But I didn't want to contradict her, not that early in the morning when there would be little point to it. If she went back to sleep, she'd likely forget the conversation completely, anyway. "That's fine. But for now try and go back to sleep – you don't get up until 8:00."

"OK."

* * *

While I am not religious, I nonetheless enjoy some aspects of the holiday season. I enjoy gift-giving, feasting, some good Christmas cheer with family and friends. Yesterday afternoon during our 'respite' break, my wife and I went out and selected a tree from the family farm – cedar, the traditional family tree – and brought it home. Now that it is settling, we'll get it decorated some time this weekend.

That's late for us, and we got a smaller tree than usual. Simple reason for this: it's less work. And right now, just about anything that's less work is welcome.

* * *

Our regular hospice nurse was on vacation this week, so the agency made arrangements for another nurse to come by and check on things. She arrived on time, bringing supplies and meds, and went in to chat with Martha Sr.

"I read that nice article about you!" she told her.

"Article?" asked Martha Sr.

Out of her sight, I shook my head at the nurse, mouthed the words "She doesn't remember it."

She nodded.

I spoke to Martha Sr. "She's talking about a nice article that was in the paper, about people who care for their loved ones at home when they get older."

"Oh, did you write it?"

It surprises me sometimes the things that she remembers. I used to write a column for the paper. "No, I didn't write it."

"But you used to write such nice things."

* * *

I've never obsessed about getting presents to people "on time" – most of my friends and family have busy lives themselves, and understand how things stand here with us. But this year we've really been caught short on planning, and our shopping has been sporadic, at best. I've been able to take care of a lot of routine things, and gotten a couple of special gifts. But for the most part I just haven't had the energy and focus to try and find the right gifts for others. And the shopping we usually do for Martha Sr just hasn't gotten done at all this year. That'll be a disappointment to some.

* * *

I walked out with the hospice nurse when she was done checking over Martha Sr. Either my wife or I usually do this, so we can go over info we didn't necessarily want to discuss in front of Martha Sr, the other staying and helping get her dressed or back into bed.

"Anything to add?" she asked.

"No, not really. We're just unsure of where we are. Not knowing is difficult."

"Well, I can't say for sure. But the end could come fairly quickly. You'll just have to let us know if you see a sudden downturn, so we can be here every day rather than just weekly."

I nodded.

"You know, you guys are doing just an incredible job in caring for her. I wish that half of our patients got even half as good care as Martha Sr is getting."

"Thanks."

And as I turned to go up the stairs, back into the house, eyes watering, she repeated: "You guys are doing an incredible job."

Then why do I feel guilty? Like I should be doing more?

* * *

"I hope I've made the right decision."

"What decision is that?" asked my wife, as she helped her mom sit up on the side of the bed.

"Well, I think it's time I went home. I've enjoyed my stay, but I think that I should be getting back."

"That's fine," said my wife, putting slippers on Martha Sr's feet. "But how about some breakfast, first?"

"That sounds nice, dear."

(Jim's blog. 1/3/08)
"She's a strong woman."

"She's a strong woman," said Lisa, our regular hospice nurse. We were standing out in front of the house, talking the way people do at such times, in spite of the 11 degree temperature and bit of cold wind. Neither my wife nor I had coats on. But it didn't matter at that moment.

* * *

I came downstairs this morning, noted that there wasn't a time marked on the blackboard in the kitchen. I went into the front room, where the health aide who stays here overnight three nights a week was waiting. I glanced at the monitor, heard Martha Sr snoring lightly.

The aide, Ruth, glanced at it as well, and then back at me. "She never called to get up to use the toilet."

"Not at all?"

"Nope. She's turned over or shifted around a couple of times, but never seemed to wake up at all."

"Huh."

"She done that before?"

"Not in recent history."

* * *

We made it through the holidays. I kept thinking that I would write about how Martha Sr was doing, but everything seemed so unsettled, I wasn't quite sure what to say. First Christmas, with my wife's brother and his family over for a big meal and to exchange presents. That went fine, and Martha Sr seemed to enjoy herself, enjoy the company. But after her nap she had forgotten entirely that anyone had been to visit.

Then she had good days and bad days. Days when she mostly slept, days when she seemed to be tracking things around her pretty well, days when even simple words escaped her understanding. Fever would spike for a day, then back to normal for two. There were no trends that were easily identifiable.

New Years eve we mostly ignored the holiday. Martha Sr wasn't aware of the date, and my wife and I weren't up for doing anything. With the home health aide coming to stay overnight that night, we just did the usual routine, went to bed as normal – and I was asleep by 10:30. A friend teased me about it by email the next day, said I was getting old. I was grumpy, somewhat resentful in my reply. I'm often grumpy these days, due to the stress. I'm glad most of my friends understand.

* * *

Lisa came into the bedroom, set down her things, handed over the package of Depends for Martha Sr. Hospice covers everything, even that. My wife helped her mom sit up on the edge of the bed as I opened the drapes for the large double window.

Lisa pulled the wheelchair over to the side of the bed, settled herself, and began going through her usual exam, chatting pleasantly with Martha Sr all the while assessing her condition, asking us questions about how she had been doing the past week. As usual, she found it difficult to get a solid pulse when taking Martha Sr's blood pressure, then her brows knit together for a brief moment. "78. Only number I can get."

She looked from Martha Sr to me and my wife. "Has she been sleeping long?"

"No, she just laid down after breakfast and getting dressed about five minutes before you got here."

Lisa nodded, continued the exam. But she was being a little more thorough than usual, checked Martha Sr's fingernails closely, then her toenails. Listened carefully to her lungs, timed her heartbeat for a long time, tested the elasticity of the skin on the back of her hand. Asked about how much she was drinking, kidney and bowel function. All the while smiling and interacting with Martha Sr, keeping her happy and engaged.

"How much is she sleeping each day now?"

My wife and I looked at each other, calculated a moment. "About 16 hours a day, give or take an hour or so."

Lisa nodded. She looked at Martha Sr, asked "Are you feeling OK?"

Martha Sr continued her smile. "Well, I think so."

"Any questions?"

She looked to me and my wife for some assurance. "No, no, I don't think so."

"Good, good," said Lisa, packing her things.

"Martha, do you want to lie down again for a while?" I asked.

"Yes, I think that would be nice."

My wife got her tucked back in bed safely as I escorted Lisa out.

* * *

Part of my difficulty in writing about Martha Sr these past days has been confusion about not just what to say, but about how I felt about it.

I'm tired. So very, very tired. As I've mentioned, this time of year usually carries something of a depressive element for me anyway. With the lingering uncertainty about where we were at with

Martha Sr's condition, I've felt a certain confusion about what I want, what to do. It is easy to understand how a care-provider will become exhausted by the process of doing what we've done for the past four or five years. It is even easy to understand how they might look to the end with a certain anticipation – not wishing for their loved one to be gone, but knowing that with the end will come release from the burdens of care-giving.

What may not be easy to understand is how the prospect of that is a little frightening. No, I'm not talking about the mechanics of death – that is fairly easy to understand when you are a mature adult with the experience of losing friends and family. Rather, it is fear which comes from a change of definition of who and what you are.

And it is fear of guilt, at least in my case. Guilt over whether I could have done more, guilt over wanting to be free of the burden of care-giving.

* * *

"Are you finished with lunch?" I asked Martha Sr, as I came into the kitchen. I had been in my office, writing this entry.

"Yes. But I need someone to unblock the wheels."

We have to keep her chair secured with a 2x2, otherwise she'll try and leave the table. I set down her after-lunch meds on the table after I removed the plate for her lunch. "Oh, I can take care of that. Here, you need to take your pills."

"Oh, OK." She took her pills.

"Ready for a lie-down?"

"Yes, I am."

I got her away from the table, removed her bib, and wheeled her into her bedroom. She used the toilet in there, then I helped her into bed. As I was tucking her in, she looked up me and said, "thank you for that delicious lunch!"

"You're welcome. Have a good nap and call when you are ready to get up."

And as I walked out, closing the door softly behind me, my eyes filled with tears.

* * *

I escorted Lisa out, after the examination. "I take it you see something?"

We walked down the front steps. "She's declined. There's congestion in the lower lobes of her lungs, and they sound rough all throughout. The low blood pressure and high pulse rate – it was over 110 – is not a good sign."

"How was her heartbeat? Same irregularities as before?" I asked, as my wife came out to join us.

Lisa looked at my wife. "Yes, but hard to tell, her heart is beating so fast it kind of covers it up."

"What do you think?"

"She's close. The end could come at any time. Hopefully in her sleep." Lisa said it in a way that was plain, honest, but sympathetic.

I nodded, looked back up at the house, the flags waving on either side of the front porch. "We were surprised she made it to new year, frankly."

"She's a strong woman."

I nodded, looked at my wife. "She is, indeed."

(Excerpt – John's blog "A Life's Worth of Memories" 03/11/08)
Wish You Were Here

One of the several songs by Pink Floyd that recall the relationship that Georgia and Kathi shared prior to my arrival and the notice-able onset of Alzheimer's is "Wish You Were Here."[11] It describes *"two lost souls / swimming in a fish bowl / year after year"* – an apt analogy, in many ways.

Kathi and Georgia had essentially lived their entire lives together. Once Kathi's father passed, they adopted an almost regular existence punctuated by the odd wild hair to travel or change it up a little. Overall, however, they had a solid routine that they rarely deviated much from. That familiarity added quite a bit of resonance to the feeling of absence that assailed Kathi after Georgia passed away; just the move to the nursing home hadn't been enough of a change to rock the boat, as it was nearby and we could visit any time.

To an extent, Georgia too had a slightly changed but ultimately similar routine; over the previous few years, she'd gotten used to seeing me and depending upon me, so although my daily visits to the nursing home – sometimes twice a day – weren't *quite* the same, they matched closely enough to her memory of my helping her get up in the morning and picking her up from her day care that she remembered me as "more recent" than Kathi, more often than not.

Kathi's job kept her busy during the hours that Georgia was the most alert; her visits didn't always remain with Georgia, who was tired by the time Kathi was able to get there. That hurt Kathi; sometimes, when we'd visit together, Georgia would ask me how Kathi was. When I'd point Kathi out to her, she'd happily exclaim "Oh, Hi!!!!!"...and then turn back to me and try to finish asking me how her daughter was. Kathi took that particular event in stride, however. It was evident that Georgia had recognized her, and that the determination to get back to the question she was asking me was simply evidence of the disconnect between Georgia's recognition and delight at seeing her daughter to her question to me about how her daughter was doing.

Dementia does strange things, and getting to know the dementia patient as well as the various characteristics of the disconnects it brings with it are important to keeping one's sanity intact.

(Jim's blog. 1/9/08)
Stellar evolution

I commented via email to a close friend yesterday about the persistent fever Martha Sr has been running, 2 to 2.5 degrees above her normal. We'd seen fevers come and go for the last several months, but this one seems to have settled in for a while. I got back this:

> *Any particular reason for it, or is she just being like a star that's going into its final flameout?*

* * *

Like my friend, I grew up after the basic mechanisms of stellar evolution were pretty well understood. What I learned long ago, and seems to still hold basically true is this: stars in the main sequence will develop, go through an initial process of fusion converting hydrogen into helium, and then will evolve one of several ways depending upon initial mass. Small to medium-sized stars will make it into the helium fusion phase (primarily producing oxygen, nitrogen and carbon), before burning out and eventually becoming a white dwarf. Larger stars can go on to greatness, however, and in the sequence of their lives (including supernova) produce all the natural elements we know in a process known as nucleosynthesis. Either way, massive amounts of material are stripped away from the star and disseminated out into the universe through explosion, solar wind, and other similar mechanisms.

* * *

What is oldest, lasts longest.

That is the basic equation to understanding Alzheimer's.

Generalizing: First, the person with Alzheimer's will lose the ability to learn new skills. Then the most recent memories will slip, and each succeeding layer of memory acquired in their life will melt away. Metaphorically, they are being deconstructed – like some great skyscraper which is slowly dismantled from the top down, floor by floor. Compare this to other diseases and injuries, which are more like an implosion of consciousness, collapsing in on itself all at once.

Because of the way the disease progresses, layer after layer of experience and memory being peeled away, the patient regresses through life, becoming once again a child in many ways. This is likely the origin of the notion that the elderly experience a "second childhood" with dementia.

* * *

Looking back over the last three or four months, it has been a difficult time. I read the posts I've made here on the topic, and am frankly surprised that things have been as bad as they have been for as long as they have been. No wonder I am exhausted, even with the extra help we're getting thanks to hospice.

Yesterday was a bad day. Whether because of the fever, or just her deteriorating condition, Martha Sr was really in a state of constant confusion about everything starting first thing in the morning. Nothing was easy, and she needed near-constant reassurance and supervision. Then, shortly after I had gotten her up from her afternoon nap, she evidently had another TIA, and for a while only spoke gibberish – complete word salad. Needless to say, this was frightening for her, and she was almost combative in response. After an hour or so she rallied, but it was still a difficult evening until we got her to bed.

* * *

We are made of star stuff.
– Carl Sagan, **Cosmos**

Ever since Sir Arthur Eddington sorted out the hydrogen fusion theory of star fuel, which led to the understanding of how the elements are created, there has been a growing awareness that we are, quite literally, the stuff of stars. All of the atoms in our bodies were likely forged in the fusion furnaces of stars now long gone.

And those atoms are shared around. Recycled. I remember seeing somewhere a fun calculation that all of us – each and every person alive – carries with them something like 200 atoms which were in the body of Jesus (or, say, Nero, Hitler, et cetera...). Whether a person is eaten by a predator, or their body allowed to decompose in the ground, or burned on a pyre, their atoms just go back into circulation and eventually make their way into all of us.

And one day our own sun will change from a hydrogen-fusing star to a helium-fusing star, if only for a little while. It will likely swell up into being a red giant, and when it does it will consume Earth, or atomize it and blast it into space.

So yes, my friend, in a very literal way, Martha Sr is exactly like a star that's going into its final flameout. And I find that oddly comforting. And beautiful.

(Jim's blog. 1/12/08)
Bits and Pieces

A brief update on Martha Sr's condition: the visit from the hospice nurse on Thursday confirmed what we'd seen this week – continued deterioration. Her BP is very low, pulse weak, and heart rate very high (all worse than they were the previous week), and her lungs have diminished capacity and evidence of fluid. Once again we have tweaked her meds and treatment procedures, but this is mostly just an effort to keep her as comfortable as possible. I think part of the exhaustion my wife and I feel is just ongoing anticipation.

I'll keep you posted.

(Kathi's LiveJournal entry. 11/8/07)
Visit

Had a very good visit with Mom *[Georgia]* today, only because we caught her right before she was to be put down for her afternoon nap. Her eyes kept fluttering as we fed her ice cream and told her how we're stripping the wallpaper in the kitchen. Her speech was more coherent than usual:

"I love you. You're so wonderful."
"Let me think about that." (followed by steepled hands and profound silence)
"You know what I think? I think yes."
"Kissy kissy!" (exclaimed as we each gave her a kiss on the cheek)
"I guess I'm feeling OK. I don't really know."

Lots of blithering and humming between statements, though. She tried to sing along with us during our bad rendition of "On Top of Spaghetti." At one point she leaned back and howled. Nurse Sandra ran in, thinking Mom was in pain. Nooo...that's her way of pretending she's a diva.

Mom's legs are very thin. I hadn't noticed it before due to the fact that she's usually in bed whenever we visit. The back of her pants legs spread out on the Geri-Chair seat. Her hands are also getting thin and veiny. Mom always had muscular hands like mine.

Her eyes, though, are a mystery. She can't track anything with her right, although she'll try to focus it on whoever's speaking. Did she lose sight from the botched cataract operation last winter? We can't tell, nor can she tell us. Her left eye is watery and glassy, but at least it tracks.

She still loves kisses and tickling. John likes to make her giggle, so he'll gently tickle her under her chin, the inside of her wrist, the inside of her knee. Her face scrunches up, her eyes become slits, and she lets out this incredible sweet giggle. She never did that "before", much less with me.

She dismissed us as usual. We wheeled her to her "place" in front of the nurses station. We started to say goodbye and Mom made a "go away" motion with her hand. "Do you still want to talk with us?" I asked. She shook her head. As we turned to go into the elevator, she was already asleep.

(Jim's blog. 1/17/08)
"I've had a very nice time this evening."

With all the dignity and presence of a southern lady, Martha Sr held herself erect, looked at me and said "I've had a very nice time this evening. And dinner was lovely. And your performance, though I'm a little ashamed to admit that I can't remember exactly what you did."

"Well, thank you!" I answered. Then I helped her finish up on the commode next to her bed, and carefully laid her down for a nap.

It was 12:45 in the afternoon. She had just finished lunch consisting of a peanut butter & jelly sandwich, Pringles, and some chopped pears. Needless to say, there had been no 'performance' by me or anyone else.

* * *

"I don't know how you guys manage it," said Lisa, the hospice nurse. She had just finished her examination of Martha Sr, and had been going over what she saw as we talked after. She'd mentioned the option to have an aide come over to sit with Martha Sr while we got out for a bit.

After my wife and I exchanged glances, I (or maybe it was my wife – these details start to slip away) said that we preferred to not both be gone at the same time at this point. Why? Well, because it feels like the end. We want to make sure one of us at least is here with her.

And it's not just us. Lisa commented that Martha Sr had never before looked so ashen, so grey. We agreed that she would come again on Monday, unless we called her sooner.

* * *

Her fever spiked about 4 degrees higher than normal last night, just as my wife and the overnight aide we have in three nights a week were getting her to bed. I was washing the dishes when my wife came into the kitchen and told me, on her way to getting a Tylenol tablet for Martha Sr. I dried my hands and followed her back to the bedroom. We got the extra pill into her, I checked her pulse and the color of her fingernails, had her look at me to see whether she could focus or not.

She couldn't.

I wondered whether she'd make it through the night.

She could.

* * *

"My mother has passed on, but Auntie has taken over for her."

"Auntie?" asked my wife.

"Yes, Auntie. She has taken over for my mom. I was waiting for my mom to come for me, but she's passed on, so Auntie has taken over..." a pause, uncertain look around the room, "... everything."

"Well, OK." My wife looked at me. We'd been waiting for this. Together, almost simultaneously we said, "Martha, if she comes for you, you can go with her. It's OK."

"It's OK?"

"Yes, when Auntie, or your mom, or your dad – when they come for you, you can leave with them."

"I can?"

"You can indeed. Until then, we're taking care of you here."

"But if they come, I can go?"

"Yes, you can."

* * *

We met with the social worker for an hour or so yesterday afternoon. She is kind, intelligent, insightful. She offered a lot of suggestions for us to consider, from a respite break (which would take Martha Sr to a skilled nursing floor at the local hospital for five days), to advice on how to better manage the stresses we're under.

None of it was useful.

Oh, it was, in the sense that had we not considered those things, it would have been very beneficial to bring it up. And neither my wife nor I were aware of the option for the five-day respite break.

But we've managed through these things long enough that I think, honestly, we're doing about all that can reasonably be done to handle the stresses, to give ourselves (and one another) what breaks we can.

And right now we're not willing to see Martha Sr off to the five-day break. Not right now. If she rallies again, and seems stable, then we'll consider it. But not when things are so shaky with her health. After all we have been through, after all we have done, to let her slip away now in the care of someone else in a strange environment would be just too painful, would feel very much like we had failed to see the thing through to the end.

Neither of us wants that.

* * *

As I got the safety rails and straps on the bed in place, Martha Sr looked up at me, concerned.

"Something wrong? Something bothering you?"

"Well, like I said, I have had a very nice time tonight."

"Yes, thank you. It is kind of you to say so."

"But I think I should be going soon. My mother and father have been on a trip, and they are looking for me."

"And when they come, you can go with them."

"But if I am sleeping," she said, that worried look on her face again, "how will I know?"

"If they come looking for you, I will be sure to tell them where you are. I promise."

And I keep my promises.

(Kathi's LiveJournal entry. 10/18/07)
"I'll See God Soon"

She *[Georgia]* has had a rather stubborn UTI since last weekend, a stubborn enough UTI that conventional antibiotics won't touch it. She's on some super-duper med with a very long name that has a zillion side effects, one of which is appetite loss. In other words, except for the ice cream we feed her, she won't eat or drink. It's driving the staff nuts.

See, this is one of the reasons why I think we shouldn't visit every day. I tried explaining this to John, but of course he lets it go over his head. If we keep appearing at lunch or dinnertime to feed Mom, then she's going to depend upon us to be there ALL THE TIME and she won't let anyone else feed her. He's over there at least twice a day, with or without me. I know he needs that "I'm needed" dependency from her for whatever reason, but he's totally oblivious as to how his presence not only drives the staff nuts, but doesn't help Mom any. Argh.

ANYHOW, Mom's been confined to bed since the UTI. She's undiapered because of it, so they have her lying on absorbent pads and such. No smells, nothing – she's not doing anything! They also can't get her into the bathroom because she needs the Hoyer, and trying to transfer her from the Hoyer to the toilet would be an accident in the making.

One thing, though, is that she's become remarkably more coherent through all this. She still confabulates, but she's making more sense. Last night she was telling us a story about how her mother wanted to buy her a new jacket because Mom had gotten a new job, and Mom kept telling Grandma not to bother spending her money. It got to the point that Grandma borrowed $ from Uncle John to buy the jacket so she could say that Johnny bought the jacket, not her. There were other stories about Grandma mixed in with this...something about Grandma throwing a customer out of the restaurant because the customer said something to Mom... another story about Mom being scared about a customer because the customer kept doing something and Mom was too scared to tell anybody (hmm)...then something about my godmother and how she kept trying help Mom care for me, but Mom wouldn't accept her help. I don't know...I lost track after awhile.

But of course the "I'll see God soon," came out loud and clear. It has been a lot lately. I really wish she'd stop saying that. From what I understand it's normal at her stage. Stevie used to do the same thing. Still doesn't make it any easier to hear, except for the point that she's made peace with it and Him.

(Email excerpt, Martha Jr to her sister. 1/21/08)
Conversation

Well, after our conversation last night, particularly the part about not having had a chance to use the "phone call to her mother" thing – it happened today! Mom *[Martha Sr]* was very confused after her morning nap this morning, apparently, so my cell phone rang about 11:20 indicating it was her. Knowing what it would be, I answered it and just chatted with her, told her to enjoy herself where she is and she could stay as long as she wants. It will be interesting to get Jim's report of how that may have calmed her (or not) or what (if any) effect it had.

Also, last night, we watched the movie "Waking Ned Devine." Have you seen that? It is a lovely little movie, set in a tiny village somewhere isolated in Ireland. Very funny at times, but also very touching and thought-provoking. When the movie was over Mom was obviously tired but also looked like she wanted to talk. I'm not sure what made me do it, but I started talking with her about her own death much more directly than I have before. I did so as carefully as I could, but I really felt like I needed to be very direct and clear (probably also influenced by the conversation with you). I told her that the nurse that comes every week does so because we think she may be dying, that we are caring for her the best we can and will continue to do so for as long as necessary. I mentioned that she often talks about people who have passed on, and told her that it would be OK for her to do so as well. That we love her very much but we want her to be happy, and if her parents come for her it is OK for her to go with them. She actually seemed to understand what I was talking about, though now and then, she seemed a little unsure, so hopefully the permission part (at least) will sink in. I dunno.

We have Lisa, the hospice nurse, coming this afternoon at 4:00 It seemed like a good idea to have her come a second time this week (and maybe every week if Mom continues this way) to touch base and check on her condition. I'll be heading home in a little while so I'm there for that.

Thanks for your call last night. Sorry if I seemed a little disconnected at times, but it was really good to talk to you.

Love to all -

(Kathi's LiveJournal entry. 10/8/07)
Humming

Mom *[Georgia]* hums most of the time now. You can't tell if she's doing it on purpose and/or if it's just another manifestation of the Alzheimer's. It's a semi-loud drone. Occasionally she'll put words together in the same drone like "Business...is...not...good..." then start counting randomly. If you count with her or call out the next number in the sequence, she'll stop counting, look up at the ceiling briefly, then string together a series of words. Sometimes she makes sense. Sometimes she doesn't. Sometimes you can't understand what she's trying to say. When it gets too confusing, give her more ice cream. That usually does the trick.

In addition to the Hoyer lift, she now has adult-sized "baby bumpers" on both sides of her bed. From the look of it I gather it's a bed-sized sling with three heavy straps on either side. The straps are attached to the "bumper" part. They must've installed it sometime within the past couple of days. By law they have to tell me if she falls out of bed or whatnot; I haven't heard anything, so until I ask the day shift, I'm presuming they're for safety.

The only clear thing she said tonight was "Kathi I love you", and "Kathi you're the best man who's ever lived." John and I always chuckle at the gender. As Nurse Marie always says, "Be glad she's saying it now because she won't say it later."

Mom's never been the frail sort, but you can tell she's getting frail. Her forearms are starting to look like sticks, the veins sticking out in all their topographic glory. Her skin has dry patches that cream won't quench. Her eyes are big, glassy, and staring off into space.

She won't be spending Thanksgiving with us this year. Nor Christmas, I'm afraid.

I also sometimes wish John would stop trying to have normal conversations with her. I know his reasoning for it, but there's just something uncomfortable listening to what becomes a monologue. You can see the disappointment in his face when he finally takes a breath.

(Jim's blog. 1/22/08)
Firewood.

I sat, my back to the fireplace, feeling the heat from the fire, listening to the pop and crackle of the fresh log I had just placed there. Across the room, the hospice nurse and my wife were sitting at Martha Sr's feet, the nurse doing her routine examination for the second time in a week.

This is new. Previously, we'd only been on weekly visits. But as it is clear that we're in the final days of Martha Sr's life, we decided to schedule an additional visit. And, thanks to how hospice works, we've the option of calling for additional visits as needed, or adding in more regular scheduled visits each week. Just knowing this resource is available is comforting.

Lisa, our regular nurse, listens, touches, looks. I am struck by just how much good medicine is still based on these simple techniques, when it all comes down to it.

As it does when you are dying.

* * *

"What do you need, Martha?"

"I need to call my mother."

I go get her cordless phone, dial the number and hand it to her while the phone is still ringing. Someone answers on the other end.

It is a brief conversation. She just wants to let her mom know that she is all right, not to worry. The voice on the other end reassures her, tells her to wait until she comes for her. She hands the phone back to me, and I disconnect. She is happy.

My wife and I had set this up weeks ago, in the event that the occasion would come that we needed it. Simple, really – an incoming call to my wife's cell phone from Martha Sr's number would be the cue that her mom needed this kind of reassurance. No need for me to say anything, contributing to the illusion.

* * *

We watched "Waking Ned Devine" the other night. A quirky, offbeat little movie that I love. The central theme is about love/friendship, played out in the story of a small village in Ireland where a local lottery winner has died before he can claim his winnings, leaving no heir. The villagers band together to claim and share the money, but as much out of memory and fondness for the departed Ned Devine as their own greed. It's the sort of movie that always leaves me with bittersweet tears.

And after, surprisingly, my wife got to talking with her mom about Martha Sr's own situation. From an email my wife sent her sister following this:

> *When the movie was over Mom was obviously tired but also looked like she wanted to talk. I'm not sure what made me do it, but I started talking to her about her own death much more directly than I have before. I did so as carefully as I could, but I really felt like I needed to be very direct and clear (probably also influenced by the conversation with you). I told her that the nurse that comes every week does so because we think she may be dying, that we are caring for her the best we can and will continue to do so for as long as necessary. I mentioned that she often talks about people who have passed on, and told her that it would be OK for her to do so as well. That we love her very much but we want her to be happy, and if her parents come for her it is OK for her to go with them. She actually seemed to understand what I was talking about, though now and then, she seemed a little unsure, so hopefully the permission part (at least) will sink in.*

Permission? To go. That it is OK to die. Often people who are in hospice need to hear this, one way or the other.

* * *

Lisa is surprised at just how cold Martha Sr's legs are. "They're like ice!"

You don't usually get that kind of reaction from a seasoned hospice nurse. And, perhaps a bit out of embarrassment, she shifted over into more clinical terminology. Blood pressure. Indications of reduced lung capacity, congestion, observation of ancillary breathing mechanisms. Compromised circulation. She asks about appetite, kidney and bowel function, signs of pain or distress, coughing. Clinical terminology or not, her voice is always concerned, compassionate. "I detect a number of changes."

We nod. Martha Sr is worried whether her lap shawl is straight.

"When she is showing signs of breathing difficulty, or coughing, use X or Y medicine as necessary."

She looks at Martha Sr for a long moment. "We want to make sure she is comfortable."

Indeed we do.

* * *

They usually won't tell you this beforehand, but there comes a point in hospice care where the usual restrictions about medicine dosage and usage becomes, let us say, somewhat more casual. The rules are in place to control the abuse of very dangerous and addicting drugs, after all. But when the end comes, no one in their right mind is going to be worrying about addiction, when there is comfort to be given.

We've reached this point. My wife and I had realized it last week, but were reluctant to act too much on this knowledge without confirmation from our nurse. No, she didn't tell us to exceed any prescriptions, but was willing to answer our questions about what medicines were suitable for what problems. So, in response to anxiety, or breathing difficulty, or coughing spasms, we add in a few drops of this solution, another one of those pills, maybe a small shot of whiskey.

* * *

My wife smiles slightly, amused, as I add another log to the fire. I know what she is thinking – she is remembering my protestations earlier in the season that we didn't want to be too profligate with the wood I had stockpiled.

Yet it is very cold out, and Martha Sr does so love a fire.

December

Passing

Death comes for us all. It is not always as easy or gentle as we would want, for ourselves or for others. Sometimes it is a struggle, as birth is. But that isn't necessarily bad.

Grief? Yeah. Maybe. Maybe you'll grieve after you recover a bit. Because now that the end has come, you no longer have the last jolt of adrenaline. It was – you were – all used up.

And in some ways, there's something worse: how you defined yourself is now over. Who are you now? You're not the person you were when you started care-giving. And you're not a care-giver. Maybe you have a job, a life, that you can try and return to. But is that still you? Is that still the job, or the life, that you want?

You think about that. In the meantime, there are still details to be seen to. And sleep to catch up on. You're not surprised by the death of your loved one – hardly. But it is still very disorient-ing, a constant sense that you have forgotten something important, or left part of yourself at the last fork in the road. Perhaps the best part of yourself.

I was "on call" with Martha Sr her last night. Actually, both Martha Jr and I had been with her almost constantly for the last couple of days, each of us taking an hour here and there to go nap. We knew the end was close, and what the likely pattern of breathing would be which would precede death.

I was afraid, as I sat with Martha Sr those last hours. No, not of her dying. I had never been with someone when they died, but we were well prepared by the hospice people. I was afraid that I wouldn't recognize the end in time, and that Martha Jr would not be there.

Martha Jr had just gone up for a nap maybe 45 minutes previously, when all of a sudden I knew it was time. I got her, apologizing for waking her so soon. She came downstairs and held her mom as Martha Sr passed.

(Kathi's LiveJournal entry. 12/6/07)
New Ways To Interact

Mom's care plan meeting went well. She *[Georgia]* now has a new roommate because Greta, Mom's old roommate, now needs a Geri-Chair and the rooms are too small to accommodate more than one. Eleanor, the new roommate, is a sweet woman with long snow-white hair who calls everyone "Patty." The nurses are still trying to figure out who Patty is, seeing that nobody in Eleanor's family is named such nor has Eleanor ever had anyone in her life with the name. *shrug*

Such as it is, people don't pay attention to their roommates. I don't even think it ever registered with Mom that she had one. Same for Greta. Gives new meaning to the phrase "everyone's in their own little world." Alzheimer's tends to do that.

The suggestion came up that John and I need to find new ways to interact with Mom. Her sight's just about shot, so anything visual is out. The nursing home has a number of portable CD players at the families' disposal, so I spent this afternoon going through my pitiful collection trying to come up with something Mom would like to listen to. I've got a number of classical CDs (mostly choral music) which she might enjoy. John's going to burn a CD of Big Band-era tunes. Poetry reading was another suggestion, in that the cadence is soothing. Now where the heck are my poetry books?

Mom was out of it today. I was told she'd been lethargic all morning and fell asleep during lunch. I found her in the hallway next to her room and roused her enough to eat a couple of pieces of fudge. She fell asleep with the second piece between her lips. I tried not to giggle.

(Jim's blog. 1/14/08)
Getting close

It's hard to say when the end will come. But we must be getting close.

How close? Days. Perhaps just hours.

Why do I say this?

Instinct. Well, that and lots and lots of small clues, details that add up to one probability, details that probably most wouldn't notice.

But among the little things are some big mile-markers. The last few days, Martha Sr has slept between 18 and 20 hours per day. When awake, she breathes with some labor, and she regularly shows signs of cyanosis. Her confusion is noticeably worse.

Couple that with what Lisa, the hospice nurse, noted on her last visit, and I've been mentally reviewing what we need to do, what we need to look out for, what I will need to tell the family. I worry that I have "cried wolf" too many times, in my effort to keep everyone informed. Well, better that than a misguided attempt at secrecy, I suppose.

So, I re-read all my posts on this subject. And went through, once again, *Dying at Home.*

I'm about as ready as I can be.

I hope.

(Jim's blog. 1/15/08)
Situation normal

Martha Sr made it through the night. And seems to be holding her own today. But her fingernails are still blue, breathing noticeably labored. To be perfectly honest, I hope the end comes quickly and with ease for her. If that sounds horrid, or cold, or heartless – well, I'd say you haven't been paying attention. I am none of those things.

We're trying to keep things as 'normal' as we can, to maintain our usual schedule, get Martha Sr up at her usual time, have meals as planned, all the normal routines. This might be a bit absurd – it feels like it to me – but consistency really does give comfort to someone with Alzheimer's. And while other health factors are now in action which will likely end her life soon, she is still very much an Alzheimer's patient.

But I am changing my schedule a bit, canceling meetings with clients, postponing this or that activity to make sure either my wife or myself are always here. We had our usual 'respite' break scheduled for this Thursday afternoon, but I worry about leaving the respite sitter here alone with Martha Sr. My clients have all been understanding about this, which is good. As I told a friend this morning, there are advantages to being a skilled craftsman in an unusual profession.

So, we wait, pretending that things are normal. Until they're not.

(Kathi's LiveJournal entry. 12/10/07)
Delirious

We got a call from the nursing home late this morning. Mom *[Georgia]* woke up with a rather high fever, a UTI, and some lung congestion. At the time the doctor was trying to figure out which antibiotic to put her on – very dicey because Mom's allergic to most of the penicillin-based suspects as well as a few others –

but he finally decided to try one she'd never been on before. He also put her on vicodin to break the fever. We weren't planning to visit her at the time, but decided it'd probably be better if we did.

Mom was delirious when we got there. She was alternating between dozing and just awake enough to open her eyes only to expose the whites. Her forehead and most of her body was warm and clammy. She didn't want any fudge. She never registered that she knew we were there. We left her moaning something unintelligible and told the nurses we'd return in a couple of hours.

When we returned nothing much had changed except they had her dressed, in the Geri-Chair, and out in the hallway. Her fever was down a little, but not by much. Still moaning and quasi-asleep. Still didn't want any fudge, but she took a few sips of lemonade. She stared straight at me at one point. I kept saying, "Mama, it's me." John kept singing the nonsense songs he'd sung with her, made funny faces, tried tickling her. No recognition.

I asked about the lung congestion. It isn't bad and it's only in one lung. There isn't a bug going around nor has Mom had a cold or anything like that. I asked, "So how does something spontaneously happen like that?" The nurse shook her head. "Sometimes there's no explanation."

Wait and see. That's about all anyone can do right now.

(Jim's blog. 1/27/08)
Plans and preparations

I came downstairs yesterday morning a little after 6:00 to discover from the home health aide that Martha Sr had not been up all night. This has happened a couple of times recently, and usually she calls or rustles around enough to indicate that she wants to get up and use the potty sometime shortly thereafter.

But not yesterday. She was quiet, sleeping until my wife and I went in to check on her. And she didn't want to get up at her usual time of 8:00, sleeping until 9:30. Then she had a light breakfast and went back to bed, sleeping until noon, when she had some lunch and then again back to bed. Then she slept until 4:30. When I got her up then, her cyanosis was the worst it has yet been, her entire fingers a disturbing deep blue, as were her feet. This indicates a level of generalized hypoxia that shows just how poorly she is doing.

At no point whenever she was awake did she know just where she was. She kept thinking that she was on a train, or wondering where her car was, asking about when she was going to go home. We played along as best we could.

* * *

I sent this to a good friend last night:

Anyway, then dishes, got Martha Sr to bed, et cetera. Now, catch up on some email, do a bit of surfing. I need to start doing some research, find a good online source for learning a bit of survival Spanish.

Why? Well...

You probably already know about the North American Welsh Choir tour to Patagonia next October. And you may know that in return for my wife coordinating all the reservations and money and whatnot on the Choir's end, she is getting her cost of the trip offset (in full, it looks like). Just in the last few days I've decided that I am going to go along.

Yeah, surprises me a bit, as well. I have no desire to go to South America. I have never had any desire to go to South America.

But Martha Sr is going to die soon. And late this year I should have decompressed from that, and been working hard for months being a good little book conservator. It will be a good time to challenge myself in a new way, get out of my comfort zone. This tour will be a good opportunity to do that. Plus my wife and I haven't had anything approaching a real vacation in a couple of years, and we didn't do anything to celebrate our 20th anniversary last October. So, this will serve that purpose as well.

So, I guess I should learn some survival Spanish. It is only cour-teous. And doing that won't hurt me, either. Neither will push-ing myself to get in better physical condition for the trip – some-thing I am planning on for all the other good reasons I know, but this will provide additional incentive.

It's odd to be thinking ahead this way, to a time when Martha Sr will no longer be with us, no longer our hour-to-hour responsibility.

* * *

She seems somewhat better this morning. She slept well last night, but wanted to get up to use the potty at 4:30 this morning (I was on-call). I checked her temperature then, and it was almost three degrees above normal. But her hands were their normal color, with just a trace of blue under her fingernails.

And she was anxious to get up and have breakfast at her usual time, though a bit reluctant to get her weekly bath after. During her bath, my wife reported a return of the more noticeable cyanosis. After, she was limp and sleepy, barely able to stay awake while we got her dressed and back into bed.

I just checked on her, helped her get settled in a new position in bed. She is getting weak enough that she has difficulty just rolling over. This time she was also worried about whether she was going to disturb the person who was sleeping next to her. I told her it was OK – they would understand.

* * *

It's odd – making plans to be gone traveling this fall, yet being very tentative about what I am going to be doing this afternoon. Like so much of my life these days, it is the exact inverse of what anyone would consider 'normal.' But so it goes.

(Kathi's LiveJournal entry. 12/14/07)
Fever

Mom's unexplained fever still hasn't broke. It's been spiking 1-2 times every day. They've added another antibiotic to the one she *[Georgia]* is already on. This particular antibiotic is an injection. In a way it's a saving grace that she's still delirious because she hardly recognizes the needle, according to the nurses.

She hasn't been eating very well, but she will drink something at breakfast. Lunch is a 2-3 bite affair. If they can rouse her for dinner, she'll eat maybe a fourth of it, then fall back asleep.

The restlessness is what gets me. You know how an infant, when lying on his/her back, squirms and kicks? Mom does the same thing. She makes "O" shapes with her mouth, holds up her arms at different angles, and alternates squirming with rocking side to side. If you ask her if anything hurts, she doesn't reply. She never opens her eyes. Her forehead is clammy and seems to alternate between hot and cool with each touch or a kiss.

Nevertheless we read her some Christmas cards she'd received at the house. Many of her old friends from church haven't forgotten her. I have no idea if she recognizes any of their names, but I'd like to think that somewhere amidst the plaque tangles there is a glimmer of recognition.

John and I are going to be splitting Christmas dinner between us when we visit her before we go to John's family get-together. Since the family dinner doesn't start until 4 and the nursing home's dinner starts at 12:30, we figure that we'll both build up another appetite between times. We've requested that the dinner be brought up to Mom's room. Even if Mom doesn't eat and/or is still delirious (which I'm praying she won't be by then), I don't see how we could NOT spend a portion of Christmas Day with her.

(Jim's blog. 1/31/08)
"You always have such a beautiful smile."

Lisa, our regular hospice nurse, arrived while we were getting Martha Sr dressed this morning. She sat and watched, observing Martha Sr, seeing how she interacted with us, how she moved, how she looked. Then she went through her usual examination, checking vital signs, listening to heart, lungs, intestines, asking the usual questions about sleep, and appetite, and signs of pain. She sat back, looked at Martha Sr, and said pleasantly to her: "you always have such a beautiful smile."

* * *

There is light snow falling, but the winter storm which had been predict-ed has missed us for the most part. The grey fits my mood.

In anticipation of the storm, and in response to the accelerated use of wood mentioned previously, I spent most of yesterday afternoon out at our farm, cutting seasoned downfall and then hauling it back home. It felt good to be physically tired, rather than just emotionally exhausted. The soreness I feel today is a reminder of just how out of shape I am, but also holds a promise that I can once again get back into something resembling decent condition. Pain isn't always bad.

* * *

The last few days have been oddly quiet. Martha Sr has slept most of the time, for all but 3–4 hours each day. My wife and I move through the house as silently as possible, even chastise the cats and the dog if they get noisy. We want her to have whatever peace and quiet she can.

When she is up, she is confused about where she is, who we are. We roll with it the best we can, though sometimes we're caught off balance and react poorly. At least a couple of times we've played the "oh, here, let me call your mother" game again.

Today at lunch she was worried about where she had left her purse – she was concerned about how she was going to pay for her meal. I told her it was all taken care of, that she didn't need to worry. She looked at me with such gratitude, the thanks not given a son-in-law of 20 years, but rather of someone offered unexpected shelter and food by a stranger on a long and difficult journey. Then we watched a squirrel play, and she laughed.

* * *

We were just getting her tucked into bed for the night. My wife leaned over the bed rails, down to kiss her mother on the cheek, as she usually does. "Sleep well. Have good dreams and pleasant journeys."

Martha Sr looked away for a moment, rather than replying, "you too, dear," as she usually does.

"Something wrong? Is there something you need, do you hurt?"

A glance, almost embarrassed. "Could you stay with me?"

It was my turn to be on-call. My wife looked at me, back to her mom. "You mean just for a little while?"

"No. Sleep here with me."

"Of course. Let me go put some things away, and I'll be back in a little while."

* * *

"Any further signs of T.I.A.s?" asked Lisa, once she was done with her exam.

"No, but she's been sleeping so much we likely wouldn't have noticed."

She nodded. "Her heartbeat is now much more irregular, and that can frequently cause a T.I.A. at this point."   ——

We nodded. The signs of hypoxia were very clear, and there was a mottling to Martha Sr's skin in places we'd not seen previously.

"Her lungs are also very crackly, breathing labored just from sitting up. Pulse is weak, blood pressure low." She looked calmly at my wife and I. "Is there anything you need? Do you want someone else from the hospice team to come out and give you a break, so you can get away together?"

My wife and I exchanged glances. We have discussed this. As tired as we are, we don't both want to be gone at this point. One of us is always here now, both of us most of the time. "I think we're fine."

"OK. But this is exhausting. I know it is." Lisa brushed Martha Sr's hair again with her hand, smiled at her. And repeated what she had said moments earlier: "You always have such a beautiful smile."

(Kathi's LiveJournal entry. 12/15/07)
Afraid To Call

Latest news is that Mom's fever broke sometime this morning. She *[Georgia]* awoke long enough to drink 2-3 glasses of the "house shake" (Ensure?) and a couple of bites of breakfast. Then she went down for the count.

When John visited her this afternoon, he found her fairly cool but still a bit clammy. She squirmed but didn't thrash. She never woke up nor responded to his voice. He left soon after.

I'm almost afraid to call to see how she's doing.

John and I had another heated discussion about my calling Extended Family to ask them the burial or cremation question. I said that Saturday night two weeks before Christmas is hardly the opportune moment to pose the question. He disagreed, saying "What if she went now? Then what? You can't keep putting off the conversation because it's going to suck even more when you HAVE to make a decision." I understand his point, but tonight? I don't think so.

(Jim's blog. 2/1/08)
Free Jazz

No, sadly, not the musical movement. Rather, the approach we now take to caring for Martha Sr. All our routines are slipping away, the carefully practiced choreography which has defined our lives for years no longer relevant.

I've been saying for a while that we were coming to a close of this chapter of her life. I've been wrong before in my predictions that it would come on this day or that, before or after a particular holiday or birthday. And so I may well be wrong again when I say that we are now on the last few pages of the book.

There is something to this of that bittersweet moment, that sense of coming to conclusions you know are there, the resolution of conversations and plot lines that you get at the end of a cherished book. She no longer needs to wait for the usual markers of the day – when to get up, when to eat, when to nap. She got up this morning, and the rest of the day has followed as best we can to her wants and desires. Lunch an hour early, and including her favorite soup even though she just had it yesterday. (Campbell's Tomato, if you want to know.) Supper about a half hour early. Bed more than an hour early. Because that is what she wanted.

Her worries we have answered as best we can, telling her that tomorrow we will see if we can help her find "the people she came here with."

Unless she finds them on her own in her sleep.

I'll keep you posted.

(Kathi's LiveJournal entry. 12/16/07)
Closer

Mom's temperature spiked again overnight and into today. It stabilized around lunchtime, then spiked again a couple of hours later. State law prohibits the nursing home from giving her *[Georgia]* an alcohol bath or compresses, but they've been putting cool washcloth compresses on her forehead, feet, and armpits. ⏤

She drinks very little – a sip or two of milk here, some water or juice there, but never finishes a full glass. If you give her apple-sauce she holds it in her mouth and doesn't swallow. Her neck and face are smooth, shiny, and puffy. This afternoon she suddenly opened her eyes, but they were vacant. She kept holding onto my hand, though.

Her lips are cracked. The aides swab them and the inside of her mouth several times daily.

I burst into tears as soon as I sat down on the bed and took her hand. I told her it was me and wished there was something I could do to make her feel better. She stirred when she heard me sob, but nothing else.

There's a portable CD player on her nightstand, courtesy of the home. I switched it on. A new-agey rendition of "Silent Night" started playing. John and I held Mom's hands and quietly sang to her.

One of the weekend nurses told me that this "fever of unknown origin" is common in late-stage Alzheimer's. I could tell she really didn't want to say it, but she admitted that, in her experience, it's usually the first sign that the physical body is beginning to break down. Given the amount of time Mom's had this fever – almost 2 weeks now – if she comes out of it, she would probably be too weak to do much of anything.

I've been in a daze since we left her. It's one of those dazes where you want to do something to distract yourself, but you lack concentration. The weekend nurse assured me that they'd call if something happens. My immediate thought? I don't want to go to work tomorrow.

I said a silent prayer on the way home, a modification of the same prayer I said about Daddy: Please, God, if you're going to take her, don't take her on Christmas Day or New Year's. Thank you.

(Jim's blog. 2/3/08)
Waiting for the train to come

"What's wrong, Martha?"

She'd been restless most of the afternoon, but each time she called or squirmed enough to prompt me to investigate, the most she had been able to tell me was that she was "uncomfortable." I tried to tweak her meds a bit, but I suspected that the duragesic patches which are supposed to be good for 72 hours were running dry half a day early.

She took a sip of water from the straw I held to her lips. She swallowed, then said: "I was just worried."

"Worried? What are you worried about – maybe I can help?"

"Well, I think I need to go shopping."

"Shopping?"

"For clothes. For when I take the train back to college this fall. I won't have time to shop once I am there."

* * *

My wife had been napping. These days, each of us does what we can to get enough sleep, whenever we can. Because while I write these entries about what I have been doing in caring for my mother-in-law, be assured that my wife does even more in caring for her mom. So we watch out for each other, try and leave time for napping.

When she came down, asked how her mom had been doing, I told her my suspicions about the patches. We'd seen evidence previously that they ran out a bit early for Martha Sr – everyone has a different speed at which they metabolize medicine, even something as supposedly stable as a transdermal patch. She agreed with my assessment, and we changed the patches 12 hours early. At worst, the hospice might complain that we had made a mistake, and not to do it again.

I didn't care about that, and I wasn't sure that it would matter – that the end would probably come before we had to worry about a new Rx for the patches.

* * *

It takes a while for the painkillers from the patches to saturate the system – there's a 'ramp up' period, once they have gone dry. This is well understood, and we have additional painkillers on hand to help get past the initial stages – what are called "break-through" medicines. We'd given her what we hoped was enough of this when we got her to bed, along with something to help relieve her breathing difficulties. For a while, she slept fitfully.

Then at midnight she woke, tried to get out of bed. I heard her (I was on-call), got dressed and went down to see what she needed. As I got her disentangled from the bed rails and onto the commode, I asked her if she was OK.

She looked at me, her eyes watery and unfocused. I never did get much of an answer out of her, but it was clear from how much difficulty she was having breathing that I needed to do something. I did – increasing the dosage of the med she takes to control this kind of spasming. This is what we've been instructed to do by the hospice nurses.

It worked. After I got her back into bed and settled, her breathing relaxed, and she started snoring loudly. She snored like that for two and a half hours, during which time I actually got some sleep. You learn what sounds are good sounds when listening to a monitor at night.

And you learn what sounds are not. I woke about 3:00 to the sound of silence. Not even a hint of breathing from Martha Sr.

I went to check, found her still breathing, but so lightly and shallowly that you could barely tell it, even when standing right over her.

Two more times before I got up at 6:00 I went to check, see if she was still with us. She was.

* * *

She wanted to get up for breakfast, so we did that. But she was breathing and coughing so hard that when she'd finished we didn't even suggest that we go ahead with her normal Sunday morning bath. Getting her dressed, she was barely able to hold herself upright in the wheelchair. When we got her into bed her breathing was again stressed, and again we gave her something to help, half a dose.

And then we called hospice.

Lisa, our usual nurse, had told me on her last visit Thursday: "Call. Anytime. We don't like surprises."

So I called. The office put us through to the nurse on call this weekend. It was Lisa. I told her how things had gone in the previous 24 hours.

"I'll be right over."

* * *

"There's significantly diminished lung capacity," said Lisa, setting aside her stethoscope. Kneeling there next to the bed, her hand gently brushing Martha Sr's hair away from her face, she looked up at us, then back at Martha Sr. "Can you say goodbye to me? I just stopped by for a moment, and have to leave now."

It took Martha Sr a few moments to understand. Then she smiled slightly, and with a weak voice said "Goodbye."

Lisa gave us another patch, this one to help control secretions into Martha Sr's airway. Some swabs for her mouth, when it needs moistening but she is unable to drink. Told us how to arrange the pillows under her to help control aspiration problems. And that we should freely use the meds which help control breathing spasms, keep her comfortable. "It'll probably make her even sleepier. But at this point, that is not a bad thing."

I nodded.

And now we wait.

(Excerpt – John's blog "A Farewell to Georgia" 12/27/07) "As I Lay Dying..."

[The following is a stream-of-consciousness text that began next to Georgia's bedside in the nursing home as she slowly passed from this mortal coil we know as life. Kathi and John are the sole narrators, alternating perspective as they passed a small computer back and forth.]

The title, reminiscent of a popular novel, sprung into my head as I sat with Georgia while she lay quietly in the bed at the nursing home. Her eyes sometimes opened, sometimes partial slits, she lay facing diagonally across the room, her eyes focused on a point just shy of the window at the far wall.

When I spoke to my wife on the cell phone a few minutes ago, I could have sworn Georgia teared up; I squeezed her hand, my fingers aligned along hers and gently tugging her listless hand. Did I just detect a few twinges in her fingers, as a response as she tried to squeeze mine? Her breathing is labored, with a scratchy rattle softly underscoring each breath.

We got the word yesterday from the nursing home that she was officially dying at this point. They surmised from her condition and rate of change that she might last a week on the outside.

We haven't been able to communicate effectively with her for the majority of the past two weeks. Three weeks ago, when I was pulling her through a doorway in her geri-chair, she caught my eyes and stuck her tongue out, then closed her mouth and smiled slyly when I mock-complained to Kathi that she was teasing me. Kathi had missed it, but caught the sly smile – an unmistakable sign that Georgia was playing with us.

I'm on her right – I should be over on her left, in the direction she's facing. I'll move the other patient's bed (it's been empty over the past two weeks) once Kathi arrives, so it'll be easier to put a chair there.

* * *

Why don't they call? Aren't they supposed to call?

I'm at work and jumpy. I've already burst into tears twice, once when I first walked in and saw Andy, the second in the freezer while Andy put the load away. I have my to-do list in front of me, but my writing is messy and keeps wavering every time I look at it. Thank god I have people here who don't need a lot of supervision.

Every time the phone rings my heart rises to my throat and my pulse pounds in my ears.

I attempt the to-do list. I can't get past the first two or three items. The floor is filled. I finish product for the cream case so the case is filled; Beverly can take care of the rest. When Steve walks by I tell him that my mother is dying and I'm expecting a phone call. He tells me to do whatever I feel is correct. Customers hold out bread for slicing; there are four women in a row waiting to place orders. I tend to each one mechanically. Am I really here?

* * *

I try to gaze into Georgia's good eye. I had just spoken to Kathi on the phone. She was getting out of work early.

I was leaving to go meet her at the house and bring her here. I hoped to precede her by a short time in order to take care of the dogs: give them dinner, top off their water and walk 'em around out back for them to go to the bathroom.

Kathi arrives when I finish caring for the dogs. I waited for her to grab a bite to eat and change, filling her in as she gets ready. We head back to the nursing home and Georgia in relative silence.

(Kathi's LiveJournal entry. 12/18/07)
Daze

John got two calls from the nursing home this morning. Mom's respiration is down to 85. She *[Georgia]* is also developing chest congestion. She's refusing all food and drink.

I have no idea why they didn't call me at work, but that's neither here nor there at the moment.

I left work and came back here to change clothes. John left the home and came back here to pick me up because I'm in a daze.

(Excerpt – John's blog "A Farewell to Georgia" 12/27/07)
"She's actively dying."

[More of our stream-of-consciousness text as Georgia passed from this life. Kathi begins this one.]

My mother's *[Georgia]* feet are mottled blue. Her toes ARE blue. I touch them and shiver. I reach over and grab her exposed hand. It is warmer and has faint blue mottling. Her cuticles are shriveled, making her nails longer than they actually are.

Her eyes are slitted open, her right eye staring in my direction while her left eye – the eye botched by a bad cataract operation, slides backward so that the lower portion of the iris only shows.

"She's actively dying," Mark the nurse replies when I ask him about her toes. "She's having kidney failure. Her blood and bile are backing up and and have nowhere to go. Her heart is weakening, so the body instinctively tells the blood to protect the internal organs. The extremities are the first to go."

They lend us a CD player and keep a respectful distance unless we need something. We brought CDs of some of her favorite artists – Gershwin's "Rhapsody in Blue", Dean Martin, and a couple of classical CD's of mine which weren't necessarily Mom's favorites, but are soothing just the same. I just hope I don't burst into tears during the Pachebel Canon like I usually do.

Mark tells me that Mom is comatose. He turns her toward me. Her eyes are slits, with her good eye staring at me. I say to her, "Mama, it's me. It's OK. I'll be fine. Mama, it's me." She never moves.

* * *

We'd begun falling asleep, Kathi at Georgia's side, holding her hand and laying her head on the bed rail.

We've sung Georgia some of the silly songs that we'd made up or shared while we'd cared for her at home.

One of the CDs that Kathi plays is a hit by Dean Martin called "You're so mean to me." We look at each other in a mix of surprise and delight – I'd made up a song very similar to it for Georgia to gently chide and tease her; this was the first time Kathi or I ever heard the Dean Martin song, but we think that Georgia probably knew of it and thought we were purposely channeling Dean when we sang our own home-grown ditty – much to her delight, and our ignorance.

* * *

I wonder if she can hear me. They say that hearing is the last sense to die, so I talk while I brush her hair, rub lotion on her arms and legs, and clean her fingernails with an orange stick. She usually flinches if I accidentally dig the stick between her nails and fingertips, but this time she doesn't. I ask her if I'm hurting her. She doesn't respond.

"Talk to her," John tells me when I'm silent. "Keep talking to her!"

I don't know what else to say to her. Small talk isn't my thing. If I have nothing pertinent to say, I'm quiet. Mom knew this in her previous life, and although she sometimes wasn't happy about it, she'd let me be.

"I don't know what else to tell her," I say. "I don't want to bitch about work. What else can I tell her except I love her and I'll be OK?"

* * *

I was trying not to make it more difficult for her, but couldn't help myself. "Talk to her," I kept saying whenever there was a pregnant pause. I kept quiet while Kathi did Georgia's nails and applied lotion to Georgia's hands and feet, and while the CDs played.

When there seemed to be nothing left to say, I started singing some of our silly songs again.

Kathi joined in, holding Georgia's hand and sporadically stroking her hair.

We completed a couple rousing renditions of "On Top of Spaghetti," "Show Me the Way to Go Home," "When the Red Red Robin Goes Bob-Bob-Bobbin' Along" (sort of – we couldn't remember all the words), and few made-up favorites.

The room was very warm; we kept drifting off to sleep.

I asked Kathi if she wanted to stay longer, or take a break and return later. She opted for the break – Georgia appeared to be stable.

I drew in close to Georgia's face, trying to focus on her good eye, and told her we were going to head out for a little bit, and maybe get some shut-eye at home. I told her we'd be back early in the morning.

I told her not to go anywhere until we got back, but silently amended it to mean "unless you need to and can't stay."

We left.

(Kathi's LiveJournal entry. 12/18/07)
Dazed, Home

We just got back from the nursing home.

I'm not going to work tomorrow.

Her toes are black and blue. The rest of her feet are mottled red-turning-to-blue up to the ankles. I know this because I peeked under the sheet.

Her hands aren't blue, but she's got the same mottling on both, going up to the wrists.

Mark (the RN on duty) told me that she *[Georgia]* no longer has the strength to close her eyes. Her eyes are slits. The good eye – her right – stares in the direction of whatever noise there is. The left – the one botched by the cataract operation last year – turns up so all you see is the white. She doesn't blink.

She reflexes if she's touched, but otherwise doesn't react. One of the aides showed me how to swab her mouth. It was the first time Mom's closed her mouth in the past few days. She grunted, but otherwise didn't react. When John tickled her toes, she jerked for a second, but otherwise, nothing.

She gurgles at the end of each raspy breath.

We brought a bunch of CDs with us – Gershwin (Mom's all-time favorite piece is "Rhapsody in Blue"), Dean Martin, Mozart, a Baroque compilation including Pachebel's Canon in D, and a Sondheim compilation. The nursing home gave us some George Winston and other meditative-New-Agey stuff. We played everything for her.

I held her hand. I kept telling her it was me, everything was OK, she needn't worry anymore.

John fell asleep because the room is quite warm.

Before we left they checked her vital signs. Her temp was down to 99, but her BP is hovering around 80/40. Her oxygen level is in the high 80s.

They're going to call if something changes. Doesn't matter when – it could be now, it could be 3AM, it could be tomorrow morning – whenever.

I called my manager at home to tell her I wasn't coming in tomorrow. I left a message on her voice mail.

"Do you want to talk about it?" John asked me on the way home.

"No," I replied. "I'm better at writing this stuff than I am saying it."

(Excerpt – John's blog "A Life's Worth of Memories" 03/11/08)
Speak To Me / Breathe

The song "Speak To Me / Breathe" – also by Pink Floyd – further described the emotional interplay between Georgia and Kathi. The singer tells the listener to breathe, to not be afraid to care, and to leave – but to not leave the singer. It echoes a piece that Kathi wrote before we were married entitled "Please Breathe." I thought of it while we sat vigil with Georgia as she lay dying on that final, fateful day. I so very much wanted Georgia to waken from her near-comatose state and acknowledge our presence, even if just to whisper goodbye to Kathi once more. It wasn't happening. Kathi stroked her mom's hair after tending to her nails and soothing lotion on Georgia's feet and hands. We'd begun to run out of things to say to keep our presence from stagnating; the warmth of the room was putting us to sleep.

I asked Kathi if she wanted to stay longer, or take a break and return later. She opted for the break – Georgia appeared to be stable. I drew in close to Georgia's face, trying to focus on her good eye, and told her we were going to head out for a little bit, and maybe get some shut-eye at home. I told her we'd be back early in the morning. I told her not to go anywhere until we got back, but silently amended it to mean "unless you need to and can't stay." We left.

I didn't tell Kathi what I thought I saw when I looked into Georgia's one good eye. I wasn't certain if it was just my own mind, my own heart, playing tricks on me. At the moment I hovered at the point where her eye was focused, when I told her we were going to leave for a little while and return in a few hours, I thought I saw a brief glimmer of mixed emotion and thoughts skitter across the surface – recognition, both of me and of "being seen" by me; fear, at the thought of being left alone; acceptance, at the realization that we'd be back; doubt, at the thought that she'd be able to hold on long enough for us to return; understanding, knowing that her daughter may not be able to take being here "in the moment" of her passing.

I felt terrible, and hoped that I was wrong, or that at least Georgia would understand that I was doing this for Kathi...even so, I couldn't help thinking that it was a horrible thing to do if there was even the slightest chance that Georgia was there, and could understand us and see through her one good eye – the window to her soul.

A few scant hours later, Georgia passed away and we were on our way back to the nursing home to say goodbye and to arrange for the local funeral home to come pick up her body.

(Jim's blog. 2/4/08)
Brief update

For all who are following things here with Martha Sr...

She has largely been sleeping/dozing comfortably, and we're doing all we can to make sure that she stays out of pain, unworried. Either my wife or I are now with her all the time. She didn't eat any supper last night, had a bit of yogurt this morning. Things seem to be winding down as well as they can be. Lisa, our hospice nurse, should be by later this afternoon to check and see if there is anything else we can do to help matters.

I will post updates as appropriate. Otherwise, do not expect to hear from me very much.

(Jim's blog. 2/4/08)
Further update

Another brief update about Martha Sr...

Lisa, the hospice nurse was here a little while ago. Based on what she sees, she said that we should expect her to pass on sometime tonight, and made arrangements to inform the people who are on call for the hospice organization. Based on her other recommendations we are also switching Martha Sr's meds over to those which can be administered in liquid form, to minimize difficulty in getting them down.

It's likely that my next update will be news of her death. May it come gently.

(John's online entry. 12/19/07)
Georgia: 1923-2007 RIP

Georgia passed away a little while ago.

We're off to the nursing home now. We've only been home a few hours.

(Excerpt – John's blog "A Farewell to Georgia" 12/27/07)
Nursing Home Goodbyes

[More of our stream-of-consciousness text as Georgia passed from this life. Kathi begins this one.]

Ruth, the night nurse on duty, is quiet as she tells me what happened. She thinks Mom *[Georgia]* passed in her sleep around midnight. She tells me to come in because there's paperwork I have to sign. She tells me she's sorry, but I half hear her. I gulp sobs while she's telling me this.

I don't want to go in there. I say this to Ruth. Ruth tries not to chuckle as she replies, I'm sorry, but you have to. It's the rule.

I pull sweatpants and a sweatshirt over my pajamas. We scritch the dogs and tell them what happened. Hubby drives us to the nursing home. It's cold outside, but I'm not registering it.

One of the aides greets us at the door and lets us in. She tells us she's sorry. We nod and get on the elevator. Ruth is waiting for us as we disembark.

"I don't know if you want to see her," Ruth says to me. "You might want your last memory to be what she looks like at the funeral home. It's up to you."

"I...don't...know..." I stammer.

She pats my hand. "That's OK. You don't have to decide now. But I need you to come in here and sign some papers while I make the call."

I give her a look.

"Oh, we don't have facilities here, if you know what I mean. Your mother is still in bed."

Oh.

* * *

Kathi is filling out papers with the nurse. I go to say goodbye to Georgia.

She's in the bed, her hand on her chest, covered in a sheet. I can see her toes are pointed.

She's yellow. Like a banana.

This is what physical death looks like.

I cross over to the bed and bend over, giving her a soft kiss on the head.

"Goodbye, my friend," I whisper.

I could feel the empty bone-deep cold beneath my lips.

Georgia hated the cold.

I went back and told Kathi that her mother was a banana.

* * *

Ruth asks me if I want to see her.

"I don't know,"I reply.

"You don't have to," Ruth replies. "You might not want to have a nightmare."

"Oh."

Ohhhhhh.

"Well, maybe. I don't know. Can I peek in there?"

"I'll come with you," Ruth says as we stand up, her arm around me. "It's OK. Ask me anything you want."

John is already in her room waiting for us. Ruth and I are at the doorway. "You don't have to do this if you don't want to," she says.

I'm shivering.

"Maybe I'll take a peek," I say.

"If you want. I'm right here."

Mom is on her back, hands folded on her belly. Her mouth is still open, but her eyes are closed.

She's yellow.

Like a banana.

I wonder if her toes are black.

"Why is she yellow?" I whisper to Ruth.

"That's what happens when you die," she explains. "It's the bile backing up in your system."

I suddenly remember a book I'd read about physical death, about how the blood pools in the low areas of body, which makes the body harder to move. The pooled areas supposedly look like huge bruises. I don't want to see if this is happening to Mom. I can't.

She's yellow.

Her mouth is open.

Why isn't she snoring?

* * *

The rest of the night is a blur.

We got back home around 3:30 am, and went to bed.

In the morning, the funeral home called. They set up a time for Kathi to come in to finalize everything: the wake, the funeral and the associated particulars.

I quietly sent out emails to key family and friends so they'd know. I posted a couple messages online and respond to a few.

The longest days are just beginning.

* * *

Oh, I have to call people. I remember Mom doing this when Daddy died. She got into a huge argument with the woman whom she thought was her best friend. The best friend passed a few years ago, so I don't have to worry about her.

I go through Mom's Rolodex while I try not thinking about what actually happens when they prepare her for the wake. I silently curse myself for having no fear of "the dark side", as in it's OK when you're discussing a person you don't know, but it's another thing when it's your parent, spouse, child, or sibling. I was an ardent fan of "Family Plots" on A&E a few years ago. The camera never showed the faces of the deceased, but they'd show Shonna, the embalmer, working the less savory aspects of preparing a body.

That's OK. I trust Al or whoever's preparing her. I know what they do. They'll treat her with the utmost respect. And, oh hell, why did I decide to let her wear the jacket that I covet?

(Kathi's LiveJournal entry. 12/19/07)
Almost Nobody To Call

It's a very weird feeling going through your mother's *[Georgia]* address book and realizing that most of the people in there have already passed. There's almost nobody to call. Who am I going to call?

I dozed off around 3AM, I think. I awoke to the phone around 7:30. My manager never got my message, so A called in a frenzy wondering what'd happened to me. I'd given him a heads up when I left there yesterday afternoon. There was a major screw up with a few orders last night. He's trying to straighten it out now.

I'm meeting with Al the funeral director at 2:30. Thank god I had the foresight to pick everything out when I went there a couple of months ago. We're shooting for a Saturday funeral, providing that the slots aren't already taken. Yeah, it's really a "first come first served" in a large Catholic parish like ours. If Al can't get one it'll have to be pushed to Monday, but he reassured me that he'll do everything in his power to get a Saturday slot.

Outfit? Check. (Mom's, not mine. Which reminds me I have to go shopping. So does John. Neither of us have dress up clothes so to speak).

The Good Attorney has been notified.

I can't make arrangements for the after-burial festivities (oh, you know what I mean, it's not festive per se, but you know people meet and mingle and eat after these things) until we get a time down for the funeral. I just realized that Ye Olde Watering Hole will be out because it's Saturday. They also don't have a function room.

John's forcing me to eat breakfast. He's making an omelet.

The dogs haven't left my side since last night.

(Jim's blog. 2/5/08)
And another update

... on Martha Sr's condition.

She made it through the night, though has been in a light coma for the last several hours at least (that's not a medical diagnosis, but seems to fit). My wife and I are still able to stay on top of her needs, and she seems to be in no pain, though her breathing is distressed and indicative of the nearness of death.

My wife and I are doing well through this, and have taken turns resting. My wife's brother was able to come and spend a good long time with his mother this morning, and we're getting plenty of support from friends and family. It's about the best one could hope for, and I will have a lot to say about the whole experience once we have a chance to rest and recover a bit.

(Jim's blog. 2/5/08)
Yet ANOTHER update

OK, I shouldn't be flip about this.

But Martha Sr continues to astonish. As noted previously, the woman is very strong. Our hospice nurse all but said (and this is no criticism of her or her judgment) that Martha Sr would likely pass last night. But she made it through. And through the morning.

And through the afternoon. Late afternoon another nurse (our usual is off today) called from hospice to see what was going on – and whether we needed any help, supplies, et cetera. The hospice people have been great.

Anyway, she is still hanging in there. She's weaker, her breathing continues to deteriorate, she's in a deeper coma than I mentioned earlier, and her fever is now 5 degrees above normal. But she is still fighting. It isn't necessarily what I would have chosen for her, but my respect for her has stepped up another notch.

So, predictions be damned. We're just sticking in there with her for as long as she's with us.

(Jim's blog. 2/6/08)
It's over

After a long and valiant fight, Martha Sr passed away this morning about 5:20. My wife and I were with her.

Memorial arrangements, and further reflections on her battle with Alzheimer's, to come later.

For now, think of her, whether in your prayers or your hopes.

(Kathi's LiveJournal entry. 12/20/07)
Plans

OK, here are the plans:

Wake is Friday from 4-8PM
Funeral on Saturday at 9AM

I'm not planning any get-together afterward. I suddenly remembered that one of John's nieces is having a family birthday party later on Saturday afternoon. Nothing was said to me directly about it, but from the way my mother-in-law hinted around about "you don't need to do anything like that" earlier – this was before I went to make the arrangements – it sounded like something else was already scheduled. I checked with John, and yep, sure enough, the birthday party.

That wasn't the reason why I decided against it. I thought about it. I spoke to Susie about it. She agreed that I really don't have the $ to do something like this. Um, yeah, after all the checks I have to write for Friday, but nevertheless...she said that there've been a few times where she's attended a funeral and there wasn't any socializing afterward. It depends on how the family's feeling and whatnot. She reminded me that her mother didn't have any get-together after her dad died a few years ago. That's true. There were only 10 or 12 of us in attendance. I said I wouldn't have any issue if she, her husband, John, and I went out for lunch afterward. That's still up in the air. We'll take it as it comes.

My cousin in Florida hasn't called me back. We found out last night that he'd just lost his brother-in-law a few days ago, and his wife is still reeling over it. That's OK.

I was surprised that my cousin Gayle left a message. We hadn't spoken since Uncle Stevie's death 2 years ago. Her mom, my Aunt Helen, also has Alzheimer's, although she's in the early stage right now. She moved Helen into senior housing down by her over the summer. We compared notes. Stevie had the same black-blue toes and mottling right before he passed. Gayle said it was the result of a UTI gone haywire, and she wouldn't be surprised if the same had happened to Mom. She added it's very common for the late stage of the disease and the physical age.

The arrangements. Gah. My head swam. I was handed piece after piece of paper with explanations and "How do you feel about this?" and "What do you think your mother would want to have done?" I have no idea! We never discussed this so I'm just going on my gut feeling here! "Here are your choice of Mass cards. Pick a saint and a prayer for the back." Ick, some of this stuff is so sickeningly glurgy I'm ready to barf! Forgive me for saying that, but really...'I will see you again in the sky!"?!? Ack! I chose St. Francis of Assisi and his prayer "Make me a channel of your peace" because it's one of the few prayers I know that isn't sentimental and truly says something. I know Mom would appreciate that.

I had to correct the death notice 3 times. They got Mom's maiden name completely wrong the first time. The second time they spelled her original maiden name – the real Greek name which she and Stevie both shortened – wrong. Her other two brothers used the original version. I expected the misspelling, so that was OK. The third time they forgot Susie and her husband, Gayle, and got the location of my cousin in Florida wrong. Good god, people! I can understand the maiden name thing, but the other two?!?

I won't go into the financial stuff. I don't have to pay it all at once, which is nice. I do have to make checks to the cemetery on Friday for the opening/closing *gulp* and for the church/organist/soloist/priest at the cemetery.

Flowers? Check. I ordered a casket spray in bright colors. Mom hated pastels more than I do.

Work? I talked to M earlier tonight. They're giving me now through Christmas off. I can have off through New Year's if I want because I've got unused sick pay coming to me. I said I didn't know if I could go that long without having something to do, but it depends. I could have a nervous breakdown after all this is over. Then again maybe I won't. M said she'll leave it up to me.

Tomorrow I get to go shopping for something funereal to wear. Whee.

I have a headache.

(Jim's blog. 2/6/08)
Obit

The following is the obit for Martha Sr which will run in our local papers. After checking with my wife, we decided to go ahead and post the information here as well, even though I have through all my posts never used her name, out of respect for her privacy. But she deserves to be now named and recognized for her long and rich life of involvement in her community and devotion to her family.

* * *

Martha Burr Bates John, 90, of Columbia passed away on February 6, 2008 at her home.

Memorial services will be held at 2:00 on Saturday, February 9, 2008 at Memorial Funeral Home in Columbia.

Martha was born on June 14, 1917 to Archie Burr and Martha Frances Breiner Bates and they preceded her in death. She was married on October 5, 1940 to Hurst John in Boonville, Missouri and he preceded her in death.

Martha was a 1934 graduate of Laura Speed Elliot High School in Boonville and a 1936 graduate of Stephens College. She graduated in 1938 from the University of Minnesota with a B.A. in Architecture. She worked as a draftsman for noted Columbia architect, Harry S. Bill, where she met her future husband. After World War II she worked occasionally, mostly for her husband, and began raising a family. During the next 30 years she was involved in many activities relating to the family, PTA President at both Benton Elementary and Jefferson Junior High School, Camp Fire leader

and local board president, Cub Scout den mother. She volunteered at Ellis Fischel Hospital for thirty years, serving at least once as Auxiliary President and was a long time member of First Baptist Church in Columbia.

She is survived by daughter, Martha K. John and husband Jim Downey of Columbia; son, John John, his wife Karen and their son, Justin all of Columbia; daughter Susan Newstead of Navarro, California; granddaughter, Miel Newstead of Philo, California; grandson, John Newstead, his wife Holly and their sons, Kai and Max, all of Navarro, California.

She was also preceded in death by her son, Lawrence Edward John; sister, Ida Frances Bates Dyer Kalb; nephew, Bob Dyer.

Tributes can be left online at www.memorialfuneralhomeandcemetery.com

* * *

Thanks to all who have sent me messages or posted comments here. My wife mentioned that some flowers would be welcome for the service, but I think we would both also welcome donations made in Martha Sr's name to your local Alzheimer's Association Chapter or hospice organization.

I'll be posting more, later.

(Excerpt – John's blog "A Farewell to Georgia" 12/27/07)
A Farewell to Georgia

[More of our stream-of-consciousness text as Georgia passed from this life. John begins this one.]

Flashback to 2003: a Bourke family gathering, a formal affair, had come up. I'd just gotten into the swing of caring for Georgia; neither Kathi nor I realized that Georgia's wardrobe was so screwed up. She'd maintained a very respectable business wardrobe, right up until Kathi and I married. When I tried to help her prepare for the event, however, I made a startling discovery – she had no idea where the key components to any of her suits were.

Neither did I.

Georgia had always taken care to maintain a well-groomed, well-dressed and appropriate appearance. I wasn't about to let her down, now that she depended upon me to help her get ready.

I realized we didn't have a shot at finding a suitable outfit, or cleaning those complete ensembles that we found hidden in the back of the closet, half-cleaned and half-not.

We made a road trip to a local mall, where I made the command decision to fully outfit her – jacket, pants, shirt and shoes.

$700 later and custom-tailored by a very helpful and supportive staff, Georgia was positively aglow with joy. The outfit looked great on her.

She looked as though she felt like a million bucks. In retrospect, it wasn't a bad exchange rate.

Kathi and I would add a few interchangeable shirts, pants and a few jackets over the next couple of weeks. Until Georgia qualified for additional care benefits, I'd have to occasionally take her with me to clients, so she had to dress the part. The clients – both home and business clients – knew of Georgia's "condition" and welcomed her. We were blessed in that regard. While Georgia would speak to the client, I'd get the work done that they'd contracted for.

Georgia was thrilled. She was "working" and helping out her daughter and new son-in-law. She felt useful again.

We went to show off to Kathi at her work. Daily, or whenever we worked in that area at least.

Kathi was both pleased and slightly annoyed. "Do you have to come by my work to show off every time you two go out together dressed like the Bobbsey twins?"

"Yep," I grinned.

Not long after the incident with the tailored suit, in an impromptu planning session where Kathi and I discussed future planning over Georgia's care and eventual passing, Kathi got very quiet.

"You realize that we're probably going to bury her in that suit, don't you?"

Yeah, I realized that, I admitted. The momentary sadness we both shared was quickly replaced by the acknowledgment of how much fun Georgia was having.

"And," I pointed out, "you can probably wear some of the same clothes, particularly the jackets."

Kathi didn't like shopping for herself, so I thought this would be a good topic-changer.

She grinned. "I already knew that. I used to steal her clothes all the time. She called me 'My daughter, the crook.'"

* * *

The thing was, that jacket fit me perfectly. I'm not a clotheshorse, so whatever I happen to find that fits me perfectly I grab. In the past it didn't matter if it was Mom's. I'd appear at breakfast. She'd look at me with narrowed eyes and a smirk and ask, "So where did you get that from?"

"From your closet," I'd chirp.

"My daughter the crook," she'd mutter. But if you looked at her sideways, you could see the smirk and the glitter in her eyes: Ah, my daughter is finally a smart ass! It's about time!

Thing is, I have no need for business clothes. I wear a uniform for work. We don't often go to places requiring a dress code of sorts. But this short dark brown tweedy jacket, double breasted with an extra pleat with hooks instead of buttons, fit me perfectly. It looked fabulous paired with an ivory cashmere sweater and black slacks. Trust me.

Which is why I let Mom have it.

Brown was her color. Our home decor is based on brown; her wardrobe, until her deterioration, was based on every premise and tint of brown imaginable. As a kid she tried convincing me that brown was "my" color because we had similar coloring: Ick! BROWN! I don't want to look like you!

But brown was her color. There was no getting around that. When Jane, the assistant at the funeral home, asked me to bring her clothes, I had no other choice. The other jackets in Mom's closet were either too big or there was nothing with which to match them. I thought about donating a brown tweed jacket of mine which I'd worn maybe twice, but neither I nor Mom had anything to match it. So it was The Coveted Jacket.

* * *

We had to be at the funeral home at least 30 minutes before the wake. I'd blown up a few pictures on the computer, particularly one of a very young Kathi and Georgia, and uploaded it to a local print shop, so I brought Kathi and dropped her off then went to get the pictures.

They hadn't printed 'em yet.

I'd received the confirmation email over an hour ago that had said the pictures were ready.

I elected to wait. How long could it take?

Back at the funeral home, Georgia was smirking.

* * *

I'd picked the photo. It'd been taken when we lived in town. I was about 4 or 5. I don't remember who took the photos, but there is a series of them – Mama and Daddy together, me and Daddy, me and Grandma, me and Mama. In the picture Mama and I are in profile and exchanging a lip kiss.

I've always been her baby girl.

I was her reason for living, especially after Daddy died. She used to introduce me as, "This is my daughter. If I didn't have her, I'd kill myself." I didn't want her to commit suicide, so I never left her.

I thought about the other wakes I'd been to, with photos and mementos festooned all over the inner covering of the casket, leaning on the edge between the upper lid and the bottom. Thing is, neither Mom nor I were overly sentimental types. We had a very small family, for one. Even if I wanted to place mementos around her, I would've been hard pressed to find enough things to keep her company.

The photo, though. Now that I know she would've wanted. Her baby girl. Her only reason for living.

* * *

4:45 pm. I'm forty-five minutes late to the wake, and I'd only been down the street at a drugstore waiting for pictures that should have been ready long ago.

When I arrived, the priest – Fr. Bob – was just finishing the short prayer service. He was then off to cover yet another engagement; another wake, I believe, out of the three more that he had for that day. December was a busy month for death.

Kathi's dad – Georgia's husband – had died on December 13th over thirty-four years before.

My youngest sister was by Kathi's side when I got there. Jane, the funeral parlor's administrator, relieved me of the pictures and placed them out on a table in another part of the room. I missed the first few sets of people who stopped in, several of whom knew of Georgia and us from our favorite watering hole – the bar side of a small family restaurant that we took Georgia to on a regular basis. "The Regulars" had all made it a point to stop in.

I was glad Kathi hadn't been left alone for too long, and had someone by her side until I returned.

She was holding up well.

In the casket, Georgia was beautiful, a picture of serenity and style, wearing an ever-so-slight smirk. It's that little hint of a smile that seemed to help Kathi the most. Only a few people were surprised at it. Many more actually thought it suited the Georgia they had gotten to know.

Kathi thought it was quite appropriate.

His First Year
The long, slow process of recovery

Your time of being a care-provider is over.

But the journey you have been on is not.

In many ways this part of the journey is just as important as having
been a care-provider. Just as most men will find themselves somewhat unprepared for the role of being a long-term care-giver to
someone with dementia, they will also likely find themselves
adrift and uncertain at the end of that intense period of their life.
Seeing how we went through the process of decompression and
re-integration may help. Do not take this as a script of what you
should do. Only accept it as a map of what we did.

This is a much more straight-forward memoir, and all the entries
are in actual chronological order over the span of a single year. You
may not believe that it will take that long to recover. Chances are,
it will take even longer. For both John and Jim, a year wasn't the
end of the journey. Writing this book in some ways meant
extending the time necessary for recovery, but it also helped to
bring it to a more satisfying conclusion.

*(Excerpt – John's blog "A Dash, A Comma and a Footnote"
2/4/08)*
"Never put a period where God has put a comma"

The concept of a comma on the pages of history may also be an
allusion to or a variant of the famous phrase "a footnote in pages
of history." Whatever the context, however, it does serve to
illustrate the simple concept of how all of history can sometimes

be condensed and distilled over time, leaving the reader with but a few words, phrases and punctuation marks to cover sometimes intricate and tumultuous periods of time.

Our time, the time we are given in which to live our lives, is fleeting at best; we can slow the pace a bit in an attempt to enjoy and capture moments of joy or delay the onset of sorrow, or we can let life carry us away as though through a series of rapids in a wild white-water stretch. In the end, we are left – if we are lucky – with a stone marker denoting simply our name and the dates of our turn at life, while the whole of our lives are condensed to the dash between birth and death.

Some of us may generate longer-lasting, more detailed remembrance and more than simply a casual mention among the worn and yellowed pages in the archives of humanity, and through such remembrance gain a measure of immortality. For those people, still, there will be a set of dates set apart by a dash to denote their start and end, as noted in Linda Ellis' poem "The Dash." For those people, will the dash serve to call up recorded pages of history that cast their former lives in a kind light, or will the light be dimmed and darkened, destined to cast a pall over the events of the period?

Those who never achieve explicit mention outside of their individual "dash" will not have to worry what kind of light is cast by their remembrance; they may live on in family stories and history passed down among their descendants, or live on within the community or culture they served without making a larger mark on human history, but the common folks – of which we are many – will often have just our contemporary loves to reflect upon our lives and the meaning which we left behind.

In any case, be the events of a life big or small, there's nothing worse than not giving oneself any meaning at all to the dash between their dates. A good mother, father, sibling or friend is, indeed, an admirable "dash" to bequeath those left living when one moves on. Live your life as you are able, and spend your "dash" wisely.

(Jim's blog. 2/7/08)
Bits and pieces

I find it odd, but somehow telling, that the obit for Martha Sr has gotten the most hits of anything I've posted on my blog previously, and as a result I've hit a new "best day" today. Ah, well.

The newspaper coverage of her passing can be found in the same issue of the Tribune which contains news about this year's Notable Historic Properties. Which includes our home.

(Jim's blog. 2/8/08)
And now, The Migraine

I was half expecting it.

As mentioned previously, I suffer from migraines upon occasion. Perhaps a bit surprisingly, the last couple of months have been fairly light in that regard. But I have one now, of the "stress-release" variety.

Last night, for the first time in the better part of a week, we cooked dinner and relaxed watching a couple of episodes of Doctor Who. I had a couple of drinks, but that's not a lot for me over the course of the evening. I fell asleep later in front of the computer, catching up on news of the world. In other words, I was starting to spin down from recent events.

I went up and went to bed, while Martha (no longer 'Jr') did the dishes and caught up on some email. I woke sometime after midnight from the pain of the migraine. Got up, went and took some over-the-counter stuff I hoped would shut it down, went back to bed. Woke up again about 4:30, pain worse. Got up and took some more OTC stuff and something stronger to give it a boost. Unfortunately, those meds include a fair amount of caffeine, so getting back to sleep was not much of an option. I laid down, let them work for a while, then got up.

It may seem odd that I would be suffering a stress-release migraine going into what is likely to be a fairly stressful and emotional weekend, what with the memorial service tomorrow and all. I'm fairly introverted, and the prospect of a large public gathering and all that concentrated emotional outpouring is rather daunting.

But that is nothing in comparison to the stresses of caring for someone with dementia who is dying. Even now, all my instincts and conditioned reflexes are concerned first with taking into account where Martha Sr is, who is keeping track of her, what needs to be done next in the usual care regimen. Yesterday, returning from errands I needed to run, I glanced at her bedroom window as I drove up the driveway, to see whether my wife had her up from her afternoon nap and had opened the drapes. This morning before grinding my coffee I went to shut the door from the kitchen in order to muffle the sound and not disturb her sleep. And those are just two of the dozens of examples I could cite from the last 24 hours. It will take months, at least, to set aside these reflexes, to fully become 'free' of the ingrained habits of years.

So, yeah, I have a migraine. Not horrid, with the meds I have in me so far, though this post may be a bit less coherent than it could be. I should still be able to play house-elf today in preparation for the visitors we will have this weekend, and to make the memorial book for the service tomorrow. If it doesn't get a lot worse I should even be able to function well during the public outing tomorrow (I got a lot of experience with that sort of thing while I owned the art gallery). But there it is - perhaps the first marker of the real change in my life. We are, after all, born in pain.

(Jim's blog. 2/25/08)
I knew these days would come

Last night we settled down with some dinner to watch a bit of Firefly, settling on "Serenity" (the episode, not the movie). At one point fairly early on, when plans have gone south at several junctures, the captain of the ship (Mal) is considering options,

trying to make the best of a not-great situation. There's this little
bit of dialog:

> *MAL: We don't get paid for this, we won't have enough money
> to fuel the ship, let alone keep her in repair. She'll be dead in the
> water anyhow.*
>
> [Mal turns to the others.]
>
> *We just gotta keep our heads down and do the job. Pray there
> ain't no more surprises.*[12]

I looked at my wife, and we just nodded to one another.

* * *

We did a hard thing. And we did it well.

Caring for Martha Sr for years somewhat warped my perspective.
First and foremost in our consideration was always what her
needs were and how best to meet them. I've often talked about
what that meant in terms of rewards and sacrifices, and I don't
intend to rehash that now.

But a couple of things have changed with her passing. First off, is
the odd sense of disorientation. I've compared it in discussion with
friends with almost having a sense of agoraphobia – a nervousness
when out in the world I've never felt before. It's really just a
conditioned reflex, and will fade as I adjust to the lack of need to
always being worried about Martha Sr.

Another thing which has changed is the need to return to something resembling a 'normal' life, with the usual requirements of
work. I don't mind work, never have. My life has never been
easy (though it certainly could have been harder), and I've never
expected it to be otherwise.

But sometimes you wonder if maybe it couldn't be just a little bit easier.

Caring for Martha Sr those last weeks was more demanding, and lasted longer than anyone expected. Getting hit with the flu so hard afterward seemed a bit gratuitous, in the sense of the universe having fun at our expense. Both my wife and I are behind on our work, and while our clients understand, that doesn't help the cash flow situation. I knew these days would come, and things would be a little rough for a while until we got settled again. But we'll manage.

* * *

We did a hard thing, and we did it well.

What has come of a bit of surprise has been how some people have responded to that. There's been some discord in the family about the disposition of Martha Sr's possessions, borne mostly out of a misguided sense of guilt, from what I can tell. It's really unfortunate, but everyone has their own way of reacting to death. If we're lucky, with time the matter will sort itself out with a minimal amount of damage.

I've also seen others in different forums who have almost felt like they had to defend their own decisions regarding a loved one who has Alzheimer's or some other debilitating illness leading to hospice care. I've witnessed those who almost seem resentful that we did what we did, because it somehow implies that they did less – that they cared less.

No. We were able to make this work out. Barely. Everyone has a different situation, and each family, each person, must come to their own conclusions, their own solutions. None is better or worse than another. Because my wife and I don't have kids, we didn't have to juggle that aspect of life at the same time. Because we live here in the same town as Martha Sr, and have professions which allow a considerable flexibility in terms of work hours, we were better able to adapt to providing care at home than most. Our solution worked for our situation – barely. Those final months were very demanding, and I will admit that I was pushed further than I would have thought was possible, and failed and succeeded in ways I never expected.

I will not judge another – this experience has taught me humility.

(Jim's blog. 2/28/08)
Transitions

Last night, my wife washed off the blackboard which hangs in the kitchen.

* * *

I just got back from a quick trip to KC to pick up the first large load of books from the seminary. Simple. Got up this morning, usual routine, jumped in the car and drove to KC. Met with the client. Selected about 60 volumes to start with, wrapped them in cling film, boxed 'em up. Put the boxes in the car, drove home, pausing to check out a new store just off the highway – and amazing myself that I didn't have to call home to coordinate the slight delay.

* * *

I sent this note to a friend:

> *Mostly I've been getting work done, at least in the afternoons. Feels good to be able to focus in and do it – a nice affirmation, and there is that joy that comes with doing something well which most people can't do. Still struggling to shake off the last effects of the flu, which is annoying, but there is clear progress.*

> *And that has been the real change this week. Each afternoon I've been able to just dive in and work. For hours. Very productively. Such a change.*

* * *

It's the little things. Yes, there are the larger changes: more sleep, no need to go around always listening to a monitor, being able to come and go as I please. Those I expected, even if they have taken some adjustment. But it's the little things that catch you unprepared.

Last night, Martha washed off the blackboard which hangs in the kitchen.

The blackboard which for years had our contact phone numbers on it. Those were first put there by Martha Sr years ago, when her memory was becoming undependable and she might need to call someone for help. Then they remained even once we moved in here, since both my wife and I still had our jobs elsewhere during the day. After I closed my gallery and moved home that was no longer the need, but by then they were an institution. More recently, long after Martha Sr had stopped using the phone, the numbers were there as a quick resource for the various respite care workers and whatnot, in the event of an emergency.

Last night, my wife washed it clean. It was time to move on.

(Jim's blog. 3/3/08)
Feeling small

Seems a bit ridiculous for someone 6'2" and pushing 250 pounds to be "feeling small," but that's about the best characterization of my emotional state today. Bit of a headache, some intestinal issues – not 'sick' exactly, but just under the weather.

And what weather. What was mostly sunny and near 70 yesterday and Saturday is cold, grey, wet and very unpleasant today. 35 for the high, sleet/freezing rain this afternoon and snow scheduled for tonight and tomorrow. The kind of day that makes the cats curl up on the radiators and refuse to budge.

Both Martha and I are feeling this. I think it is just part of the natural let-down, the ebb & flow of recovery from being care-providers for so long, of grieving. I cross-posted the transitions post (with some additional explanatory material) to Daily Kos yesterday, and it generated some really good discussion. But I think it left me feeling a bit wrung-out. For the longest time I have been able to attribute any mild depression or exhaustion to the stress and demands of care-giving, but the fact remains that I do have a mild bipolar condition. I suspect that for a while things are just going to oscillate before reaching some kind of equilibrium once again.

So, take it a bit easy today. Maybe go watch Blade Runner or something this morning, then see if I can accomplish some more conservation work this afternoon. One step at a time.

(John's blog, 3/11/2008)
What I've Been Up To . . .

For over a month now, I've been trying to assemble a piece in tribute to Georgia that tied together some music with some of the memories that those tunes invoked.

I've finally completed it, in two parts: *Stir of Echoes* and *Musical Deconstruction of a Life's Worth of Memories*:

Stir of Echoes

> *Sometimes within the brain's old*
> *ghostly house,*
> *I hear, far off, at some forgotten*
> *door,*
> *A music and an eerie faint carouse*
> *And stir of echoes down the*
> *creaking floor.*
> – Archibald Macleish, "Chambers of Imagery" [13]

Kathi's mother – my mother-in-law – passed away December 19th, 2007, at the nursing home where she had lived for less than a year. I affectionately referred to her as "Mumsie" and had served as her primary caretaker from the day Kathi and I married until the time we moved her into the nursing home. Truth to tell, I continued the role even afterward, working to ensure due diligence in her care and facilitate understanding and communications between Georgia, the staff and us.

The house felt quiet, somewhat empty, when we moved Georgia to the nursing home. I felt somewhat empty, somewhat relieved, and a little as though I had betrayed not just a friend but a person who had grown to depend upon me to be there to help her.

There are so many ways to second guess the decisions one makes in life, regardless of whether it pertains to something major or minor. With major decisions – those which impact not just your life but the lives of others – the tendency to second-guess can explode exponentially into a multitude of "what-ifs" and "if onlys" until the mind and spirit strain under the weight.

We were spared some of this.

Some of it.

We missed Georgia, but were no longer able to care for her at home without assistance, and we didn't qualify for the assistance we needed. It was the best thing we could do to ensure the high level of care we'd established for her, albeit at a cost of a level of interaction that I still regret today.

In the aftermath of her passing, as days stretched into weeks and the weeks into months, we've come to believe that she gently lingers with us in both memories unbidden and incidents of awkward recognition – her life spirit, echoing through the halls of body, mind and abode. It is a reassuring feeling, comforting on several levels even while a touch spooky and otherworldly.

* * *

A minor New England Haunting

Animals are uncanny in their ability to discern unseen changes in life around them, as well to apparently determine when one of their human family has passed beyond the veil of mortal life. Both our dogs Ember and Jack have reacted to us as though they realize that Georgia has passed; Jack, the younger but much larger dog, appeared to sense it more keenly. Perhaps it was due to his own experience with death, or perhaps due to the oddly coincidental nature of his own arrival in our lives. Whatever it was, from the very night that Georgia had passed, he's been spooked about going into her room, a room that he formerly always tried to get into.

He acted as though someone was there, and was freaked that he couldn't see the person. In addition to the animals, both Kathi and I have experienced a few interesting moments.

Initially, after Georgia's passing, we'd kept her bedroom door shut most of the time. Part of this – most of the reason, initially – was to avoid reminding Kathi of her mom by confronting her with the open door to her mother's room, particularly at night. Now, it's open most of the time except when it's really cold outside, when we need to try and conserve heat. But the door, when shut, didn't always stay shut. Sometimes, when Kathi or I would walk by it, it would pop open just the way it did when Georgia would apply a little strength to the knob to unstick it and pull sharply. The first time it happened to either of us, we each jumped nearly out of our skins. Sometimes, when all of us are downstairs, we'll hear someone moving around in Georgia's room upstairs, sounding just like she did when we'd all still lived here – long before she'd had to go to the nursing home. The first time this happened, I thought it was either Jack or Kathi, until I turned and saw Jack next to me. Ember was on Kathi's normal chair in the living room, so I called out to Kathi to ask her what she's doing, and she answered from the computer room around the corner – thus accounting for everyone in the house, and leaving me momentarily dumbstruck about the footsteps pitter-pattering 'round up in Georgia's room. Sometimes, we hear something fall as though it was knocked over. At first, still raw with grieving, Kathi was very upset by these events. She wrote about them elsewhere, but made an explicit reference to some of the creaking:

> *My husband, the dogs, and I jump when we hear the creaks in the kitchen ceiling. Above is Mom's bedroom. Her door slams shut and randomly pops open. I run upstairs and slam it shut, wedging a chair under the knob. "What if she wants to come out?" my husband asks.*

Kathi didn't find the question amusing in the least.

We made it through our first Christmas without Georgia, then the first New Year, and the end of January brought Georgia's birthday – the first one without her to blow out the candles. "The Firsts" are always hard, learning to adapt to the unexpected absence of a loved one and to retrain the body, mind and spirit to acknowledge the loss, incorporate it and continue.

I recall something Kathi had written, similar to our stream of consciousness memorial to her mother, about making it through difficult periods by operating in an almost otherworldly form of autopilot. Her thoughts, about the day of her mother's funeral:

> *I'm numb, but the show must go on. You get dressed in the same outfit that you wore to the wake – black-and-white tweed jacket, fuchsia turtleneck wool pullover, black pants, black boots. You do last night's dishes. You check your websites, hoping there's nothing to answer because you really don't want to deal with questions or condolences right now. The car will be picking you*

up in a few minutes. Your husband is upstairs getting dressed. The dogs know something's going on, so they hunker down, looking at you to make sure you're OK. Everything's ready. The car pulls up. The driver, Fred, is a neighbor, whose wife was friendly with your mother. You used to play kickball with his daughters. You arrive at the funeral home. The pallbearers and secretary greet you and lead you to Mom. Guests arrive for the morning prayers. You're asked to go to the car so Al, the director, can line up the procession to church. Inside you know that somebody's closing the lid. Mom always disliked the dark, but there is nothing you can do. You sit in the back seat making random conversation. You think of premature burial and the subsequent horror, but you also know that once the mortician drains the bodily fluids, there's no way anyone can remain alive. Then you think of how comatose your mother was the last day and a half of her life and how, basically, on her last day, she was a breathing corpse. You bite your lip and stare out the window.

The show must go on. No stopping and getting off, no slowing the ride down – just sometimes disengaging your direct conscious participation or focusing it elsewhere. Next month will be the first time my wife and I will celebrate our wedding anniversary without Georgia. We'll have been married five years. Sometimes, "first" sucks. Nary a day goes by that doesn't contain within it some echo of Georgia, particularly for Kathi. Her mother was a constant presence in her life for over forty-odd years; the simplest of things, from daily chores to simply crossing into the kitchen, evoke a flood of memories. Kathi was experiencing this for the second time in her life – the first time, the loss of her father when she was only thirteen poked a hole in her routine that her mind and heart tried to wrap itself around:

After Daddy died, I used to perch in my chair at the kitchen table, turned toward the side door. I would look up at the clock above the sink. Daddy always left work by 3 PM at the very latest and be home before 4 because there was no way he'd let himself get caught during rush hour. He'd bang open the side door, up the stairs and into the kitchen, kissing Mama hello then telling her whatever deals he and Joe had done during the day.

I sat there every day waiting for him. He'd arrive in his favorite navy suit, the suit we'd buried him in. He'd look exactly the same way he did before the cancer ravaged his body. I'd jump up and run up to him, hoping that he'd pick me up and whirl me around like he did when I was very little. Of course I knew he really wouldn't show up. He was in a big metal box six feet under the surface of sacred ground in a town near where Mom grew up. But that didn't mean there was a chance he couldn't show up. Stranger things had happened...why not Daddy?

That one event – the loss of her father to cancer – shaped the life that she and her mother built from that point forward. It was a loss that dealt them a harsh blow, but they muddled on through it, through the pain and the loss, for each other. Now, Kathi finds herself coping with the loss her mom, an event she dreaded even with her understanding that this was how life was meant to be – parents raise children, children grow to adulthood, parents age and pass onward, and the cycle continues across the ages for as long as there are parents and children to perpetuate it.

Of course you have a totally different perspective as an adult. You know that once there is death, that's it. Nobody will come walking through the side door looking exactly as they did in their prime. You will never hear the voice in real time again. No more hugs, no more touches (or, in Mom's case, back scritches). You feel vaguely disconnected, as though you're floating in space like a balloon with only a slender line tethering you to somewhere unseen far below. You're somewhat comfortable with this vague space place, which even makes you more disconnected. And that big unspoken empty place deep in your gut. It's the place some people mention, but nobody can truly describe.

When somebody has been a fixture in your life for decades, their disappearance makes you even more disconnected. I come home from work. My husband and the dogs are upstairs, but once my hand starts to open the kitchen door, I expect to see Mom at the sink or doing the Herald cryptoquote at the table. If I stumble downstairs with a basket of laundry, I first wonder why the light isn't already on, then, as I descend the basement stairs – Mom? Where are you Mom?" Oh, there you are, folding my socks! Or repotting your plants! Or rewiring one of your lamps! Mom? Mom?

At one point during our care-giving of Georgia, shortly before we had to turn to the nursing home for assistance, Georgia had asked Kathi if she remembered her father. Kathi answered carefully, honestly but with an eye toward guarding Georgia's feelings. Her memories of her father were fading, and we thought Georgia was partly concerned that Kathi's memories of her would fade too. Georgia knew that her life was coming to an end, and she didn't want to be forgotten.

Toward that end, she also tried to convince Kathi to bury her in the local cemetery instead of the plot that she held where her mother and her husband were buried; she was afraid we'd never visit her.

In the same breath, sometimes, she'd also threaten to never leave.

As I mentally review the various and sundry strange events and incidents that have occurred since she passed on, I can't help grinning to think that she has found a way to make good on her threat – her promise.

* * *

Music and Memories

Georgia was always a big fan of Hollywood movies and Broadway musicals. In addition to those, she was a fan of classical music – a big fan. One of the ways I kept her mind engaged while care-giving had involved taking an old popular song and making up whole new lyrics to them. Sometimes, the tune and lyrics were catchy enough that in spite of the advanced Alzheimer's Disease, Georgia would occasionally break out into spontaneous bits of the tunes. Music plays a big role in life and in memory; there's mathematics in music – structure, elegance and sweeping beauty that evokes powerful emotion and tells epic tales. "Fearful symmetry" and the "Music of the Spheres" combine, often stretching to the limits of the extreme and the sublime. When I write or tell a story, I often tie certain key, complex scenes to a piece of music so that I can assist my ability to remember it whenever needed. This has helped when I've lost all my paper and electronic backups of stories, and had to recreate from scratch. It has also helped me with regard to my memories of Georgia. I composed a play list for this piece, in fact, that helps me recall aspects of my life, inter-action and observations of life with Georgia and Kathi. Different parts of the different songs each called out to a specific set of memories of Georgia, of Kathi and of the life we shared or the life they'd shared preceding my arrival. Here's the playlist:

> *Unwell* by Matchbox Twenty
> *Mother* by Pink Floyd
> *Nobody Home* by Pink Floyd
> *Ice Cream* by Sarah McLachlan
> *Wish You Were Here* by Pink Floyd
> *Hold On* by Sarah McLachlan
> *Speak To Me / Breathe* by Pink Floyd
> *Angel* by Sarah McLachlan
> *Here With Me* by Dido
> *Someone to Watch Over Me* (written by Gershwin,
>   performed by Sinatra)
> *Silent Lucidity* by Queensryche
> *I Will Remember You* by Sarah McLachlan
> *Elsewhere* by Sarah McLachlan
> *Is There Anybody Out There?* by Pink Floyd
> *Learning to Fly* by Pink Floyd
> *Fly Me To The Moon* by Bobby Darin (and sometimes the
>   Frank Sinatra version)

The words in the lyrics and the melody of the music, taken together, evoke memories and build a picture of Georgia's presence and her life that – from my perspective – will always help me to remember her with warmth and a smile. The playlist now serves as my own personal invocation to a stir of echoes close to my heart and soul.

* * *

Musical Deconstruction of a Life's Worth of Memories

Georgia had confided in me, more than once, that she was afraid that she had kept Kathi from living her own life; that was one of the major ironic conflicts within her. She didn't want to be alone, but didn't want her daughter to lose out on living a full and complete life. She couldn't understand why Kathi hadn't married before now and why she wasn't going to have any children – Georgia wanted Kathi to have someone to watch over her when she got old, particularly because women live longer than men. (She didn't mean to dismiss me so easily, but she was being practical.) Kathi screamed the moment the phone rang at the house when the nursing home called to tell us Georgia had passed, even before I'd answered it.

For some reason, the song "Silent Lucidity" by Queensryche[14] began to echo in my head.

> There's a place I like to hide
> A doorway that I run through in the night

The strange echoes that reverberate through the house and within our minds reflect the sense that those who have departed the physical form of life may yet linger among us, keeping an eye on us from their special otherworldly location. Kathi had experienced something like this before, although she now speaks of it as if it was probably just the overactive imagination of a child:

> When my uncle – Mom's oldest brother who lived with us – died, I moved into his tiny bedroom off the upstairs bathroom. I don't know why I did. My bedroom was twice as large and perfectly fine. Maybe I was afraid he'd be forgotten, and the only way I

could honor him was to sleep in his room. A couple of months later, as I fell asleep, I suddenly bolted with the feeling that something was watching me. The curtains next to the bed made shimmering shadows from the streetlight. Toward the door, for a split second, stood a shadow in my uncle's shape. I jerked. The shadow disappeared. I never fell asleep that night.

We also had several strange happenings occur shortly after our oldest dog, Missy the Malamute, passed away – now nearly two years ago. Georgia and Missy had established a very strong bond over the years they were together. In many ways, Georgia's ability to remember Missy a year after we'd said our final goodbyes made it seem as though the big dog was still looking in on her from wherever she was.

I- will be watching over you
I- am gonna help you see it through [14]

Now, as we find ourselves – and the dogs – reacting to Georgia-like sounds and bumps in the night, we are comforted more than spooked by the thought that our home may yet offer comfort to the spirit of those who have gone before, and give them an opportunity to keep an eye on us from their special vantage point.

There's a somebody I'm longing to see
I hope that she turns out to be
Someone who'll watch over me
– Someone to Watch Over Me (Gershwin / Sinatra)[15]

We found special significance to this song after Missy had passed away; now, with the thought that Missy had been watching over both us and Georgia, and now had Georgia safely with her, the song provides me with a sense of quiet security that both Missy and Georgia may yet be keeping an eye on us all.

Kathi wondered aloud once if, since she was having difficulty calling her father's face to mind, he would still remember her when she dies. The words from Sara McLachlan's "I Will Remember You"[16] come to mind:

I will remember you
Will you remember me?

Sometimes, the thought of being forgotten can hurt us even more deeply than the thought of death.

It's funny how we feel so much but we cannot say a word
We are screaming inside, but we can't be heard

Kathi lost her mom twice – first to the wasting of Alzheimer's Disease, and then to the physical passing from this realm. Since the funeral, however, she's found something interesting and – at times – a little unsettling: she hears her mother's voice in her head as she goes through her day.

I catch myself doing something the exact way she did it. I cut sausages into disks and sauté them for spaghetti sauce. I pile the dirty dishes on the counter and wash them in order. I'll suddenly get a burst of energy and do x number of chores at once, not stopping until I silently hear her voice:

"What the heck are you doing? Will you PLEASE RELAX AND STOP WORRYING? You're NOT me! That's MY job!"

Her voice follows me from walking the dogs to work to talking with people and back. The funny thing is that now I can confide in her, something I was never able to do while she was bodily here. Until the Alzheimer's softened her spirit, she was an indomitable force you never, ever questioned. I spent most of my childhood cowering before her. Mama, what should I do? I don't know what to do.

"You know what to do."

No I don't! Why aren't you here?

"I am here. Why didn't you ask me when you were younger?"

Because I was afraid of you.

"I'm sorry, baby. I never realized that until after you were an adult. I love you. I kept forgetting you were just a kid."

Kathi found it odd, at first, but now finds the voice of her mother within her to be a comfort. She's not sure if it's simply her own mind providing the comfort, but in the long run – does that matter?

"You're never going to forget me. I'm going to be here until the day you join me."

Yes, Mama, I know.

"[You may think that] My job may be done where you are, but it's not."

I know.

"If it bothers you, I can go away. I can play bridge with your uncles or spend time with Daddy or chat with my girlfriends."

I've already lost you twice, Mama. I don't want to lose you again.

It was a mental and emotional tug-of-war within Kathi that was captured by another Sarah McLachlan song, "Elsewhere":[17]

can't you see I've got to
live my life the way I feel is
right for me

With Georgia tucked up inside her heart, her soul and mind, Kathi can now move onward, growing and changing and becoming without fear of leaving her mother behind or forgotten. The next three songs, taken collectively instead of individually, pertain to

Georgia's new existence in my mind. Tentatively at first, she casts about to become familiar with her new surroundings...reminiscent of "Is There Anybody Out There?" by Pink Floyd

As she's getting her bearings, she comes home here to check in on us, grounding herself in a sense before spreading her wings...again, bringing to mind another Pink Floyd song, "Learning to Fly."

Once she's got a feel for it, she's off – the song "Fly Me To The Moon" was a favorite of her husband's and reminiscent of the songs and music that Georgia enjoyed all her life; I like to think that whenever she's not popping back here for a visit that she's off visiting her husband, her parents, her friends and – of course – playing bridge with her brothers, who have long been saving a place for her at their table. In the meantime, Kathi and I listen to the songs and music that lead to the stir of echoes within the walls of this house and the hallowed, haunting chambers of imagery within our minds.

And so I throw the windows wide
And call to you across the sky... [18]

(Jim's blog. 4/11/08)
Grief

It is enlightening, if sometimes dismaying, to discover what sorts of things motivate people. I have found that one of the most reliable ways of doing this is to see what sorts of motivations they perceive in others – what motives they attribute for a given behavior.

Case in point: our caring for Martha Sr. I had mentioned previously that there was some discord in the family about the distribution of her estate. And what at the time seemed to be a misplaced guilt (that still may be the base motivation, actually) causing this has now manifested as a perception that we cared for her over the last five years out of some financial motivation. Yes, it seems that some people thought that we did what we did in order to benefit from a more favorable disbursement of her estate.

Sigh This is so wrong that it took me a while to really wrap my head around it.

As I told a friend via email this morning:

> *Needless to say, this is not why we did what we did – honestly, no amount of money (well, no reasonable amount of money) would be sufficient inducement for me to have cared for someone like that for so long. It was done out of love – for her, and for my wife.*

And I've been thinking more about it. Why? Because I like to understand my own motivations, and to keep them as honest and clean as possible. I'm an idealist, and try to approach the world that way, knowing full well that the world is not an ideal place and that reality will likely not be kind to my approach. When my motivations are questioned, either directly or by events, I like to step back and reconsider – and will make changes if necessary to insure that my motives are clear.

We were favored by Martha Sr in her will. Not to a great degree – the value of it was less than I could have earned in the intervening years, had I been working rather than caring for her. And it was considerably less than would have been spent on either hiring full time care-givers, or moving her into a nursing home for that time. But because this additional benefit was there, some made the assumption that this was our motivation for caring for her. And this has caused the discord mentioned above.

So, after discussing the matter with my wife, we're going to wipe out the benefit, just split up her estate equally and without consideration. It is not worth the grief. We didn't do what we did for money or property – we did it because it was the right thing to do, and we could. Removing the benefit should resolve in anyone's mind what our motivation was.

Everyone grieves in their own way. We may have wiped the slate clean, but that doesn't mean that the grieving process is over. Not by a long shot. There are still sympathy cards on the mantelpiece. There is still a sudden slight panic over where the monitor is when I forget for a moment that Martha Sr is gone. There is guilt over the times we failed in some way, and joy over memories of happy moments Martha Sr had even in those final difficult days. And there is a profound gratitude I feel in having experienced this role of being a care-provider.

I think that I am richer for this experience than others who have not been through it. I sometimes wonder whether the tendency to put people in nursing homes is partially done out of a fear of grieving – to create a distance from a loved one who is reaching the end of life, and so to mitigate the pain of loss. If so, those who take that path have indeed curtailed the amount of pain that they would feel, perhaps even cut short the time needed to completely grieve. But they have also cut themselves off from a remarkable human experience.

(Jim's blog. 4/16/08)
Funky

Sorry I haven't posted much the last couple of days. Honestly, I am in a funk – the sort of deep-seated inertia which comes after completing a protracted project. On one level, it is just the down-turn from the ballistics testing project I was working on with a couple of friends. But more, it is the still lingering exhaustion from care-giving.

Which is not surprising. You can't expect to recover from years of poor sleep and intensely caring for someone else 24 hours a day in just a few weeks. Particularly not when we're still very much dealing with resolution of the estate (strangers are here right now going through things, giving us estimates on the value of some items) and trying to play catch up on professional and personal obligations. We collapsed immediately following the memorial service for Martha Sr, but then tried to pretend that we were recovered, to get on with the life which had been put on hold for so long.

But now it feels like it is catching up with me again. Like how a battery can get a 'surface charge' quickly, but also wears out again quickly. I need a prolonged period of recovery and recuperation. That, however, is not likely to happen. There are books to repair, bills to pay, years worth of things to catch up on.

So, forgive the slight break. I'm not burned out – I still have a lot to say, to do, to write about here. I'm just tired.

(Jim's blog. 4/29/08)
A personal triumph I thought I'd share

This afternoon I was getting ready to take some books back to Special Collections at MU, and since it was still a bit cool out, thought I'd toss on a nice leather vest I have. This is a vest which was a gift a couple of years ago, designed for concealed carry, and which I find to be very useful for other purposes as well. Anyway, I put it on, and noticed something...it felt a little loose.

Hmm.

Now, I knew I had been shedding weight since Martha Sr had died, as a natural function of getting regular sleep, more exercise, and not eating to excess as a function of stress. Pants fit better, I'd taken my belt in a couple of notches, all those sorts of things.

But this vest was a new one. For the first time in a couple of years, I could actually button the thing up, and it felt comfortable. Excellent.

I have no illusions about getting back into the sort of shape I was twenty years ago, when I was literally in "fighting trim." But in the last three months I've probably shed close to thirty pounds. If I can lose another twenty, I'll be happy – thirty would be just about ideal, particularly if I can change some of what remains from fat and slack muscle into toned muscle.

Anyway, just a small personal triumph I thought I would share.

(Jim's blog. 5/8/08)
Sleep is the default

It's now been three months since Martha Sr died.

You'd think by now that I'd be caught up on sleep. You'd be wrong. As I look over the last few month's posts I note that time and again that I mention sleep. It is still the default that I want more, more, more. Even when I've gotten a good night's sleep, and am not fighting any kind of cold or flu, a nap in the morning or afternoon tempts me. For someone who thinks of himself as energetic, productive, it kind of goes against the grain. For someone who has a backlog of work running to years, it can be a little maddening.

Yet, sleep is still the default.

* * *

My sister called the other day.

"Thirty pounds? Wow. Be careful."

I assured her that I wasn't trying to overdo anything. That it was just my body moving back towards a natural set-point, as mentioned in that blog post.

But she has a good reason to be concerned: in our family, weight loss is one of the markers for the onset of the family genetic curse, Machado-Joseph disease. To be honest, this is one of the major reasons that I have always felt a little comfort in being a bit over-weight – it provided some sense of protection against the disease (which was very poorly understood or even known as I was growing up). That's not how it works, of course, but it was always there in the back of my mind. If you'd lived with seeing what the disease does, you'd be willing to risk obesity, too.

* * *

Go back to any of the entries from last year under the tag Alzheimer's, and you'll see that one of the most common things I talk about is just how tired I was. For years – literally, years – my wife and I had taken turns being "on call" each night, lightly dozing while listening to a baby monitor in Martha Sr's room. On those nights we'd barely get anything which amounted to real rest. When we weren't "on call" sleep usually came, but wasn't as easy or restful as it could have been – having your partner there more or less awake next to you all night wasn't that conducive. Sure, there were naps whenever we could squeeze them in, but I would still say that my average sleep per 24 hour period was probably about 5 hours, maybe 6. Things did improve once we had a health aide three nights a week, but by then we were in hospice care, which had its own stresses and demands.

* * *

From Yahoo News yesterday:

People who sleep fewer than six hours a night — or more than nine — are more likely to be obese, according to a new government study that is one of the largest to show a link between irregular sleep and big bellies.

* * *

The research adds weight to a stream of studies that have found obesity and other health problems in those who don't get proper shuteye, said Dr. Ron Kramer, a Colorado physician and a spokesman for the American Academy of Sleep Medicine.

"The data is all coming together that short sleepers and long sleepers don't do so well," Kramer said.

The study released Wednesday is based on door-to-door surveys of 87,000 U.S. adults from 2004 through 2006 conducted by the National Center for Health Statistics, part of the Centers for Disease Control and Prevention.

Surprise, surprise.

* * *

I've got a pretty strong work ethic. And it was shaped by conventional standards: get up, go to work for 8 -10 hours, come home. That's not how I work – hasn't been for years – but it is still the baseline instinct for me, the initial criteria I use for whether or not I am "getting things done." So it is frustrating to feel sleepy and want a nap. That doesn't pay the bills, get the backlog under control, get the next book written or the ballistics research written up.

Three months. Seems like a long time. And our culture doesn't understand grief well, nor leave a lot of room for recovery that takes time. We expect people to "get over it," to take a vacation and come back refreshed. It is part of who we are – part of who I am.

But I try to listen to my body. It is naturally shedding the excess weight I put on, now that regular sleep and exercise are again part of my life. Realistically, it is only halfway done – I've another 30 pounds or so to go to get back to a point which I consider 'normal' (though that's still about 20 - 30 pounds heavy for me, according to the 'ideal'). Does that mean I have another three months of wanting naps all the time? Yeah, maybe. Maybe more. I'll try and give it that time.

I'll try.

(Jim's blog. 6/24/08)
Detox

I worked over six hours yesterday. Yeah, I took a few breaks, but still. Something of a milestone.

* * *

Humans are remarkably adaptive creatures. We can adjust to a wide range of environmental conditions, accommodate significant changes in diet, accept shifts in social structure. Just look around the world and you'll see what I mean, from variations in culture in response to climate to how people cope with extreme conditions such as war and famine.

There can be a toll to such adaptations, of course, depending on what they are, how long they last, and the particular individual or society.

In caring for Martha Sr I slowly changed my routine and focus to better meet her needs, so most of the changes I went through in that time were barely discernible from day to day. Over the four plus years of intense care-giving, however, both my wife and I underwent a very substantial shift in what could be considered our normal life.

I've mentioned some of those changes previously – the weight gain, the loss of concentration, the lack of sleep. But I haven't discussed the operative mechanism behind all those changes: stress. Specifically, the physiological changes in hormonal balance which come with prolonged stress – the so called stress hormones of cortisol and norepinephrine. Most people know these as the 'fight or flight' reflex effects: boost in blood pressure and heart rate, heightened sensory awareness, a slight time dilation. It is our body's way of preparing us to survive a threatening situation. It is a very powerful experience, and can even be a bit addictive – anyone who characterizes themselves as an 'adrenaline junkie', who gets a kick out of doing dangerous things or watching scary movies, is talking about just that.

The problem is, those stress hormones come with a price – they exact a toll on the body. For most people, occasional jolts of this stuff isn't really dangerous, but for someone with a heart condition or an aneurysm waiting to blow, such an event can kill. That's why you see those warning signs on roller coasters.

And consider what happens to someone who slowly ramps up their stress hormone levels over a prolonged period. That's me. My formerly excellent blood pressure and heart rate is now scary bad, and has been for a while. I'm lucky that I started this in good condition – but think back to the episode last year when I wrote "Beats Having a Heart Attack," and you'll see what kind of effect the excessive stress hormone levels had. In the final year of care-giving, my system became saturated with stress hormones – my 'fight or flight' reflex changed from being related to a sudden threat to being an ongoing condition. I adapted.

So now I am in detox. That's what the last few months have been all about. Slowly adapting back to something resembling normal, at a very basic physiological level. More sleep. More exercise. Better diet. As I've discussed recently, I have started to see some real changes. But as a good friend who is also a doctor reminded me recently, it will likely take a year or longer to make this transition, for my endocrine system to settle down. Recently I have taken some additional steps to help this process, in terms of changes to diet and food supplements. But it is a long and winding road I need to walk now.

* * *

I got up about 3:30 this morning for a potty run. Stepping from our bedroom into the bathroom, I froze: there was a light coming up from the downstairs that shouldn't have been there. I quietly backed into the bedroom, put on pants and glasses, grabbed my cell phone, a pistol and a powerful flashlight.

I'm no 'macho guy' or wanna-be hero. The smart thing to do if you have an intruder in your house is to batten down the hatches where you are, call 911, and let the police deal with it.

But what if you just left a light on by accident?

I was about 90% sure that was what happened. So, carefully, I went to investigate. Checked the house completely. Everything was safe and secure. The cats were confused by what I was doing up so early.

I went back upstairs, hit the head, put away the various items I'd picked up, and crawled back into bed.

And have been awake since.

After an hour or so, I just got up. Because I knew I wasn't getting back to sleep anytime soon. That's the problem – the stress hormone receptors in my brain are so adapted to a regular high dose of adrenal squeezin's that they hungrily lap the stuff up when it comes their way.

* * *

I worked over six hours yesterday. Yeah, I took a few breaks, but still. Something of a milestone.

Six hours may not sound like a lot. After all, most people are expected to work eight or more hours at a time, with a couple of paltry breaks.

But for me, regaining the ability to focus in, to concentrate and work for that length of time is a real improvement. It shows that I am making progress in detoxifying my system, of readjusting the endocrine balance.

Today is going to be a bit of a bitch, though, thanks to the early-morning jolt of adrenaline. But I know how to handle it, and hopefully it won't cause too much back sliding. We'll see.

The road is long and winding, and I must take it where it leads.

(Jim's blog. 7/17/08)
More tears

Been a long week. I mentioned the other day that it had been a rough day for me personally. That was the 37th anniversary of my mom's death in a car accident. It's always an emotional day, but it hit me harder this year than it has for a long time, probably because of Martha Sr's death early this year.

In addition to that, we're in the midst of doing a massive re-arranging of the house, following the division of the household possessions. It's more than a bit of a juggling act, because at the same time we're having to deal with things still here that no one in the family wanted. The chaos of having my home environment thus disrupted is hard on me, but the whole thing is harder on my wife, who now has the unenviable task of going through all her mom's remaining things and deciding what to do with it all. Because with each dress, each photograph, each trinket, there is emotion, made tangible. To shed these things feels a little bit like abandoning the memory of her mom.

* * *

Whew.

I just finished going through and editing all the posts related to caring for Martha Sr, up to her death. It's something I've been working on the last couple of days, part of the preparation for getting that material in shape to be a book I am collaborating on with someone else (more on that later).

Almost a hundred posts. Something like 40,000 words.

And an untold number of tears.

Wow. She was a remarkable woman. It was a phenomenally rewarding experience. I hope that I am able to convey that. I hope that what I have to say will help others get through, perhaps even to cherish, the time they spend caring for a loved one this way.

But for now, I'll have a drink, and cry.

(Jim's blog. 7/22/08)
"...we were not alone..."

I mentioned in passing last week that I was working on all my care-giving posts for a book. Here's a bit more about that project, as it is tentatively shaping up.

Sometime last year, when I cross-posted one of those entries on Daily Kos, I discovered that there was someone else there who was in pretty much the exact same situation: caring for a beloved mother-in-law. For a variety of reasons, it is fairly unusual to find a man caring for a mother-in-law with dementia. We didn't strike up what I would call a friendship, since both of us were preoccupied with the tasks at hand, but we did develop something of a kinship, commenting back and forth in one another's diaries on that site. Our paths diverged – he and his wife eventually needed to get his mother-in-law into a care-facility, whereas my wife and I were able to keep Martha Sr home until the end. But the parallels were made all the more striking by those slight differences. In the end, his "Georgia" passed away about six weeks before Martha Sr died.

Recently this fellow and I picked up the thread of our occasional conversation once again. And discovered that both of us, independently, had been thinking of writing up a book about the experience of care-giving. It didn't take long before we realized that together we could produce a more comprehensive book, and a lot more easily, drawing on our individual experiences to show similarities and different choices. A few quick emails sorted out the pertinent details – basic structure of the book, that a portion of the proceeds from it will go to the Alzheimer's Association (or them and other related organizations), some thoughts on publishing and promotion – and we were off and running.

For now, I'll just identify him by his first name: John. By way of introduction, check out this excellent post of his at ePluribus Media, where he very neatly explains the *why* of our decision to write this book:

> *Special thanks to Jim Downey for the supplying the links to the video and to his blog, and just for being him; my wife and I took comfort from the fact that we were not alone in our situation, and that we knew at least one other couple who were going through a very similar experience to our own.*

That's it right there. Millions of Americans are facing this situation today, and millions more will in coming years as the baby-boomer generation ages. I'm not a scientist who can help find a cure to the diseases of age-related dementia. I'm not wealthy and able to make a significant difference in funding such research. But I can perhaps help others to understand the experience. John and I are going to try, anyway. I know that my wife and I found comfort in knowing that we were not alone in this. So did he and his wife. If we can share that with others, and make their experience a little more understandable, a little easier, then that will be a worthy thing.

Wish us luck.

(Jim's blog. 7/24/08)
The choices we make

Almost a year ago I wrote this:

> *There's a phenomenon familiar to those who deal with Alzheimer's. It's called "sundowning." There are a lot of theories about why*

it happens, my own pet one is that someone with this disease works damned hard all day long to try and make sense of the world around them (which is scrambled to their perceptions and understanding), and by late in the afternoon or early evening, they're just worn out. You know how you feel at the end of a long day at work? Same thing.

* * *

We cared for Martha Sr for about four years. Well, we were here helping her for a couple of years prior to that. But the nearly constant care-giving lasted for about four, growing in intensity during that time, culminating with nearly six months of actual hospice care.

That was a long time. But my wife and I had each other, and it could have been longer. From a piece titled "Hospice"[19] that ran on Weekend America on 7/26/08:

> *That same day, a hospice patient named Michelle passed away. She was only 50 years old. She'd been battling MS for over 20 years. Debra is dispatched to her home.*
>
> *The little brown house is shrouded by trees. Stray cats eat free food on the rusted red porch. Inside, Michelle lies in her hospital bed with her eyes slightly open. Debra's there to help Michelle's husband Ross. He quit his job in 2000 to take care of his wife.*
>
> *"So eight years," Debra says.*
>
> *"She was permanently bedridden," Ross replies. "This is the way it's been. But like everything in life, it all comes to an end I guess."*
>
> *His voice sounds steady when he speaks, but his eyes are full of tears as he remembers his wife.*
>
> *"I've never seen a women fight something like she did," Ross*

*says. "She spent years on that walker because she knew when she
got in a chair she'd never get out. The pain it caused her."*

*Ross talks for more than an hour. Debra listens and commiser-
ates. It's at these moments, even more than when she's providing
medical care, that Debra feels her work is appreciated.*

Appreciated, indeed.

(Jim's blog. 7/28/08)
Stress? What Stress?

Some years back a good friend sent me a postcard from Florida
with the image of a tri-colored heron's head. On the card, the
heron is looking straight at you, top feathers standing straight up,
and above it in bright blue 'electric' lettering are the words
"Stress? What Stress?"

It's been tacked to the wall next to my desk here since. And it
has been something of a standing joke between my wife and I.
When things have gotten bad from time to time, one of us will
turn to the other and simply say in a squeaky, high pitched voice
"Stress? What Stress?"

* * *

A month ago I wrote about slowly coming down from the prolonged adrenalin high which was being a full time care-provider.
Doctors have known for a while that such long term stress was
hard on care-providers. It'll drive up blood pressure, screw with
your sleep habits, and even compromise your immune system.
Now they have started to figure out how that immune system
mechanism works. Last night I caught a piece on NPR's All
Things Considered [20] with UCLA professor Rita Effros about her
research on this mechanism. Relevant excerpt:

So, in the short term cortisol does a lot of really good things. The problem is, if cortisol stays high in your bloodstream for long periods of time, all those things that got shut down short term stay shut down. For example, your immune system.

...

But let's say you were taking care of an Alzheimer's spouse, or a chronically ill child – those kinds of situations are known now to cause chronic, really long-term stress - let's say years of stress.

...

(These care-providers) were found to have a funny thing happening in their white blood cells. A certain part of the cell is called the telomere, which is a kind of a clock which keeps track of how hard the cell has been working. Their telomeres got shorter and shorter, and it has been known for many years that when cells have very short telomeres they don't function the way they're supposed to function.

What happens is this: cortisol inhibits the production of telomerase – a protein which helps to lengthen and buffer aging effects. From an abstract on Eurekalert[21] about professor Rita Effros' work:

BACKGROUND:
Every cell contains a tiny clock called a telomere, which shortens each time the cell divides. Short telomeres are linked to a range of human diseases, including HIV, osteoporosis, heart disease and aging. Previous studies show that an enzyme within the cell, called telomerase, keeps immune cells young by preserving their telomere length and ability to continue dividing.

FINDINGS:
UCLA scientists found that the stress hormone cortisol suppresses immune cells' ability to activate their telomerase. This may explain why the cells of persons under chronic stress have shorter telomeres.

IMPACT:
The study reveals how stress makes people more susceptible to

illness. The findings also suggest a potential drug target for preventing damage to the immune systems of persons who are under long-term stress, such as caregivers to chronically ill family members, as well as astronauts, soldiers, air traffic controllers and people who drive long daily commutes.

* * *

io9 picked up on this story[22], and gave it a nice Science Fiction spin:

Stress runs down the body's immune system, which is why people with high-stress jobs or events in their lives are vulnerable to illness. Now a researcher at UCLA has discovered the link between emotional stress and physical damage — and she's going to develop a pill that will allow you to endure stress without the nasty side-effects. And there may also be one good side-effect: Extreme longevity.

It turns out that when you're under stress, your body releases more of the hormone cortisol, which stimulates that hyper-alert "fight or flight" reflex. While cortisol is good in small doses, over time it erodes the small caps at the end of your chromosomes known as telomeres (the little yellow dots at the end of those blue chromosomes in the picture). Many researchers have long suspected that telomeres would provide a key to longevity because they are quite large in young people and gradually shrink over time as cells divide.

Rita Effros, the researcher who led the UCLA study, believes that she can synthesize a pill that combats stress by putting more telomerase — the substance that builds telomeres — into the body. This would keep those telomeres large, even in the face of large amounts of cortisol. It might also make your body live a lot longer too.

Curiously, this clue about telomere length and aging is exactly the mechanism I use in *Communion of Dreams* to reveal that the character Chu Ling is a clone. Genetic testing reveals that the telomeres in her cells are much shorter than would be expected from a child her age, leading to the understanding that this is due to the fact that she has been cloned.

Ironic, eh? No, no one is going to think that I'm a clone. But I find it curious that the same mechanism which I chose for a major plot point pertaining to the health of the human race in my book is one which has been clearly operating on my own health.

(Jim's blog. 8/2/08)
"I live to serve"

I had sent a note to a friend that contained something which I thought may have been of interest to his students. He said thanks in return, and I replied (jokingly): "I live to serve."

His reply:

> *Man, we got to break you of that. Is there a 12 step program for former care-givers out there? I kid just a little here ...*

Actually, it's an interesting idea ...

(Jim's blog. 8/9/08)
Been busy

I took some books back to Special Collections yesterday afternoon. As I was unpacking items, one of the staff members asked how I was doing.

"Pretty well. Been busy."

She looked at me for a long moment. "You look...rested."

* * *

On Wednesday, in response to a friend who asked what I had going on, I sent this email reply:

> *Need to do some blogging this morning, then get settled into the next batch of books for a client. Print out some invoices. Also need to track down some camera software and get it loaded onto this machine, and finish tweaking things here so I can shift over the last of the data from the old system and send it on its way. Need to work on learning some video editing, and start uploading clips from our ballistics testing project to YouTube. Then I can get going on creating the rest of the content for *that* website. Play with the dog. Should touch base with my collaborator on the Alz book, see where he is on some transcriptions he is working on. And then prep dinner. In other words, mostly routine. Yeah, I lead an odd life.*

An odd life, indeed.

* * *

The chaos continues. Yeah, we're still in the process of completely re-arranging the house, and of seeing to the distribution of Martha Sr's things. Looks like there'll be an estate auction in our future sometime next month. But that's good – it means that things are moving forward, heading towards some kind of resolution.

As mentioned in passing in the email cited above, I've been shifting over to a new computer system I got last week. My old system was starting to lose components, and was becoming increasingly incapable of doing things I need to be able to do. Well, hell, it was 7 years old, and was at least one iteration behind the cutting edge at the time I bought it. Thanks to the help of Martha, this has been a relatively painless transition – though one which has still taken a lot of work and time to see through.

And one more complication, just to keep things interesting:

Martha is moving her business practice home. This had been the tentative plan all along, once Martha Sr was gone, and for a variety of reasons it made sense to take this step now. She'll be able to devote more of her energy to seeing to her mom's estate, hastening that process. And she's going to take on the task of shopping my book around agencies and publishers. Now that there have been over 10,000 downloads (actually, over 11,000 and moving towards 12,000), it would seem to be a good time to make a devoted push to getting the thing conventionally published, in spite of the problems in the industry. We're hoping that she'll be better able to weather the multiple rejections that it will take, and I'll have more time and energy for working on the next book (and blogging, and the ballistics project, and – oh, yeah – earning money for a change).

* * *

She looked at me for a long moment. "You look...rested."

"Thanks!"

It says something that with all I've been doing (as described above has been fairly typical, recently), I look more rested now than I have in years.

Actually, it says a lot.

(Jim's blog. 8/19/08)
Declined

As I have noted, I have been fairly busy of late. And in looking back over the last couple of months, I can see a real change in both my energy level and my ability to focus – it's no longer the case that I want to nap most of the time. Yeah, I am still going through a detox process, still finding my way back to something akin to normalcy – but there has been a decided improvement. Fewer migraines. More energy. A willingness to take on some additional obligations.

So I had to debate a long time when I was recently contacted by a site wanting to expand their scope and impact. They were wanting me to do a column every two weeks, more-or-less related to Science Fiction (giving me a lot of latitude to define the scope of the column as I saw fit). They have a lot of good ideas, and seem to have a pretty good handle on where they want to go in the future. And the invitation was a real compliment to me – not only did they say nice things about my writing, but they have a good energy and attitude which is appealing.

But I declined the invitation. Why? Well, to a certain extent it's like Bradbury says: "You have to know how to accept rejection and reject acceptance."

I may come to regret this decision. It could possibly have helped my writing career, at least in terms of landing a conventional publishing contract. And I know from writing my newspaper column that the discipline can do good things for me – forcing me to address a specific topic rather than the more general musings I post here and at Unscrewing The Inscrutable. But I really do have a lot on my plate right now, and they are all things I want to do well, rather than just get done. Blogging here (which is really quite important to me). Participating at UTI. Crafting this book about being a care-provider. Getting the ballistics project website up and running. All the book conservation work waiting for me. Eventually getting to work on *St. Cybi's Well* again. And enjoying life. There's been precious little of that these last few years.

So, I declined.

(Jim's blog. 8/26/08)
There are times . . .

There are times in your adult life when you just hunker down, get stubborn, and see to the end whatever unpleasantness you are experiencing. The last few weeks have sort of felt that way. Hell, the last few years have *been* that way. And a reasonable argument could be made that my entire life would qualify. It's like that old paraphrase of the laws of thermodynamics: "You can't win. You can't even break even. And they won't let you quit."

Anyway, back to the present. I mentioned the beginning of last month that we were engaged in some moving chaos. Well, it's gotten worse since. We've been getting things ready for the auction house to haul stuff away for an auction next month. And my wife is now moving her architecture practice home. This latter had been the long-term plan all along, once Martha Sr was gone, but for various reasons it has become necessary for this to take place now. Meaning more boxes, more moving of furniture, more crowding of space as things are shifted and re-shifted, juggling this and that in such a manner that the three-dimensional puzzle all works out the way it needs to. But at least I'm getting regular exercise.

Oh, that other thing I mentioned in moving chaos, about having just delivered the first big batch of books? Well, I still haven't been paid for that work. Some kind of screw-up in the business office, people on vacation, yada yada. Which is a problem . Because unlike my private clients, who have to put down a 50% deposit on work, my institutional clients get billed when the work is completed. Meaning that I am effectively out about 4 months of pay (because I first did a batch of work for Special Collections, and then got started on the next round of books for the seminary). If there's one thing worse than being unemployed, it is working but not getting paid for it. What should be the start of getting back on my feet financially, after years of minimal income due to care-giving, has become an unexpected crunch, thanks to the ineptitude of whoever was responsible for processing my invoice. Thanks, buddy – I owe you one.

sigh

Anyway, soon my wife will be out of her office, and the auction house will collect things. Eventually I'll get paid by my clients. Things will get better. But for now, it's just a matter of hunkering down, getting through this. As always.

(Jim's blog. 8/29/08)
Wow

Quick update: I did finally get payment for the conservation work, and on Wednesday we finished getting Martha moved out of her office. By next Wednesday the bulk of the estate stuff will be gone for the auction, so things will eventually settle out here at home. This is good.

And my wife and I are getting ready to leave for the weekend. All weekend. Just going. Sure, we've made arrangements for someone to check in on the pets regularly, but that is all the arrangements we needed to make in order to be gone. Which is rather a substantial change from how my life had been the last five or six years. Wow.

Have a good weekend.

(Jim's blog. 9/10/08)
Selling memories

Martha teared-up as we went over the statement from the auction house.

* * *

I've mentioned previously the chaos of the last few months, as we went through distributing Martha Sr's household items between family members and then packed things up to go to a local auction. Well, things are starting to get sorted out and put away now. And we gave away my old computer on Freecycle to someone who needed it. So, while it still feels like we're knee-deep in boxes, we've been making real progress.

But as I said, it has come at a price: tapping into my energy reserves. Another component of that is that I think I have developed a respiratory infection. I've had awful problems with allergies all this year, but in the last couple of weeks things have compounded. I'm scheduled to see a doctor tomorrow for a general check-up (since I just turned 50 and haven't had one for a while), so we'll see if there is something else going on.

* * *

I charge $100 per hour for my conservation services. Oh, I usually don't bill for all my time – there's prep, and clean-up, and distractions, and breaks – but that is my rate. So I use that as a rough rule-of-thumb when considering whether it makes economic sense for me to do this or that thing myself (like working on my car). Now, a lot of times I do decide to do things like yardwork or gardening, because they get me out of the house or give me pleasure. But still, that calculation is there, running in the background.

And so it was as we packed up things for the auction last week. I knew that it would probably be more financially sensible to let someone else do it (the auction house will have their people wrap, box, and load things at a flat rate less than mine), or just not bother taking the time to individually wrap up glasses and old dinnerware. I knew that it was unlikely that most of the stuff we were sending to auction would generate much. But I just hate to waste things, to see them damaged, when they are perfectly good and serviceable.

* * *

Martha teared-up as we went over the statement from the auction house. After all the costs were factored in, and the split with her siblings, our share would come to less than one hour's worth of my time doing conservation work or her doing architecture work.

But that wasn't why she was ready to cry. The money didn't matter, not really. It was because the memories associated with those things were still so strong. Yeah, even the silly chipped dishes and the aging salmon-colored loveseat. And holding the statement and check from the auction house in her hand, it was one more bit of her mom she had lost, along with all the others which had slipped away over the years.

Letting go is hard.

(Jim's blog. 9/12/08)
Learning the cost

I mentioned in a comment the other day that I had a doctor's appointment, and expected to find there that I had a respiratory infection that needed treatment. Well, I did, and I do, and now I've started a 10-day regimen of antibiotics.

But that's not the reason why I made the appointment two weeks ago.

* * *

Almost a year ago I wrote a very raw and painful post titled "Beats having a heart attack." Here's the crucial passage:

> And as I stood there at the sink, washing the dishes, thinking favorably on the option of having a heart attack, it sunk in that I was done. I mean, I'd been considering that a heart attack might be the best solution to my problems. Yeah, a heart attack. Hell, at 49, I'd probably survive it. It'd come as no surprise to anyone, given the kind of physiological and psychological stress I'm under. No one could blame me for no longer being a care-provider for someone with Alzheimer's.

Well, I didn't have a heart attack. And I wasn't done. We made it through six months of hospice care for Martha Sr - easily the most demanding period of care-providing. But that doesn't mean that there wasn't a cost to me, physically.

* * *

I sat in the exam room, waiting to meet the new doctor. My face was flushed, my heart racing. I was having a low-grade anxiety attack.

No big deal, right? Lots of people get nervous around doctors.

But I don't. Hell, I put myself through grad school working in an outpatient surgical unit. Because it was a remote location far from the central supply facility for the hospital, they had established a large sterile storage area adjacent to the 8 surgical theatres. For five years I manned that storage area, keeping the surgical teams supplied. And I was in and out of operations constantly, bringing necessary sterile supplies to the surgical teams. Even my designated break room was shared with the surgical staff. In that five years I got to see and know a lot of doctors in almost every imaginable medical situation, as well as personally. I've never been nervous around doctors since.

The doctor knocked and then came into the room. I was sitting on the exam table, still fully clothed. I hadn't been told to undress or anything by the aide who had parked me there half an hour earlier, so there was no modesty issue connected with my anxiety.

"Hi, I'm Dr E."

"Jim Downey. Pleased to meet you."

She held out a hand, relaxed. "Likewise. What can we help you with today?"

I shook her hand, then passed to her a book I had been browsing through. One I had seen on the shelf there in the exam room. "This was my life for the last 5 years."

The book? *The 36 Hour Day: A Family Guide to Caring for*

*Persons With Alzheimer Disease, Related Dementing Illnesses, and
Memory Loss in Later Life*

* * *

I've talked about the stress of care-giving before, and how I am now
in a detox period from a prolonged norepinephrine saturation. As
I wrote in June:

> *The problem is, those stress hormones come with a price – they
> exact a toll on the body. For most people, occasional jolts of this
> stuff isn't really dangerous, but for someone with a heart condition
> or an aneurysm waiting blow, such an event can kill. That's why
> you see those warning signs on roller coasters.*
>
> *And consider what happens to someone who slowly ramps up
> their stress hormone levels over a prolonged period. That's me.
> My formerly excellent blood pressure and heart rate is now scary
> bad, and has been for a while. I'm lucky that I started this in
> good condition – but think back to this episode last year, and
> you'll see what kind of effect the excessive stress hormone levels
> had. In the final year of care-giving, my system became saturated
> with stress hormones – my 'fight or flight' reflex changed from
> being related to a sudden threat to being an ongoing condition.
> I adapted.*

That was why I made the doctor's appointment. And the reason I
was nervous was because I was afraid of what the cost I had imposed
on my body actually was.

* * *

Dr E took the book, looked at it. She nodded, then looked at me.
"Tell me about it."

We talked.

We talked about the care-giving, when it ended, what I had tried to do to care for myself during and since. She looked over my records, asked a few questions, did a few of the typical exam things doctors do to confirm their innate understanding.

"Well, let's treat this respiratory infection." She paused, looked at me. "You know, your blood pressure is quite high."

Actually, my blood pressure was scary bad. When the aide took it earlier, she was startled by how high it was. Let's put it this way – it's in the range where if it were just a bit higher, hospitalization would be indicated in most cases. If I walked into an ER with that blood pressure, people would start rushing around.

"Yeah, I'm not surprised." I told the doctor what I've said in those posts cited above.

She nodded, realized that I knew what I was talking about. "How would you feel about starting a drug therapy to get it under control?"

"What did you have in mind?"

"Beta blocker." She looked at me. "You may not need to be on it forever. The other things you are doing and recovery from the care-providing might be sufficient – later. But for now, I think it would be wise."

It was the right call. Beta blockers act specifically to counter the effects of stress hormones, especially norepinephrine.

"Sure. Let's do it."

* * *

So, that's part of the cost of care-providing, documented by medical authority. It's too early to say whether this drug therapy will be sufficient. I do still need to shed weight (though I'm now only about 20 pounds over what was my 'normal' weight about ten years ago), and keep an eye on diet and exercise, control stress, get plenty of sleep. And there's no way to say how much long-term damage I did to my system by my period of high blood pressure (which increases the risk of stroke, dementia, heart disease and kidney damage). There's no indication yet that there's been any long-term damage, but...

I'm still glad I did it.

(Jim's blog. 10/5/08)
Happy anniversary

"I'm glad it was just the two of us. Seems appropriate."

* * *

My wife's family settled in Missouri in the Nineteenth century. I don't know (or I should say, don't remember) all the details, but they wound up south of here in Maries County. They started a small community which no longer survives, and a church there that does. The family still meets in the church annually for a John Family reunion.

I've mentioned previously my own connections to the southern part of the state, and how much I enjoy going there. Particularly this time of year, when the air is crisp but not cold, when there is fall color starting to settle onto the trees. It's the reason Martha and I decided to get married in October.

So there was some pleasure in the drive today down highway 63. But still, we both cried.

* * *

I spent some time this afternoon reading journal entries from my partner in writing, dating back to the early onset of his mother-in-law's Alzheimer's. Raw stuff. Honest stuff. Bits about some of the early signs of declining mental ability, confusion about where she was, what was happening. How he and his wife were trying to cope with it. And now and then, when Georgia had a particularly bad period, or her health required hospitalization, wondering how long it would be before she passed away, how long he would be able to see through the role of care-providing.

Thing is, this was *two years* before her actual passing.

Sometimes, the only way you can keep going is if you don't know how long you'll have to do so. If you knew the true length of the road ahead, and the condition of it, you'd be too likely to give up.

* * *

This evening I'll fast after dinner. I go in in the morning and have blood drawn for tests, and later this week I'll meet up with my doctor for a follow up to my earlier exam. We'll find out what things other than my blood pressure need attention. We'll also see if I need to do something in addition to the beta blockers mentioned in that post – possibly, though my bp is down 50/20 already. This is a huge improvement, though I have about that much further to go to get to 'normal.' Yeah, like I said, it was scary bad.

But I've begun to notice other improvements. I sleep longer, better. There are even nights when I don't wake up at 3:00, listening hard for the sound of Martha Sr's breathing over the baby monitor.

* * *

"What are you thinking?" Martha asked.

I watched leaves skittle across the road, tumbling in the draft of the car ahead. A wide and glorious vista opened to the north, ridge after ridge of green, little clusters of other colors here and there. "Lots of things."

Yeah, lots of things.

"I'm glad it was just the two of us. Seems appropriate."

She nodded.

"I mean, we were with her pretty much on our own. It just seems appropriate that it was the two of us to bury her cremains." I paused, thinking of the memorial service. That was for the family, for the friends. We'd decided on making the trek to the family church, where there is still half the graveyard reserved for family members, on this day, because it was the her parents' anniversary.

I'm an atheist, and I don't believe in the survival of the soul or any such. But it seemed like the appropriate day to bury Martha Sr, there next to her husband. And that Martha Jr and I should be the ones to do it.

I now know how long the road is, and in what condition. But I am glad I drove it the full distance.

Happy anniversary, Martha and Hurst.

(Jim's blog. 10/11/08)
Learning the Cost, Part II

As I mentioned the other day, I've been very busy getting ready for our trip to Patagonia, including some long hours to wrap up  work for clients before I leave.

But I took some time out for a follow-up visit to my doctor. A good thing that I did.

* * *

As I sat waiting in the exam room for my doctor to come in, I looked around. All the usual stuff. But high up on top of a cabinet, only barely visible from where I sat on the exam table, was a wooden box. Some light-colored wood, perhaps pine or a light oak. It was a bit battered, but in decent shape, about the size of loaf of bread. Not one of those long loafs of sandwich bread – a short loaf, of something like rye or pumpernickel.

One end of the box bore a large seal, the sort of thing which was popular in the late 19th century. Big outer ring, inner motif of a six-pointed star, cross-hatched on half of each star arm to indicate motion or something. Center of the star had three initials: JBL. Around the ring was more information: "TYRELLS HYGIENIC INST. NEW YORK CITY U.S.A. PATENT JANUARY, 1894 AUGUST, 1897 JUNE 1903." Outside the ring, one in each upper corner, and one below in the center were three words: "JOY. BEAUTY. LIFE."

* * *

I'd gone in first part of the week to have blood drawn, for tests my doctor wanted to run. I still have the bruise where the aide who drew the blood went a bit too deep and punctured the back of my vein.

My doctor looked over the lab results, looked up at me. "Not too bad. LDL is a bit high, so is your HDL, which helps. Fasting blood sugar also a bit high, but not bad. I think we should give both of those a chance to settle out some more, as you continue to get diet and exercise back completely under your control. The rest all looks pretty good – liver & kidney function, et cetera. Nothing to be too worried about."

She handed over the sheaf of papers to me. "But I want to do something more about your blood pressure. It is still dangerously high, though you seem to have made some real progress with the beta blocker."

Yeah, I had – I'd been testing it. And it was down 50 points systolic, 20 points diastolic. About halfway to where it should be.

"Would you be willing to try something else? Another drug?"

Echo of the first conversation we had on the topic. "What did you have in mind?"

"Calcium channel blocker," she said. "We could still increase the dosage of the beta blocker you're taking, because you're on the low end of that. But I would like to see how your system responds to this additional drug, also at a minimal dosage. Then we can tweak dosage levels, if we need to."

Another good call. "Sure, let's try it."

* * *

My doctor returned with my prescriptions. "Do you have any other questions?"

I pointed at the box up on top of the cabinet. "What's the story behind that?"

Caught off-guard, she looked at the box, confused.

"I mean, what was in there? Is there a particular reason you have it?"

"No, not really. Nothing's in there. I just came across it at an antique shop some years ago." She looked at me. "Why?"

"There was an author in the 60s & 70s who wrote a lot of stuff I like. Philip K. Dick. He had a lot of health issues, and I can imagine him sitting in a room not unlike this one, looking at some variation of a box like that." I got down off the exam table. "One of his most important books was made into the movie *Blade Runner* in the early 1980s. In that movie one of the major characters goes by the name Tyrell, and he has a connection to...um, the medical industry. I just thought it an interesting coincidence."

"Oh." She was completely lost. I've worked with doctors enough to know that they do not like this feeling. "Well, we'll see you after your trip, check out how the new meds are working, OK?"

"Sure."

(John's blog, 11/7/08)
The Chestnut Tree

Georgia passed away last year, on the cusp of December 18th and 19th. Next week is Kathi's birthday; a little more than one month later is the first anniversary of her mother's passing.

Today, Kathi ran across a video – it is a sweet, special memory of the special bond between a mother and daughter called "The Chestnut Tree." [23]

It reduced her to tears.

(Jim's blog. 12/24/08)
Mincemeat mice play puppets all the time

No, I don't know what it means.

It was one of those things I woke up thinking in the middle of the night, a week or so ago. So I wrote it down.

Why did I wake up in the middle of the night, thinking such a thing? Good question. It was about 3:00, the usual time I would wake and go check on Martha Sr the last couple of years of her life. And even though it's been almost a year since her death, I still wake about that time fairly often. I try and get back to sleep, and usually succeed. Because I know sleep is important to my recovery.

I've mentioned several times the steps I am taking to get my health under control, and why. For the last six weeks now my blood pressure has been stable in the 145/85 range. Still high, and next month when I see my doctor we may need to tweak my dosages again, but about 90/40 points better than it was three months ago. The meds I'm taking, a beta blocker and a calcium channel blocker, are doing their jobs and helping me detox from my cortisol and norepinephrine overloads, but I'm not past it all yet. My waking at night, even occasional bouts of insomnia, are evidence of that.

And researchers have added another level of understanding to just how dangerous this sleep disruption is:

Morning Edition, December 24, 2008: [20] *The human heart requires a certain amount of sleep every night to stay healthy, and that link between sleep and heart health is stronger than researchers suspected, according to a report in the Journal of the American Medical Association.*

* * *

When they put it all together, the researchers got a surprising result. Among these healthy, middle-aged volunteers, those who averaged five or fewer hours of sleep had a much bigger incidence of silent heart disease.

"Twenty-seven percent of them developed coronary artery calcification over the five years of follow-up," Lauderdale says. "Whereas among the persons who slept seven hours or more, on average, only 6 percent developed coronary artery calcification."

In other words, the sleep-deprived people had 4.5 times the risk of heart disease — and that's after researchers subtracted out the effects of other known coronary risk factors, such as high cholesterol, high blood pressure, diabetes and smoking.

It remains to be seen why too-little sleep is linked to clogged

coronaries. Maybe it has something to do with stress hormones.
Lauderdale says other studies have shown that depriving people
of sleep raises their levels of cortisol, one stress hormone.

I don't yet have any indication of serious heart disease. The
preliminary checks from visiting the doctor over the last few
months haven't turned anything up, but she has been mostly
concerned with getting my blood pressure under control. We'll
be doing a more complete exam in the new year, now that this
other issue is less of an immediate concern.

That's not to say that I expect that we'll find anything. But neither
would it surprise me if we did, given what else I know about
what the stresses I've placed my body under over the last five
years. I've been my own puppet, dancing at all hours.

Maybe that's what it means.

(John's blog, 12/28/2008)
Whispers of Memory

A year has passed now – has it already been a year?

Georgia passed away as midnight rolled the calendar from
December 18th to 19th last year. It was only recently that we
started to gather her things and put them away; some donated
(lots of clothing), some to the trash (old mattresses and old
furniture)...some things, of course, staying where they'd been for
years.

> *The roses in the window box*
> *Have tilted to one side*
> *Everything about this house*
> *Was born to grow and die*
> – **Love Lies Bleeding**, lyrics by Bernie Taupin [25]

Some things just seem to need to stay a bit longer.

We've got – and will keep – the wonderful old quilts that Georgia made over the years. Her comfy chair and hassock, in the front room – that's also going to stay a while, in spite of getting on in years. Most times, it even has a throw she knitted or one of her quilts hanging over the top of it. Kathi used to sit in the chair after Georgia would go to bed; now, she sits in the way Georgia did, at an angle, as if ready to snooze.

We've had reminders of Georgia crop up constantly, of course. It's not unlike one or the other of us to reminisce about her or quote one of her favorite sayings or songs, or to mimic some of the more vibrant interchanges we'd had during our years of care-giving, before she had to go to the nursing home.

The dogs, too, still remember Georgia. It's fitting, as she remembered them right up until she could no longer communicate. They were an odd lot.

Ember was Georgia's fur-coated alarm clock. She would be waiting at Georgia's door every morning at the same time, waiting for me to open the door and let her in to go discharge her duties. She would go in, gently stop and scratch her neck at the foot of Georgia's bed – the rattling of her collar appeared to be part of the routine – and then softly leap up at the foot of Georgia's bed and walk along edge. She'd bend over Georgia's sleeping form and lick her face, or – if the face wasn't accessible – begin licking any exposed skin, usually a forearm. Georgia would awaken with a smile, and after cuddling the little dog for a few minutes she'd rise and go to the restroom. She slept in the master suite, and had her own bathroom; the fact that she'd lived in the same room for 40+ years made going to the bathroom at night very easy.

Before Georgia had become truly wobbly, Jack used to come into the bedroom while Georgia in the bathroom and wait for her to come out. She would wobble out with a slow shuffle, and he'd greet her by slapping his forelegs and paws on the ground playfully.

Georgia would chuckle and protest, "I can't play with you – I'm 83 years old!"

Jack would cock his head, accept the gentle rebuttal and go jump up on Georgia's bed to wait for her to get ready for the day.

We all had routines. By sticking to the same morning routine, it was relatively easy to manage everyone.

It also formed lasting memories.

We hadn't realized how much the dogs had bonded to Georgia before she had passed. Kathi and I figured it out just a few short months ago, when we took a walk with the dogs and encountered someone who triggered a few whispers of memory within all of us.

It started simply enough...

Jack, the five and a half year old Alaskan Malamute, stopped cold and focused intently on the elderly woman across the road.

Something about his stance spoke of memory and recognition, mixed with a touch of uncertainty.

He turned his head this way and that, then made a tentative play-slap on the ground.

The elderly woman grinned and began wobbling toward him.

He bounced with joy and tried vainly to close the gap.

As I watched, I realized that he thought she was Georgia, who he had not seen in the flesh for many months. The grin and the wobble appeared to confirm it for him: he *really* wanted to go say hi, his tail wagging a mile a minute.

"Jack, NO!"

He relented, slightly.

"Jack, c'mon *walk*...we're going to the park."

He grudgingly acquiesced, stealing glances back toward the woman on the sidewalk across the street. The elderly lady looked a tad disappointed and confused...she had an air of uncertainty, like she didn't know if she had done something wrong.

Like Georgia sometimes looked, especially toward the end.

I grinned and smiled, hoping the effort of keeping Jack under control wasn't contorting my face strangely, and called out that he loved making new friends, but he might accidentally knock her over because he didn't know his own strength. She grinned back, a little uncertain and hinting disappointment, but with more understanding than she'd had before. She no longer looked like she was thinking of crossing the street to us.

Half an hour later, we walked back along the same area. The elderly woman was still across the street, now one house further down from where she'd been.

Again, Jack focused on her as if he was still trying to confirm the memory. He made a couple test pulls to see if he'd be allowed to close the gap, but I held him close with the leash. No go.

We walked home.

When Georgia passed away, Kathi and I wrote a special farewell to her by passing a small pocket computer and keyboard back and forth while we sat at our favorite watering hole. In similar fashion, on the day I recorded the encounter above, I passed the computer to Kathi and she recorded her observations and thoughts in her own words, below. We got interrupted and she never finished her thoughts...but I think that, at the point she left off, that was pretty much all she had at the time.

The encounter had touched both of us deeply.

I saw her before Jack did. She stood in front of the house that used to belong to the old fire chief, the house with the elaborate flowering backyard I used to sneak peeks at as a kid. Short, stout, with short gray hair, her dress billowed in the slight breeze as she stood motionless on the sidewalk, facing the other side of the road.

Ember and I stopped short as Jack lingered along the side, staring at the woman. My husband gave a slight jerk to Jack's leash, but Jack stayed still, his tail wagging furiously as he gazed at the woman.

"C'mon, Jack," my husband murmured.

Tail wagging, Jack gave a happy yelp, slapping paws on the pavement. Ember pulled me below the young dogwood, so I craned my neck to see the woman beaming at Jack. She started to totter across the lawn into the street.

Jack yelped, trying to drag my husband over to meet her.

I looked up.

The woman.

Jack.

Mama.

Several months had passed before we noticed that the dogs both adopted a desire to sit in Georgia's old chair.

Ember's first forays into it were really unique – she pawed and pulled and scratched to lift and push the main cushion to one side, and lay on the chair without the cushion beneath her.

That was where Georgia used to stuff things she didn't want us to know she had.

Jack followed suit – in terms of jumping into the chair in spite of his size, not in terms of pulling up the cushion. He didn't seem to care too much about that.

When they first started getting into the chair, it was odd...we hadn't realized that they didn't do that before until they had started doing it, and even now they don't seem to get into it to lounge about the same way they do on other furniture.

Perhaps it's just projection on the part of Kathi and I, but they seem to think of the chair differently than other furniture they'll get up on. True, Kathi and I both sit in it from time to time, so they are probably picking up our scents more than any reminder of Georgia, but still...the feeling of a different significance lingers.

Jack won't go near the toys (stuffed animals) that Georgia had with her at the nursing home; Ember gets very somber and gives them a sniff, then a tap with her nose, and then walks away from them even now. It could be the scent of death – Georgia had the toys with her when she died – or the scent of the nursing home, or other patients.

Both of them – and both Kathi and myself – give a start when we hear an odd noise upstairs, and all of us are in the living room together. We're still jumpy from whenwe were all Georgia's care-takers, of course.

Jack sometimes whines at one of the closets in Georgia's old room, which Kathi and I have finally moved into. It's got my clothes in it now – it could simply be that he wants to make the foot of the closet his new "malamute cave."

He's like that.

He likes to cover any of my clothes with his fur and dander while they hang in the closet, so he's probably just upset that he hasn't figured out how to open this closet door. My former closet was much easier – it didn't close all the way, so he could nose or paw it open.

But still...the incident with the elderly woman reminded us that our two furry companions also lost someone special to them, even tho they'd only visited her once or twice while she was at the nursing home.

They still remembered Georgia, and different things would trigger and stir the echoes of memory within them.

We're pretty good at judging their expressions and actions; whether we project what we want or think upon them or not, we're still certain that they remember and miss Georgia just as we do.

I still can't believe that it's been over a year now.

Peace.

> *the flowers that you painted on the chair*
> *and the cushions that you made for the chair*
> *they make me feel like you are here*
> *and when you go*
> *I'd like to curl up in the arms of the empty chair*
>
> *to be with you...*
> – **Empty Chair** by Lynne Belle-Isle and Laszlo Szijarto of naked i [26]

(Jim's blog. 1/2/09)
Busted

We had an Open House here for our neighborhood all afternoon yesterday. Which meant a lot of cleaning and prep beforehand (we're still dealing with all the leftover stuff from the estate division for Martha Sr), the crunch of which has occurred in the past week. And then I was on my feet all day, pushing my extrovert batteries to the limit of their endurance by playing host to strangers in my home. In short, by the time everyone left and we got the worst of the mess cleaned up and put away, I was exhausted.

A bit over a week ago I wrote about getting an assessment of my health here sometime after the first of the year. As it happens, a couple of days later I had reason to wonder whether I needed to do so in a more immediate manner, thanks to a clear-cut case of peripheral edema which was the result of being on my feet a lot, more or less in one location. Now, the beta blocker I am taking is a known culprit with this kind of swelling, and I have seen some problems with it off and on over the last couple of months. But this time it was really bad. Made me wonder whether it was evidence of a much more serious problem with my heart. First chance Monday of this week, I called to see about getting in to see my doctor.

Naturally, she is out of the office until next week.

Sigh.

Well, rather than have to go through and explain everything about my life and condition for the last few years to another doctor, I decided that I would take some reasonable precautions, but just make an appointment with my doctor for next week. And I have no real regrets about doing so – if something serious happens, I can go to the ER about three minutes from here.

Anyway, all of this is a bit of prep for explaining what I decided to do last night. Following the clean-up from the party, and getting a bit to eat, I was beat but my legs were aching – both from being on them for much of the day, but also from making about 50 trips carrying boxes up to storage that morning and the day before. I also had some significant swelling again. A friend suggested a soak in the sit-up jacuzzi tub we'd installed for Martha Sr a couple of years ago, and I thought it sounded like a good idea. Before bed, I went in, got things ready, and climbed into the tub.

As I sat back in the tub, which is really pretty small (to fit into a little nook in our downstairs bathroom), my left elbow came back and smashed a plastic cup containing ice-water. It's one of those 16-ounce 'to-go' cups you'll find at about any pizza place, intended to last longer than a disposable cup so you can see the logo for the place where you got it. No big deal, right?

Well, not exactly.

But sorta.

See, this one was a nice red. Only one in the house like it. Meaning that during parties or whatnot, it was easy for me to find *my* cup, if I set it down and wandered off to do other things. By tacit agreement with my wife, this had become 'mine' – she didn't use it. Bit silly, really. You know how it is.

So, it busted. Caught it perfectly positioned against the wall, the entire force of my body sitting back focused on it. Didn't explode or anything dramatic, and I wasn't doused with a lot of ice water. But it busted beyond repair, a couple of chunks of the red plastic dangling, nice crack around the top.

Coming at the end of the New Years Day celebration, I couldn't help but sit there and reflect on the appropriateness of the busted cup, as the tub continued to fill around my aching legs.

As I've said before, I'm not religious. But many years ago I was a fairly serious student of Zen, until I figured out that for me that was a bit of a contradiction in terms. And from that time I still carry along some perspectives that I have found valuable. One of them is about the inherent ephemeral nature of all things.

So I sat there in the tub, thinking about my poor broken cup.

And about my aching legs, and what they may signify. And I felt touched, in a funny way. Letting the cup go – letting it stand as an unintended metaphor for the past year and the changes and costs it has seen, was easy. Allowing that same attitude to seep into me as the water covered me was somewhat more difficult, but eventually worked.

I may find out Tuesday that I have a serious heart condition. That the cost of being an Alzheimer's care-giver for those years was higher than I or anyone else expected. Or I may not. Either way, my wife and I will cope with the news, the facts, and move on with our life to the best of our ability. Because unlike my special red plastic cup, I am not busted.

Happy New Year.

(Jim's blog. 1/6/09)
Not busted

Thought I would follow up with a brief note, now that I am just back from seeing my doctor.

After going over everything reasonably carefully, she's of the opinion that there's no evidence of heart disease, that the various symptoms which had caused me concern can all be traced to my blood pressure meds. So we're going to tweak those. But she was adamant that I did the right thing in being concerned and coming in to see her. She also complimented me on managing to lose weight over the holidays. Not a lot, but even a few pounds loss rather than a few pounds gain is a good thing.

So, there's that. I don't need to worry about being fragile – just keep doing what I am doing. Not busted.

Cheers!

(John's blog, 1/24/09)
Land of the Lost...and Found

Sometimes as we putter through life, we come across something that triggers an avalanche of memories. Such was the case last Sunday, January 18th, as I worked with Kathi to get a few things done around the house. We still have gobs of things left to be done since Georgia's passing; we hadn't gone through what appeared to be the nearly infinite piles of things that were left behind, sometimes hiding bits and pieces of our own lives intermingled with bits and baubles that Georgia had collected, stacked, sorted, unsorted, re-sorted and reassigned as her dementia grew and worsened.

As Kathi and I tried to get an old sewing machine to work so that we could finish a project hanging curtains in the living room, Kathi handed me an envelope with my name on it.

I hadn't seen it in nearly two years, but recognized it instantly. It was from early summer 2007, from one of the editors at ePluribus Media: badges (plastic name badges that looked like stylish credit cards).

The badges had been intended for use at DemocracyFest 2007, where I was slated to give a presentation along with another citizen journalist. The badges had disappeared from my perpetually cluttered office within a day of receiving them, forcing me to question my sanity as I tore apart the office for several days – backwards, forwards and sideways – trying to locate them.

I felt horrible at the thought of having lost them so quickly and expeditiously. They were professionally produced, and had been sent to me for safeguarding since I was (theoretically) the most logical choice: I was going to drive us both up to the conference.

Fortunately, both of us had old badges from attending Media Giraffe; I was able to finesse them to look acceptable. Still, I was at a loss to explain the disappearance of the brand-spanking-new set.

I never thought to check Georgia's room, nor did I expect to find the envelope wedged in between elements of an old Singer sewing table amid the pins, bobbins and spools of thread.

The discovery was bittersweet in some respects, as we realized yet again the fog that was enveloping Georgia – a very meticulous, detail-oriented woman who demanded perfection in everything she did – was quite likely wreaking more havoc with her than we realized at the time. Hindsight is 20/20, as they say.

We're constantly referring to Georgia, of course; she's only been gone a little more than a year now, and we're still making little discoveries about her, about ourselves and about life. And finding that our house, as well as our hearts and minds, are serving us well as lands of the lost and found.

(Jim's blog. 1/28/09)
Getting fixed

"Say, while you're here, maybe you can take a look at this piece of artwork I have. It was given to me by the artist, a friend, but it seems to be coming away from the frame."

This is part of the price of having owned an art gallery and having done framing. Friends and family ask these questions. But it could be worse – I could be a doctor.

"Sure, be glad to."

* * *

Email from a friend, following my post about depression:

I hope you've turned the corner on the inertia and are getting back into it. Got meds?

My reply:

Lets see – yeah, a couple of different ones for my bp. For the depression? Nope – the state of treatment there is still less than a crap shoot, in terms of finding something that works. And since I am not paralyzed by it, and know how to work my way out of it over time, I'd rather spend the time doing that than mucking around with random chemicals on a "try this for six weeks" basis.

* * *

I sat in the recliner, just enjoying the picture created by the fair-sized window on the wall across from me. All I could see were trees – no sky, no landscape beyond – just trees.

But what trees!

Coastal redwoods. And only three or four of them. About 25 feet outside the window, so I was only getting a partial view, mostly of that rough, somewhat shabby but oversized bark. With a couple of horizontal branches to make the composition more interesting visually.

"Nice view out this window."

"Yeah, we sited the house to do that."

My wife designed this house. It was good to be staying there.

* * *

On the flight out I sat and thought. For a long time. Listening to music, eyes closed. The Southwest jet was only about 2/3 full, so my wife and I had plenty of room in our three-seat row. I could just relax, spread out a bit, and think.

I don't do that often enough. Usually, I am reading, blogging, watching something, having conversation. Or I am working – whether at my conservation bench, or playing house elf, or doing something else. But I seldom sit and just think.

Or listen to music. I got out of the habit while caring for Martha Sr. It was difficult to do, since so often I had to be listening to the baby monitor we used to make sure she was OK.

I used to really enjoy listening to music. Just listening, thinking.

* * *

"See, it's pulled away from the frame."

I looked at the piece. We'd hung it off an open door so that I could examine it easily while it was suspended. Abstract, large pieces of torn paper, colored in pastel tones of blues and greens and beiges. The pieces had been heavily gessoed then painted with a thinned-down acrylic. To add some surface effects, the mounted pieces of paper were rolled and folded such that they created a high relief of some five or six inches. All this tied onto the base sheet (also gessoed and painted), which was adhered to a piece of foamcore. This was then mounted by construction adhesive to a strong boxed-"H" wooden frame which you couldn't see from the front. The whole effect was pretty good, if you like abstract art. Overall, the piece was about 3 feet wide by 5 feet tall.

"Yeah, I see what you mean. The top part has curled away from the frame, peeling away."

"You can do whatever you need to. I've got some Gorilla Glue – maybe that's strong enough. Or, if you want to screw the piece back onto the frame, I can get some paint to blend in and mask the screws. Whatever you think it needs."

I looked at the piece again, hanging there. Pulled a bit, knocked off a chunk of the bead of adhesive. "Let me think about it."

* * *

They tell you to expect it to take a year to recover. You don't believe them.

But they're right.

Oh, that doesn't relieve you of the duty to try and get your shit together more quickly. To try and get past the soul-aching exhaustion that comes with having fought the good fight for so very, very long. You have to do that. It is absolutely necessary.

But it isn't sufficient. It will still take a year. Or longer.

* * *

I sat in the chair, looking out the window. I had changed my position ever so slightly – now, on the extreme right, I could see about half of the large bird feeder. We had filled it and hoisted it up that morning. Now maybe a dozen Steller's Jays were mobbing, taking turns at the feeder, flicking in and out of my picture.

If you know Bluejays, you know these guys. Smart. Stubborn. Survivors.

Sometimes, being a little stubborn is what's needed. Stubborn in a smart way. While several of their number kept some larger crows away, the others would eat. Then they'd swap. Smart.

* * *

"We'll get what we need when we're out. Is there an art supply store in Ft. Bragg?"

"Yeah, Racine's. Downtown." My sister-in-law looked at me, a little quizzical. "I'll be happy to talk with the artist and get some paints and do the touch-up, if you just want to remount the piece with screws or something. There's no reason you have to try and match what she used."

"I won't need any paints. Nor any screws."

"What are you going to do?"

"Well, the problem isn't the adhesive. The problem is the lamination."

"Sorry?"

"See," I pointed at the back of the piece. "There's just this piece of foamcore. There's nothing to balance the force of the paper mounted to the other side. Rather than trying to force the whole thing back, which will probably result in snapping the foamcore backing, we're going to dismount it entirely. Then I will put a layer of stiff cloth on the back, using an adhesive similar to the gesso on the front. I want to go to the art supply store, since they'll either have the PVA I want, or I can get some gesso and use that."

"Will that work?"

"Yup. It's a basic process from book conservation, just applied on a larger scale than I usually do it. Same thing as getting the balance right on the cover of a book – cloth on the outside, paper on the inside. It stops the bookboard from warping."

* * *

It's been a year. Or it will have been next week, when I'm on the east coast.

On the day I'll meet my co-author for the care-giving book, as it happens. Talk about serendipity.

Nothing magical about that. But anniversaries have meaning.

* * *

I can't quite explain how it changed. But somewhere along the way out to California I found something. Whether it was in the music, or the thinking, or just the quiet place in my head that resulted from an enforced relaxation for several hours, it was there.

Stubbornness.

Not the stubbornness which saw me through the long years of care-giving. That was different. Defiance in the face of the disease ravaging Martha Sr.

No, this was less about simple survival, and more about...well, joy, I guess.

I wasn't swept away with feelings of overwhelming happiness or anything. But there was a sense that joy could once again be mine. Not just satisfaction in work. Not just enjoyment of life. But joy in being able to create. Maybe not yet. But the possibility was there for the future.

A smart kind of stubbornness.

* * *

We turned the dining room table into a workbench. I laid down newspapers, then we positioned large jars to support the artwork from the front without damaging the high-relief rolls and folds of paper. I needed access to the back of the piece, and this was the only way to do it.

First, I cut away the frame. Some of the facing of the foamcore came off with the frame, but not much. Then I removed all the remaining old adhesive from both the foamcore and the frame itself. I set the frame aside.

Then I mixed up the straight PVA I'd found at the art supply store with water, 50-50. Set that aside.

I took the piece of light cotton duckcloth I'd gotten, and cut it into three strips, each about 2 feet tall and as wide as the foamcore. I laid out more newspaper on the floor. I laid a strip of cloth on the newspaper. And using a 4" plastic putty knife, I poured/spread the PVA across the cloth. It was necessary for it to be completely saturated, the fibers completely relaxed. I waited for a minute for this to happen. Then I picked up the cloth by one edge, and took it to the table. I draped it across the foamcore, and spread it out smoothly, making sure to have good adhesion.

I repeated the process with the other two strips of cloth, overlapping them a few inches.

"Now we wait," I told my sister-in-law.

"For what?"

"For it to dry overnight. If the cloth shrinks the right amount as the PVA dries, it will cause a balancing force to the gessoed paper on the other side, and the foamcore will flatten out. If it is not enough, another application of PVA in the morning will help get the balance right. If it is too much, I can spray it with water and let the adhesive relax. It's just a matter of finding the right balance."

She looked at the contraption sitting on the table. She said nothing, but it was clear she was skeptical.

* * *

I had been waiting around for something to happen.

Well, no, I had been trying to figure out how to force something to happen. And being very depressed that I couldn't do it.

I was being stupid stubborn. Forcing myself to work. To write.

To try and find some happiness in this or that.

It was, perhaps, a necessary stage. Just to show myself that I had the stubbornness I needed, even if it was applied ineptly.

But there was a better path. A smarter path. Just relax, and start walking.

* * *

I poured myself a cup of coffee, walked over to the table.

The foamcore was almost perfectly flat. A slight rise on one corner where the cloth was stronger than the minimal amount of paper on the other side, but that would flatten out just fine.

I sipped my coffee, glanced out the window. From that vantage point I could see the whole bird feeder. There were crows there now, arguing with one another.

Sometimes you just need to understand your way out of problems.

(Jim's blog. 2/15/09)
My eyes keep leaking

As I had mentioned, week before last I was off to the NE for a combination of business and pleasure. Pleasure in seeing a friend, checking out the Mark Twain House (more on that later), and then business and pleasure in going up to Boston to meet my collaborator on the caregiving book. That meeting went exceptionally well – almost frighteningly so. As I said in the following email exchange with a friend:

> *I am curious how the co-author gig is going. Do you feel like it's a good partnership? Do you finish each other's sentences or anything or have you carved up spheres of influence on the work?*

As a matter of fact, it is almost a little creepy how much we *do* finish each other's sentences and think alike. This was our first time to meet in person, and particularly in the brainstorming session about the book it was really weird how much we tracked along identical lines. We did come up with a structure for importing our respective prior writing into the joint book, and that is the next stage for us. But we also have a pretty good handle on how to proceed with the explanatory/ interstitial material which will be needed.

This past week I've been fighting a low grade but fairly annoying and persistent chest cold, which has sapped a lot of my energy for much beyond what I *had* to get done. But I took yesterday easy, and this morning felt like I could get started on working on the book, using the new framework we had sorted out. It's an interesting approach: we've established a metaphorical "year" that is meant to encompass the arc of the Alzheimer's disease as experienced by a care-provider, going from initial suspicions to the eventual death of the patient. Then there will be an afterward which will be about the process of recovery from being a care-provider. Each month of the metaphorical year will contain excerpts from correspondence and blog posts, intertwined with additional explanatory material as needed.

So this morning, after an initial chat with my co-author about the formatting software (I'd had no experience with anything which was designed for multiple authors to work on remotely) to get me oriented, I started to excerpt and upload many of the blog posts which I have had here about caring for Martha Sr. It's gone pretty well, and I made a fair amount of progress. But one problem keeps cropping up – my eyes keep leaking for some mysterious reason, to the point where it is difficult to see the screen in front of me. Maybe I should chat with my doctor about that.

End Notes

1. Kolata, Gina. New York Times, "Rules Seek to Expand Diagnosis of Alzheimer's." July 13, 2010. http://www.nytimes.com/2010/07/14/health/policy/14alzheimer.html

2. Thomas, Rob. Matchbox Twenty, "Unwell". © EMI Music Publishing, March, 2005.

3. Thomas, Rob. Matchbox Twenty, "Unwell". © EMI Music Publishing, March, 2005.

4. The American Geriatrics Society. Eldercare at Home, Chapter 28 "Dying at Home." http://www.healthinaging.org/public_education/eldercare/28.xml

5. Sting. The Police, "Synchronicity I and II". © A&M Records, June, 1983.

6. Waters, Roger. Pink Floyd, "Nobody Home". © Columbia Records, December, 1979.

7. Waters, Roger. Pink Floyd, "Nobody Home". © Columbia Records, December, 1979.

8. National Institutes of Health website, MedlinePlus, information about TIA http://vsearch.nlm.nih.gov/vivisimo/cgi-bin/query-meta?v%3Aproject = medlineplus&query = Transient + Ischemic + Attack + &x = 0&y = 0

9. McLachlan, Sarah Ann. "Ice Cream". © Arista, February, 1994.

10. Waters, Roger. Pink Floyd, "Wish You Were Here". © Capitol Records, September, 1975.

11. Waters, Roger. Pink Floyd, "Wish You Were Here". © Capitol Records, September, 1975.

12. Whedon, Joss. Firefly, "Serenity". © 20th Century Fox Television, December, 2002.

13. MacLeish, Archibald. The Happy Marriage, "Chambers of Imagery." Public Domain, 1924.

14. Degarmo, Chris. Queensryche, "Silent Lucidity." © EMI America, 1990.

15. Gershwin, Ira. "Someone to watch over me." Public Domain. 1926.

16. McLachlan, Sarah Ann. "I Will Remember You" © Arista, 1995.

17. McLachlan, Sarah Ann. "Elsewhere." © Arista, December, 1994.

18. Waters, Roger. Wright, Richard. Mason, Nick. Gilmour, David. Pink Floyd, "Echoes." © Harvest/EMI, October, 1971.

19. http://weekendamerica.publicradio.org/display/web/2008/07/26/hospice/

20. http://www.npr.org/templates/story/story.php?storyId=92975996

21. http://www.eurekalert.org/pub_releases/2008-07/uoc--usi071508.php

22. http://io9.com/5025594/an-anti+stress-pill-that-prevents-your-body-from-aging

23. http://www.youtube.com/watch?v=VsS4Tk-lrxo

24. http://www.npr.org/templates/story/story.php?storyId=98674086

25. Taupin, Bernie. John, Elton. "Love Lies Bleeding." © MCA Records, October, 1973.

26. Belle-Isle, Lynne. Szijarto, Laszlo. naked i. "Empty Chair." March, 2008.

Made in the USA
Charleston, SC
18 August 2014